Since only social science materi
and nonmathematical English
used, the only background
needed for this book is a basic
course in social research, and in
statistics. Given this background,
students in related fields, such as
home economics or education
will find this book suitable.

The text is self-contained enough
so that a student can begin programming without taking a
course, or read it simply for a
better understanding of the
basics.

The workbook can also be used
generally to give students in a
variety of programming courses
practice in handling these basic
procedures. Answers are given to
determine whether the student
understands each point involved,
or if it is necessary to study a
point further. The exercises are
arranged as a continuing stimulus
to move ahead into programming. At no point will the
student find material he cannot
understand.

Frequently, a text will describe a
complete process and give a few
broad exercises at the end. These
exercises may be too vague to
work out because the student
does not understand some aspect
of a whole process, but cannot
tell which aspect he is having
trouble with. Thus, he may become so discouraged he leaves
programming.

Social Research
and
Basic Computer Programming

Social Research and Basic Computer Programming

By

ELWOOD W. GUERNSEY, Ph.D.

Associate Professor of Sociology
University of Alberta
Edmonton, Alberta, Canada

CHARLES C THOMAS • **PUBLISHER**
Springfield • *Illinois* • *U.S.A.*

Published and Distributed Throughout the World by
CHARLES C THOMAS • PUBLISHER
Bannerstone House
301–327 East Lawrence Avenue, Springfield, Illinois, U.S.A.

© 1973, by CHARLES C THOMAS • PUBLISHER

ISBN 0-398-02591-6

Library of Congress Catalog Card Number: 72-81700

*With THOMAS BOOKS careful attention is given to all details of
manufacturing and design. It is the Publisher's desire to present books
that are satisfactory as to their physical qualities and artistic possibilities
and appropriate for their particular use. THOMAS BOOKS will be true
to those laws of quality that assure a good name and good will.*

Printed in the United States of America

BB-14

To my wife

JENNY

and my parents

VIRGINIA AND ELWOOD

PREFACE

This is the first of several books designed to present basic computer programming to social scientists. Using the Fortran IV programming language, this book shows how programming is applied to social science in a way that should be useful for professional researchers and teachers as well as for graduate and undergraduate students majoring in one of the social sciences. An accompanying book of exercises, entitled *Workbook in Basic Computer Programming (Fortran IV)*, is available as an aid to understanding programming and its uses in social science.

The author is a sociologist; however, the situation regarding computers seems similar enough throughout the social sciences, particularly in the teaching of programming, so that if sufficiently general, the same material on basic programming can serve students in these as well as in related areas. Bearing this out is the fact that when an earlier version of this book was used to teach programming to students majoring in sociology, political science, psychology, and home economics, the students seemed to respond favorably to the material and to learn from it.

This book differs in several ways from conventional computer programming texts and manuals. It uses exclusively social science material in explanations and illustrations, and it is much simpler, moving more slowly and concentrating more on the basic aspects of programming which are most important for the social scientist.

Such differences reflect the writer's disagreement with the kind of training in computer programming which is now generally available to social scientists. The purpose of these first few pages is to explain this disagreement and to show how the nature of this book is shaped by the teaching philosophy behind it.

This book is the result of two convictions: (1) There is a vital need for more creative use of computers in social science; yet (2) much of the current training in computer programming discourages people in the social sciences and even drives them completely away from computers.

Ironically, this second point is largely due to the fact that so few social scientists have as yet learned computer programming. This means, for example, that most programming courses are taught by people in other fields which make wider use of computers than the social sciences. So if a social scientist wants to learn programming, he is very likely to find himself in a class taught by a mathematician or physicist or chemist, or even by a professional programmer. Since an instructor tends to use the terminology of the field he is most familiar with, this means that the social science student must also have an extensive background in math, or physics, or chemistry, or whatever, if he is even to understand what his instructor is talking about. And since many of the people in social science do not have this kind of background in other fields, they are at a disadvantage right from the beginning.

Furthermore, the people teaching programming tend to emphasize the application of computers to problems in their respective fields. So if a social science student is taught by someone from outside the social sciences, he will probably get little suggestion as to how computer programming is used in the kind of work this student is interested in.

This has two unfortunate effects. One is that it leaves the social scientist with a whole body of information which he must try to find out for himself how to use, if he lasts that long. Secondly, it means that while learning programming, he is given little of the encouragement that comes from seeing a direct use for what he is learning.

Also, there is a tendency in teaching programming to present a great many complex things about computers in a relatively short time, so that while a student is still struggling with the fundamentals, he is also overwhelmed by a number of advanced facts of no immediate value to him. This not only makes it difficult to master any one thing; it also quite often tends to give the student the overall picture of programming as much too hard for him.

This is perhaps one problem students in other fields share with social scientists, yet even here students in other fields have an advantage in the fact that if they have difficulty, or simply get discouraged, they can go to the computing center where they will probably find a more advanced student in the same field who can help them out. But again because the social sciences have so little contact with computers, if a social scientist goes to the computing center for help with a problem, he is likely to find himself surrounded by consultants from math, physics, chemistry, etc., so that he has the same problem of communication he encounters in his classroom.

In short, taught by people in other fields, given explanations in terms he is not familiar with, beset on all sides by new ideas, many of which have little seeming relevance to the work he is interested in, it is understandable that a social scientist might be so frustrated that he gives up on computer programming.

That we have not overstated the problem here is suggested by the number of students who have gone precisely this route. It should be remembered that many social science students are interested enough in programming to try it. Yet it should also be remembered that they, like probably the majority of other citizens, are intimidated before they begin by the computer's reputation for mystery and complexity. It requires only a few disappointments, or a few weeks of total incomprehension, to seem to confirm this reputation. And as we have just seen, there are many things about the current training available to social science students that are almost guaranteed to produce just such disappointment and incomprehension.

It is true that a few hardy types manage to overcome all these problems, either by unusual determination or by sheer good luck, as in the case of the author who had a close friend who was a mathematician/programmer. Yet social science will make little real use of computers if it continues to rely on a few exceptions like this; rather, we must find a way to break the circle that now finds so few social scientists learning to program because there are so few people in their own field who can teach them; and so few who can teach, because there are so few learning.

In this writer's view, breaking this circle requires a very different approach to teaching programming to social scientists. Recognizing that, for a variety of reasons, we now have a definite psychological barrier between social scientists and computers, we must concentrate less on the abstract content of programming, and more on the student's reaction to, and interest in, what he is learning. We must try to keep frustration to a minimum, which means making each step as rewarding as possible, while trying to delay disappointment (inevitable for a beginning programmer) until after the student has had a chance to see that he can handle programming.

It seems to this writer that we can do this if we make use of three principles which are fundamental to successful teaching, but which for some reason have been largely ignored in present efforts to teach programming to social scientists: (1) Students should have teaching materials they can understand; (2) they should have some reason for learning; and (3) they should be *rewarded* for learning.

The first of these points suggests that if social scientists are ever to really come to grips with computers, they must have teaching materials designed as much for their particular requirements and backgrounds as most current materials are oriented toward students in other fields. The second point means that students must be shown the value of what they are learning, i.e. in terms of that magic word, the *relevance* of it. Specifically, they must see how they can relate programming to social science, and they must see this right from the beginning.

The third point suggests that since programming is a complex skill, it must be taught in the way that has proven itself in teaching things like music or language: that is, introducing the student to just one or two ideas at a time, and drilling him in these ideas until he has thoroughly mastered them. This gives the beginner two kinds of vitally needed *reward*. Psychologically, the fact that he can successfully do each set of exercises gradually builds his confidence that he can actually meet the challenges of this new skill; practically, having learned each point well enough, he can use it to produce results which are simple at first, but become increasingly sophisticated.

This book attempts to combine these three principles in a text on basic computer programming that would be suitable for a wide range of social science students. The book is written in nonmathematical English, so it can be understood by someone without an extensive background in math, chemistry, physics, etc. When more specialized terms are used, they are drawn from material the student should be familiar with; that is, the body of concepts and procedures basic enough to be fairly common throughout the social sciences.

In addition, there is a direct and constant emphasis on applying programming to the problems and procedures of the social sciences. One advantage of this is that it encourages the student by showing him, right from the beginning, a relationship between his programming and the work he hopes to use the computer in. Secondly, it can save the student considerable time he would otherwise have to spend later in figuring out, by trial and error, exactly how to use his programming in his work. Finally, it lets us take advantage of the fact that the concepts involved in programming and the concepts involved in social science turn out to be quite similar, though this similarity may not show up on the surface. By pointing out how a particular concept in programming relates to its counterpart in social science, we can use what the student already knows about his own field to help him understand an idea in programming.

In order to simplify the task of the beginner, this book tries to keep to a minimum the number of new ideas a student is confronted with at any one point in his learning. That this is possible, while still giving the student both a sound foundation for further learning, and the tools he needs to get some initial results from the computer, is because of two often overlooked facts about computer programming. One is that only some features of computers are immediately necessary to a beginner in social science programming. We can concentrate on these at first then, skipping for the time being those things of more interest to the astronomer or physicist, for example.

Secondly, there is the fact that the more advanced aspects

of computers are in no way essential to an understanding of the basic ideas. So by leaving the more advanced things until later, we can further minimize the number of concepts the student must cope with at any one time. Simultaneously, this lets us avoid two real dangers: the danger that a student will be so overwhelmed by a sheer number of facts that he will not learn any of them well, and/or the danger that he will get the picture of programming as so very hard that he will be discouraged into quitting.

A related reason for beginning with an emphasis on the most basic concepts of programming is that these are actually the most difficult, since this is where the student makes the transition to thinking in *computer terms*, which is somewhat different from the way we are used to thinking, despite the underlying similarities. Until the student has made this shift and has mastered the basic ideas, there is no point in his learning about the more advanced aspects of programming.

Our emphasis on mastering the basic facts, together with a concern for the attitude of students, accounts for another way in which this book differs from an approach often used. Often a beginning student is given a program to run in the first day or first week of his training, on the grounds that to have immediate contact with a computer will inspire him. Here this is not done, for two reasons. One is that even the simplest program includes a number of ideas, such as input, output, and formats. It is unlikely that all these ideas can be mastered in a few days, so that in running a program very early a student is engaging in an exercise which is largely incomprehensible to him. Furthermore, if anything goes wrong, he is helpless; and things do go wrong, even if only because the computer picks this particular time to malfunction. At the early stages, all the student knows is that a program has not run, and he does not know why. Disappointment over a failure at this point, coming before the student understands what is involved and before he has done anything that gives him confidence that he can solve programming problems, can be so frustrating that it can actually make the student drop out of programming. Since the amount of learning derived from running a program which is not understood is small, the risk seems unworth the benefit. Here, therefore, the material is presented in such a way that not until after a number of chapters will the student be ready to run a program.

This delay has two advantages. By then the student will have worked enough exercises to build his confidence that he can work out programming problems, and this will help compensate for the discouragement should a first program not run. Secondly, by this time the student will have a good idea of what he is doing when he does run a program, and some idea of what to look for, or at least what questions to ask, if he does have trouble.

Doing the things this book tries to do (that is, discuss basic points in detail, show how they apply to programming, and include many examples and illustrations to help in learning them) means this book takes much more space than a conventional programming text. Therefore, in order not to sacrifice the very detail valuable to students, it was decided to use several volumes, of which this is the first. Here the student is introduced to the logic of using computers, and to the fundamentals of writing programs and submitting them to the computer. We also show how to read a few figures into the computer, do arithmetic with them, and write out the answers. Here we also see what is involved in decision-making on a computer, and we see how these things are applied to basic data processing procedures like the frequency distribution, and summing. In short, this book is an introduction to the basic concepts, to lay a foundation for further programming.

Another volume will begin where this one ends, introducing arrays and DO loops and their application to various data processing and statistical techniques widely used in the social sciences. The overall effect of the combined books hopefully will be to (1) aid the student in moving from basic to more advanced use of computers in his work, and (2) leave him with an interest in continuing into even more advanced programming, having a solid basic foundation that will make this possible.

Because we are dividing the material into several volumes, readers familiar with computers will find this first book does not mention many of the features discussed in more conventional programming texts. These features are important; this is the reason for going to an advanced volume to cover points we do not have space for here. In the event that a reader is interested in brief summaries of these other features, or is simply anxious to see other treatments of the points covered here, some other programming texts and manuals are listed in the bibliography here.

This book can be used with a course on programming for social scientists. If such a course is available, it should by all means be taken, because having an instructor to answer questions is too great an opportunity to pass up. However, in many small social science departments, and even in some larger ones, there is no one who can teach programming. Therefore, the writer has also tried to make this book self-contained enough so that a student could read it and begin programming even without taking a formal course, although he would need to consult with people at his local computing center.

Also, since the book is reasonably nontechnical, it can be read simply for a better understanding of how computers fit into social science, or even to pick up enough of the basics of programming to be able to discuss it with people specializing in it.

In summary, we have tried to write this book in a way that will show that programming need not be as frustrating as many beginners find it; rather, that it can be immensely pleasurable, offering the same kind of appeal as chess or checkers or bridge. In the great precision and rigorous logic required by the computer (and rewarded when it appears) there is a refreshing contrast with the vagueness and improbabilities of everyday life.

We have also tried to show that if presented properly, there is nothing particularly difficult about programming. There are a lot of details to keep in mind, and it takes time to learn these details, but there are no concepts or ideas which are difficult to grasp, as long as the ideas are presented in logical sequence, with adequate explanation and illustrations. So we have tried to touch on only those points which are the most important for the students we are interested in, and we have tried to explain these points in the best way for them, even if this means an approach different from the kind often used in programming courses.

Furthermore, with the accompanying workbook we have tried to make it possible for the reader to thoroughly understand (and to know he understands) each point before going on to the next one, so he will always have a solid foundation on which to build further knowledge. But to accomplish this, it is strongly urged that, regardless of whether the book is being used independently or in a class, each set of exercises be worked out before moving on to the next point.

After each discussion in this book is a reference to the related exercises in the workbook. The answers to some of the exercises are given at the end of the workbook, so the reader can tell whether he understands the point covered in a set of exercises, or whether he should go back and study that particular discussion again.

The importance of this general approach is that it may begin to do something which in the author's view is vital to the continuing growth and contribution of the fields making up the social sciences; that is, make programming something that both appeals to and is accessible to virtually every social scientist who is interested in it. Hopefully this will be a step toward the kind of use of computers in our fields that there now is in math and in the physical and biological sciences. If we can move in this direction, perhaps we can then begin to find that more and more social scientists can take programming courses from their own colleagues, can find social scientists in university departments and computing centers who can offer their colleagues advice and help with programming problems: in short, can find ourselves enjoying the same advantages in learning computer programming that students in other fields now enjoy.

The approach employed in this book and in the accompanying workbook may be viewed by some programmers as *too easy*. But this is exactly the kind of material the author wished for when he was just beginning in programming, and it is also the kind of material he would like to use in teaching a programming course for social scientists. This is why it was written.

ELWOOD W. GUERNSEY

INTRODUCTION

When we in the social sciences look at the use we are making of computers, we see a striking paradox: Computers are becoming tremendously important in virtually every area of our society, and we are greatly concerned about the social implications of this; yet we social scientists are often reluctant to use computers in studying that society and we tend to ignore the basic implications of computers for what *we* do.

The explanation of this paradox seems to be that most of us have not learned the process of giving instructions directly to the computer, the process we call *programming* a computer. Yet ·this is the best, and probably only, way to really understand what the computer is and what it can do.

Without this understanding, the social scientist may react to computers in a variety of ways. He may simply decide not to get involved with something so frighteningly strange and mysterious. If he does try to use a computer, however, he may either underestimate what it can do, so that he makes only marginal use of its abilities, or he may overestimate what the computer can do, so that when it fails to live up to his inflated expectations he rejects it disappointedly.

These differing views of the computer have in common two things: They all lead to making at best only partial use of it, and they all stem from a lack of the kind of understanding of computers that comes from learning to program them personally.

Part of the reason, of course, that so few social scientists have learned computer programming is that most of the instruction in it has been aimed at students in mathematics and the physical sciences: a condition this text is designed to alleviate somewhat. But another factor is that many social scientists subscribe to a set of stock arguments for *not* learning computer programming. These reasons circulate so widely that you must sooner or later meet them, and while reading this book suggests you are presumably at least thinking of learning to program, these arguments against programming may seem persuasively logical excuses for avoiding a hard and sometimes frustrating job.

These arguments against learning to program, therefore, are of interest to us for two reasons. One is that they seem to have a marked bearing on the use our field makes of an impressive research tool. The second is that they bear on your personal decision to invest considerable time and effort into developing a skill that many people, probably including teachers and/or colleagues, may argue you do not need or should not have.

Unfortunately (in the sense of not presenting both sides of the picture) you will probably hear the arguments *against* learning to program much more often than you hear the arguments in favor of it, for this reason: The arguments against learning programming make excellent sense to one who does not program, whereas the arguments for learning it make sense only to one who *has* learned to program. Since most social scientists are not programmers, it follows that there is little attempt to present to social scientists the arguments in favor of their learning to program. Yet these arguments are compelling, and you should know them as well, if only because this will give you a better idea of what you can expect to gain from the time and effort you are about to invest. Therefore let us begin with a brief recounting of major arguments for and against social scientists learning to program.

PROGRAMMING LANGUAGES CHANGE

Computer programming is the process of giving to a computer certain instructions about what data to read, what operations to perform on this data, how to present the results to us, and so on. These instructions are written in what is called a *language.* Very briefly, a programming language consists of two things. One is a set of rules for preparing instructions to the computer. These are comparable to the rules of grammar in a spoken language like English. Then there are words and symbols in which these instructions are phrased. These are comparable to the vocabulary of words that make up a spoken language.

The language we are studying here is the widely used one called Fortran IV. Fortran is the name of the language, just as English is the name of a language; the IV after the name Fortran means we are using the fourth *version* of this language.

This idea of *versions of a language* leads to one main argument against learning to program. This argument is that programming languages change; that is, there are periodic changes in the words and rules used in giving instructions to a computer. Therefore, why waste time learning one language (that is, one set of words and rules) when there will soon be a new set along? The implication here is that when a language changes we will again be left unable to use a computer, just as if we had never learned a programming language in the first place. This argument also suggests that if we want to continue using a computer, we must be learning one new language after another, and this will take so much time we will have little time left for our main interests: for example, the research in which we want to use a computer.

This argument that programming languages change does contain an element of truth; there are periodic modifications in a language. However, this is not a matter of such drastic change that we are suddenly left unable to use a computer; rather, it is a gradual process, so that with very little effort we can keep up with each change as it occurs. This is illustrated by the Fortran language we are concerned with here. Before this fourth version, the version in wide use was the second, called Fortran II. The change from one version to the other was mainly a matter of adding new features to make the language more powerful, to allow a programmer to do more things with it. But basically, the two versions of the language are so similar that with a few minor changes, a programmer could continue in Fortran II while learning the new features in Fortran IV.

In short, learning to program is the real job; keeping up with changes in a language is nothing, in comparison. And logically, it must be this way, because of the thousands of programmers already in government, business, and science. If programming languages changed too abruptly, all the computer-based processes in every area of society (industry, government, science, etc.) would grind to a halt while every programmer stopped to learn a new programming language. Therefore, even new computers are designed to use existing programming languages.

IT TAKES TOO MUCH TIME

Another argument against learning to program is the time it takes. But this is misleading, because once we learn a few basic principles we can begin writing simple programs. It is not necessary to learn programming completely in order to get practical benefits from the time invested in it.

Furthermore, as a programmer gains experience, he finds that programming takes less and less time, while its results become greater and greater. One reason for this is that most procedures in social science are built around a few basic operations. For example, several statistics involve a cross-tabulation, so if we once write a program for a cross-tab, we have this start on any of those statistics using a cross-tab. Also, of course, each program that is written adds to the skill that makes writing the next program quicker and easier.

PROGRAMMING IS ONLY FOR MATHEMATICIANS

It is also said that programming involves so much math that only mathematicians or physicists can do it. Nothing could be farther from the truth. Many of the data-processing procedures in social science require little more than adding one and one, yet they lend themselves beautifully to computers. In general, doing something on a computer requires no more math than doing the same thing by hand.

THE SOCIAL SCIENCES ARE NOT EMPIRICAL SCIENCES

Another reason for not learning to program computers is the more general one that the social sciences are not, or should not be, empirically oriented; that is, they should emphasize ideas, not numbers, and therefore should not use computers at all.

This argument reflects a misunderstanding of computers. It is true that they handle numbers rapidly and in great quantities, but putting numbers into a computer does not mean we lose control either of the numbers or of the computer. There is nothing in this combination that gives numbers greater power; they are still just numbers, to be treated any way the social scientist believes numbers should be treated.

Conversely, by minimizing the amount of time he must devote to them, the computer can ultimately free the social scientist from being so concerned with numbers. This gives him more time to do that which the computer can not do: read, reflect, and reason out what these numbers *mean* about the things they represent.

PROGRAMMING HAS MANY RULES

Another argument against learning to program is that it imposes on the programmer a too-rigid intellectual discipline, which eventually dehumanizes him, destroying his creativity and leaving him little more than a machine himself.

It is true that there are certain definite rules and procedures in programming. These result from the fact that the computer does not (in the sense that we do) think. It executes simple, exact, instructions rapidly and with great precision. But it can only function properly when it is given these instructions with equal precision. So we must be absolutely precise in our instructions to the computer, and we must give it these instructions in a specific form.

Occasionally a student reacts to the rules of programming with the question, Why must I do it this way? He feels it is *unfair* for the computer to *arbitrarily* expect certain kinds of instructions. It should be *willing* to accept whatever kind of instructions its human master feels like giving it; otherwise, the machine is dictating to the man, not vice versa.

This discipline is part of the price we pay for the benefits the computer offers us. If someone objects that this price is too high, this reflects his personal evaluation of what is appropriate behavior for him. If he objects to discipline in principle, then he will object to the computer because of the discipline it imposes.

It should also be remembered, however, that the result of this discipline is a much greater freedom from the kind of clerical tasks that now take so much of our time in research, and a freedom to do things that previously have not been possible because of such limitations as the amount of help available, or the number of variables we can keep track of by ourselves.

HIRING A PROGRAMMER

We have saved for the last probably the two most popular arguments against learning to program. These arguments are popular because they seem to offer a way to get any desired benefits from the computer without going to the trouble of actually learning to program it personally.

One of these arguments is that a social scientist can always hire someone to do his programming. But actually this is often not true, for several reasons. For one thing, most professional programmers are drawn not to the social sciences, but to the *glamor* programming, in mathematics or the physical sciences, or to the money, in business or industry. Also, there is the fact that many social scientists work in smaller schools which have small computers, but not a well-staffed computing center with a stable of programmers. A social scientist in such a school may be forced into his own programming if he wants to use the computer.

Even if a programmer is available, however, there is often great difficulty communicating with him about the job to be done. Since most programmers do not have a background in social science, they will not understand the language we use to explain the project for which we want programs written. Furthermore, unless we understand the language the programmer uses, we will not understand what he is saying about our work. This lack of understanding has occurred so often, and has been so frustrating for all parties concerned, that it has led to considerable ill will between social scientists and programmers. This in turn has seriously limited the use of computers by social scientists.

Obviously, if we have access to a person in our own field who is also a programmer and who will write programs for us, this problem of communication is greatly minimized. But relatively few social scientists are computer programmers, and those who have this skill are more likely to use it in their own work, rather than spend time writing programs for other social scientists.

There are two reasons for this. One is that professionally these researchers are rewarded for work they produce, with the aid of computers; there is probably much less recognition for the help they give other social scientists who are unwilling to make a comparable effort to learn programming. Secondly, and probably more important, the social scientist who knows how to program is likely to become so intrigued with using the computer to do exciting new things in his own work that he would simply find it dull to help a nonprogramming social scientist, who is likely to still be doing conventional things in the standard ways, merely wanting them programmed to get them done faster. This would take much of the excitement and challenge out of programming.

But even if we find a social scientist who can program, and who is willing to write programs for us, it is still not the same as doing our own programming, because no one else can be as familiar as we are with every aspect of our work, nor care as much about it.

CANNED PROGRAMS

Another popular reason for not learning to program is the *canned program*. This is a program already written to perform a certain operation. Theoretically, a nonprogrammer decides what operation he wants the computer to perform, gets that canned program, adds his data, and has his results.

However, despite their surface appeal, there are several disadvantages to these programs. For one thing, since such programs are written by other people, a researcher may have great difficulty getting one to work with *his* data. So using these programs often takes longer and is more work than writing one's own programs. Furthermore, some sets of data simply will not work at all with a canned program because of the practical limit on how many different combinations of sample size, number of variables, number of response categories, and so on, one program can handle.

A third problem is that we are limited to the procedures for which programs have been written. Most programmers work in such fields as math or physics. If these fields use a procedure also used in the social sciences, then we may find a program for it. But various scaling techniques or certain kinds of ordinal statistics social scientists find useful would probably not be in these canned programs because other sciences would have little use for them. And even if canned programs written for another field are useful, this means the social scientist is using *hand-me-downs* from other sciences: hardly the way to build pride in one's own field or to demonstrate the right of social sciences to a respect comparable to that granted the physical sciences.

SUMMARY

In sum, the arguments against social scientists learning to program seem to fall into two general categories. One category we might term *philosophical:* for example, that social science should not be too empirical, or that man should not subject himself to a discipline imposed by a machine. Therefore, the response to these arguments must ultimately be in terms of personal values, and the individual's view of himself and his science.

The other category we might call *practical:* covering such diverse arguments as the amount of mathematical background necessary, or the time to be saved by hiring a programmer or using canned programs. Since these arguments about *saving time* are probably the ones most often advanced, we should note that the experiences of many social scientists suggest that hiring a programmer or using pre-written programs may well turn out to be more time consuming, for reasons indicated above, than if the person had learned to write his own programs in the first place. So it seems that time must be spent one way or another to get results from the computer. If this time has given the social scientist programming knowledge he can use on future problems, he would seem to be farther ahead than if it has only resulted in one hired programmer comprehending one problem, or one canned program made to work.

Ultimately, however, the significance of the problems of hiring and communicating with programmers, or of trying to use canned programs, is not the time involved. Neither is it the fact that these problems may hinder the progress of any one research project. Rather, it is that the experience can be so frustrating that the social scientist involved may develop a negative view of computers and turn his back on them entirely. What this amounts to, then, is that the attempt to take a *short-cut* to the use of computers may end up denying the social scientist all the contributions they could make to his work.

ACKNOWLEDGMENTS

I would like to thank several people whose advice and encouragement at various times helped make this work possible: Dr. Lewis Killian, who as Professor of Sociology at The Florida State University really started it all; Dr. Charles Grigg, Professor of Sociology and Director of the Institute for Social Research at Florida State University, who introduced me to the use of computers in social research; Dr. Gordon Hirabayashi, who as Chairman of the Department of Sociology at the University of Alberta offered more support than he realizes; and Vera Randall, of Columbus, Ohio, who remains for me the model of a dedicated and inspiring teacher.

E.W.G.

CONTENTS

		Page
Preface		vii
Introduction		xvii
Acknowledgments		xxvii
Chapter		
One.	WHAT IS COMPUTER PROGRAMMING?	3
Two.	NUMBERS: INTEGER AND FLOATING POINT	14
Three.	VARIABLES AND CONSTANTS	23
Four.	INPUT	35
Five.	OUTPUT	85
Six.	LABELING OUTPUT	141
Seven.	ARITHMETIC	169
Eight.	WRITING AND SUBMITTING A PROGRAM	204
Nine.	TRANSFER OF CONTROL AND DECISION-MAKING	238
Ten.	COUNTING AND SUMMING	268
Bibliography		305

Social Research
and
Basic Computer Programming

Chapter One

WHAT IS COMPUTER PROGRAMMING?

The first step toward becoming a computer programmer is to discard any awe or apprehension about the machines. It is true that computers are very complicated. But like a well-trained dog they do a few things superbly well, but really do very little in comparison with their human masters.

WHAT CAN COMPUTERS DO?

Computers do not think. They are merely useful tools. They can do simple arithmetic operations with blinding speed. They can compare characters: One character is, or is not, the same as another. They can even make numerical comparisons: One number is equal to another, or larger, or smaller. But obviously a machine which does nothing more than this kind of thing can not solve problems in the sense that the human being does, any more than a desk calculator can.

THE COMPUTER IN THE RESEARCH PROCESS

We do not gain greater intelligence simply by using a computer; it does not give us solutions to problems we do not know how to solve. Using a computer does not allow us to do anything we could not do with a desk calculator, just as a calculator does not let us do anything we could not do with a pencil. However, the computer does let us do things much faster, and it is this element of speed that makes the computer so important, because it allows us to do *more* things than we otherwise could.

Yet by itself, this speed is meaningless; the important thing is what *we* do with this speed. The emphasis is on *we*, because we (as human beings, researchers, social scientists, or whatever) are the key element in the whole computer process.

The computer itself is actively involved in the research process at only one point. Prior to using a computer, there is the choice of a research problem. This is a choice the researcher must make, on the basis of logic, theory, past research findings, his own professional interests, and so on. Having a computer handy may influence his choice of what to study or how to study it: for example, it might lead him to use more data, or to do a more intense small group analysis. If the researcher knows he will be using a computer, this may even influence such details as how many columns on a data card are allotted to each variable, or how many decks of cards to use for a set of data.

Ultimately, however, the social scientist must make all such decisions; the computer can not do it for him. The same is true of deciding which statistics are most appropriate for the data, how to design a procedure to get the desired data, and so on. In all these things, the computer is a factor only marginally.

Once these decisions have been made and the data gathered, coded, and punched on data cards, then and only then does the computer actively enter the picture. The researcher gives it the set of numbers making up the data, and a program (a set of instructions) telling the computer what to do with those numbers. The computer follows these instructions (we say it *runs* the program) and returns the results. Then the researcher must decide what these results mean in terms of his study.

In perspective, therefore, despite the glamor of its reputation, the computer represents only a small part of the research process. The social scientist, not the computer, is the basic factor throughout. What the computer does with a set of data, how much data to give it, what form the answers are to be in, how complex the whole project will be, these are things we human beings must decide according to our knowledge of the best way to handle a particular problem. These are the things that require the real thinking, not the mere following of certain precise instructions, regardless of how fast those instructions are followed. After all, we would probably not allow a clerk at a desk calculator to make all these decisions for us. And the computer is far less able to do it than he is.

WHAT IS A COMPUTER PROGRAM?

The set of instructions we give the computer, telling it what to do with a set of data, is a *program*. Every program, regardless of how complex it is (that is, how complex an operation it instructs the computer to perform) is built up out of a few basic kinds of instructions.

Each instruction, also known as a *statement,* is given to the computer on a punched card just like the cards we punch data on. A complete set of these cards makes up the program we give the computer.

Each instruction, or statement, is a relatively simple way of telling the machine to do one thing. One kind of statement tells it to read a data value. Another kind tells the computer to perform some mathematical operation. Yet another kind has to do with the *flow of the program.* That is, an instruction of this type tells the computer which of two operations to do first, or whether to skip part of a program under certain conditions. Then there are statements which instruct the computer to print out a line of results. Finally, there are certain statements which merely give it the information it needs in order to carry out other instructions. For example, an instruction of this kind might tell the computer where to find the data values on a data card it has been given.

At its simplest, then, a working computer program could consist of no more than five simple instructions to the computer. One would tell the computer to read in some data, the second would tell it what form the data are in, the third would call for some computation, the fourth would tell the machine to write out its answer(s), and the fifth would tell it what form to put the answer(s) in.

There are two vital things to remember about these instructions to the computer. First they must be absolutely specific, covering every operation to be performed. For example, we do not tell the computer to find an *average* of a set of figures. Even something this elementary means nothing to a computer, because it is actually a combination of several separate steps. To find an average the computer must be instructed to read a figure, then read a second figure, then add the second figure to the first, then read a third figure and add it to the total of the first two, and so on. The computer must even be told when to stop adding, and then told, in a separate instruction, to do the necessary division.

The second point concerning these instructions to the computer is that if we forget to give the computer an instruction, or give it a vague instruction, it does not *guess* what we want, as a clerk might. Nor does it come and ask what we want done. Rather, the computer will simply stop working and indicate something is wrong with its instructions. Then it is up to us to find out whether we gave it a wrong instruction, or left out an instruction, or whatever.

PROGRAMMING LANGUAGE

These instructions to the computer are written in a programming language. As indicated earlier, a language is a set of words and symbols, together with certain rules governing the way these words and symbols are assembled in an instruction. The Fortran language we are studying here has been designed to be as similar as possible to the verbal and mathematical languages we are already familiar with. It uses the plus and minus signs to show subtraction and addition. It uses words like *write, read, do, if,* and *go to* in the instructions to the machine, and these words mean exactly what they mean in English. The only difference is that because of the way instructions are presented to the computer, all letters used are capitals: WRITE, READ, DO, and so on.

Different Programming Languages

There are several programming languages. The Fortran language is oriented toward mathematics, as the name itself suggests: it stands for *FORmula TRANslation.* Therefore the physicist or astronomer can use this language in working out the orbits of atomic particles or of planets, respectively, and at the same time this language is also admirably suited to the data processing and statistical procedures of the social sciences, where numbers represent such things as questionnaire responses, or census totals.

There are other programming languages as well. For example, one designed for business purposes is named COBOL, which stands for *COmmon Business Oriented Language*. This is useful for such things as handling the bookkeeping of a firm: for example, keeping track of great numbers of credit statements. The arithmetic involved is fairly simple, but many verbal items (names, inventory labels, addresses) must be kept track of and manipulated.

In addition, there are various other languages designed for various purposes. However, the fact that these other languages exist does not mean we are wasting our time with Fortran. For one thing, Fortran can handle all the numerical procedures of the social sciences, and with some special features, it can also handle verbal data, as in content analysis. Secondly, these other languages do not replace Fortran; they coexist with it. Thirdly, if we want to learn another programming language, knowing Fortran provides a big headstart. The difficult thing to master in programming is not the actual procedures or symbols used, but the concepts themselves. Therefore, if it is quite simple to go from one version of a computer language to another (say from Fortran II to Fortran IV) it is not too much more difficult to go from one language to another. We would already know what we want the computer to do: the *logic* of a program. Thus learning a new programming language would mean learning only a new set of grammatical rules and perhaps symbols, rather than having to master an entire new set of concepts.

Machine Language

The computer does not itself *understand* the instructions given it in the Fortran language, or in any other programming language. Rather, it *speaks*, as it were, a separate language of its own. This *machine language* is not in the form of words and numbers, as is the language we write our programs in. Rather, it is a series of coded impulses. Each program written in a language like Fortran must therefore be converted to the language the machine understands. This conversion is done in a separate part of the computer, which literally *translates* the language the programmer uses into the language the machine understands.

This translation process may seem an unnecessary step, but it has several advantages. One is that it lets us use a language like Fortran, which is much easier than the complicated language of the machine itself. Secondly, it lets us have several different programming languages, each of which can be translated, by its own separate translating unit, into the one language of the machine.

The program we write in Fortran, the one we can understand, may be called a *source* program. It is the *original,* or the *source* from which the computer gets its instructions. It is also also possible to get a program in its machine language form punched on cards. This *machine language program* is meaningless unless one has studied the internal workings of a computer. Therefore, at this point we will mention only two aspects of it that are important for us. One is that we want a program in this form *only* after the program is completely finished; that is, when no more changes are necessary in the program. Upon reaching this point, ask someone at the computing center how to get a machine language version of a program. Doing this will save time whenever the program is used thereafter, because in this form a program is understood directly by the computer, and therefore need not go through the translation procedure each time it runs. This can save considerable computer time, because translating a Fortran source program into machine language can take as long or longer than the calculations in some programs.

The other point in this connection is that a language like Fortran is useful a great many places, whereas different computers have different kinds of machine languages. Therefore, when moving from one place to another, be sure to take programs in the Fortran form.

INTERACTION AT THE LOCAL COMPUTING CENTER

As a new programmer moves farther into programming, he finds that he occasionally needs help or advice. For one thing, there is some variation in the way different computers operate, in their characteristics, and limitations. There is also variation in the way different computing centers set up the procedures for using the computer. For the beginning programmer this kind of variation should not present much of a problem, but as his programming becomes more advanced, he will begin finding out certain things about his particular computer, such as how large a number it can handle, how many numbers it can hold, whether certain features of the programming language can be used with it, whether any special features have been added to it, and so on. These things are learned by asking consultants at the computing center. But to repeat, while this kind of variation exists, it should present little problem for the social scientist who is just beginning with programming.

Also, in learning programming it is often useful to have expert help in such things as finding errors in programs, or keeping up with minor changes in a programming language. Usually a computing center will have some provision for giving outside programmers this kind of assistance. But to benefit from this assistance, we must be able to talk to the people at the computing center.

This is one of the real benefits of learning to program: being able to speak to the people on the best terms with computers. We can hardly expect these people to learn the language of every field, from library science to astrophysics, which deals with computers. So we must learn their language if we wish to talk to them. And like other people dedicated to a field, computer people seem for the most part happy to talk shop with us: *if* we speak their language.

Yet a note of caution should be included here. Many social scientists when first going to a computing center seem to sense a certain coolness toward them there, and this has been discouraging. In part this may be due to the fact that there is something of a subculture centering around computers, and like any subculture, this one may be a little skeptical of outsiders who seem to know so little about its language or its procedures. However, if this writer's experience is at all typical, the social scientist should find increasing tolerance, and even perhaps a welcome, as his programs become more complex and as his knowledge of programming and computers increases.

Furthermore, of course, as more social scientists learn to program, beginners should be increasingly able to find assistance right in their own departments. This would take much of the discomfort out of learning to program, not only because of the technical help thus available, but also because it would help minimize the psychological stress often present in the early stages of programming. Remember that the beginner is facing a number of strange ideas. If the people presenting these ideas are also strangers, and speaking an unfamiliar language, the stress is that much more marked. But if these new ideas are encountered among familiar surroundings, they seem much more manageable.

Also, having programmers right in one's own department means there are sympathetic *shoulders to cry on*. As odd as it may sound, this is a very important point, because often when hunting for a particularly obscure mistake it helps to do nothing more than talk for a moment to some other programmer. Only people who have gone through this experience realize the importance of sitting quietly while a friend or colleague releases his frustration in a few well chosen words.

THE TIME FACTOR

To speak of mistakes is to raise another important aspect of programming: the time it takes, and how this time affects the use of the computer.

It often happens that writing a program for a particular procedure takes longer than doing that procedure once by hand. The point of a program, however, is that from then on that computation is a matter of seconds or minutes, whereas if it is done by hand, there is the next one to be done by hand, and the next one, and so on.

Furthermore, the time required to write and polish up a program is not continuous time. Rather, a programmer might spend perhaps an hour (more or less) each day. He submits a program to the computer, gets the program back and corrects the errors that show up, gives the program back to the computer, corrects any new errors, and so on.

The period of time between submitting the program to the computer and getting it back is known as *turn-around time.* This may be anything from a minute to overnight or longer. But in general, programming usually involves a period of work, and then some waiting to see the results of that work. This is why it is said that programming takes more *calendar* time, whereas doing a series of calculations by hand takes more of our *personal* time. We might get a series of results a few days sooner if we did them by hand. But if we wait a few days to get those results from the computer, we have time to do other things. For example, doing the statistics for a particular research project might take 30 hours at a desk calculator, so we could get the results in three days, say. Doing the same thing on a computer might take eight days, but during those days perhaps only ten hours of *our* time would be involved.

This time factor must be kept in mind when planning to use a computer. The researcher must begin writing programs early enough so that the programs will be ready when needed; and this *lead time* must include a few extra days in case the computer is *down,* that is, being worked on.

However, this is not such a nuisance as it might sound. Remember that at the outset of a research project the researcher has decided what kind of data to get, what statistics to use, and so on. And these decisions indicate what kinds of programs will be needed.

Gathering, punching, and coding the data would probably take long enough so that there is plenty of time to get the programs written before the data are ready to go into the machine. And it is possible to do the programming while also doing these other things, because working on programs takes only part of each day.

With more experience, the beginner increasingly finds that for an earlier project he has already written one or more programs that can be used on a current project. Also, with more experience there is increasingly a feeling for how much lead time a particular program or set of programs will require. But at the start we might offer this tip. If the first major programming can be in connection with a project which has no real time limit, so much the better. If a project must be finished by a certain date, however, remember that the programming will take longer, in terms of days, than a beginner expects, simply because he does not realize how many *bugs* can crop up in a program.

But while requiring this foresight, the computer offers major compensations. One is that we probably put in less time overall on a project. With proper planning, the computer can handle many of the time-consuming clerical chores, eliminating the endless hours with a counter-sorter or a desk calculator. Also, we probably end up doing a better job, if only because we can try things that would have been impossible without a computer.

A CONCLUDING NOTE

In closing this discussion, remember that no book, and no programming course, can really teach programming. Like any language, programing language is something learned only by using it. So above all else, it is necessary to run programs and run more programs. Make errors, find and correct them, and go back for more. Indeed, it is often said that learning to program is mainly a matter of learning to find errors and correct them.

But while doing this (which can make a beginner feel for a time as though he were working for the computer, and not vice versa) never forget that the computer is merely part of a system. The machine itself is part of what is called the *hardware* in the system. Then there is the *soft-ware,* which includes such things as the programming language used on the machine. A central part of this total system is the programmer, who contributes the purpose and knowledge without which the other parts, as important as they may be, are meaningless.

Therefore, this text assumes that you, the reader, know what you want the computer to do. You know what kind of research projects you are interested in. You know how to acquire appropriate data, what data processing or statistical procedures to use, and how to interpret the results. If you know all that, then what we will try to do here is show you how to use a valuable tool to good advantage in doing these things.

Chapter Two

NUMBERS: INTEGER AND FLOATING POINT

The Fortran language has two main kinds of numbers. One kind, which has a decimal point and a decimal part, is used for such things as measuring, or doing arithmetic which can produce fractional parts. The decimal part can be zero, in which case the zero need not be present. This kind of number could look like any of these:

72.	−72.	72.0	−72.0
16.4	−16.4	.5	− .5
0.5	15.0	− 0.5	+ .8

(Plus sign is optional)

We call this kind of number *real*, or *floating point*. The term floating point refers to the fact that the computer moves, or *floats*, the decimal point around inside the computer. That is, the computer automatically keeps track of the position of the decimal point as it does a computation involving fractions or decimal values. All we do is show how many decimal places (if any) are in the data going into the computer, and then specify how many decimal places (if any) we want in the answer the computer gives us.

The other kind of number, used for such things as counting, or for labeling categories, is called *integer*. This is a whole number, a number without a decimal part, and it is written without a decimal point. These would be integer numbers:

$$2 \qquad 7 \qquad -139 \qquad +5136$$

(Plus sign is optional)

This kind of number is also known as *fixed point*, because the decimal point (although it does not physically appear) is always *thought of* as coming just after the right-most digit. It is

14

thought of as being *fixed* in that position, in other words, although it never actually appears there. Examples of numbers like this in everyday life would be telephone numbers, or the numbers on automobile license plates. Such numbers can be *thought of* as having a decimal point after them, but the decimal point never appears because fractions are never used.

TRUNCATION WITH INTEGERS

A *very* important thing to remember about these integer numbers is that if we try to do arithmetic with them, and end up with a fractional part, it will be *truncated;* that is, the fractional part will be simply dropped off. Therefore, if we use integers in dividing 8 by 5, the answer is not 1 3/5 or 1.6. The answer is 1. Consider these examples which use integer values (they are integer because no decimal points appear):

10/3 does not equal 3 1/3, but does equal 3
15/4 does not equal 3 3/4, but does equal 3
12/7 does not equal 1 5/7, but does equal 1
149/50 does not equal 2 49/50, but does equal 2

The fractional parts resulting from divisions like these will be ignored by the computer because the numbers involved are integers; that is, they have no decimal points. So if such divisions are desired, they must be done with decimal numbers (floating point numbers).

It is obvious from the above examples that *truncation* is not the same as *rounding off*. Truncation means the decimal part of a number is completely dropped. Even if the decimal part were only 1/1000 short of the next higher whole number, the decimal part would all be chopped off. Thus in arithmetic using integer numbers, the value 4.999 would not be rounded up to 5. Rather, the value would be treated as though it were simply 4.

This characteristic of integer numbers may seem pointless, but in advanced programming it has a number of valuable uses. For the moment, however, remember that integer numbers can be dangerous, because if we are not careful in using them, the truncation can lose information we actually want.

This is our first encounter with the fact that using a computer does not automatically protect us against *human* error. If we instruct a computer to use integer numbers, it will, even though we really *meant* for it to use decimal numbers. Such an error in instructing the computer would produce an error in the results because the computer executes *wrong* instructions just as faithfully as it does *right* ones—as long as the technical rules of the language are followed. The computer will divide 15 by 6 just as readily as it will divide 15.0 by 6.0, but the answer will be 2, rather than 2.5. So if we desired the latter operation, but inadvertently instructed the computer to do the former, by simply forgetting to include the necessary decimal points, the error is ours, and ours alone.

SIZE LIMITATIONS

For both integer numbers and decimal numbers there are size limitations. These limitations take two forms: A limit to the number of digits used in writing a number, and a limit to the magnitude, or size, of a number. This difference between the *number of digits* used to express a value and the *magnitude* of that value is equivalent to the difference between asking: *How many digits does it take to write the value?* and asking *How large is the value?* For example, the values 10000 and 99999 both use the same number of digits, but the magnitude of the second value is larger. By the same token, the value 10000 uses more digits, but is of a smaller magnitude, than 10^8.

The reason for limiting the size of numbers this way lies in the way numbers are represented in a computer. Most computers are *binary* devices, which means information is stored in them in a series of tiny *cores,* with each core working something like a tiny switch which can be either *on* or *off.* This is comparable to a light switch turned on or off. These two conditions are the reason for using the term *binary,* with the *bi* meaning *two.*

For each different item of information stored in the computer's memory, which is the entire set of these cores, there is a specific combination of these tiny *switches.* The items of information placed in this *core storage* need not be numbers, incidentally; they can also be characters making up verbal data, or they can be the instructions to the computer itself which make up the computer program.

A larger number requires more of these tiny cores to represent it. Therefore, given the practical limitations on the physical size of a computer (that is, a limit on how many of these cores can be built into a computer, since each of the cores takes a certain amount of space) the designers of a computer have a choice: They can allow the computer to handle larger numbers, but fewer of them, or they can limit it to smaller numbers (each taking fewer of these cores) which means the computer can handle relatively more numbers. So for each computer the maximum size of its numbers is a compromise designed into it by its producers. This compromise takes the form of deciding how many of these tiny cores (also called *bits*) are to be included in one set. Each set of bits is called a *location,* which can be used to store one item of data. Therefore, the fewer bits in each location, the smaller the number we can store in any one location, but the more locations and therefore the more numbers we can store in the computer.

The distinction between the number of digits used to write a value, and the magnitude of that value, is due to the fact that the computer can use some of the cores, or bits, in a location to represent an exponent. So in one location, we can use fewer bits for a base value, and use some or all of the remaining bits to represent a power to which that base number is raised. This obviously makes possible much larger values (even though the number of digits used in writing the base number is small) than if all the bits were used for digits in a number having no exponent. For example, 10^8 uses fewer digits, but is larger, than 1000.

The internal workings of the computer make up a highly complex subject, and a major reason for developing a language like Fortran in the first place is to free the user from worrying about these aspects of the computer if he does not choose to. So having shown why there is a physical basis for the limitations on size of numbers, let us merely offer some guidelines on how to limit the size of numbers.

Larger computers, logically enough, may permit us to work with larger values than smaller computers. But since some readers of this book may use a smaller computer, we will offer limits here which are both conservative and easy to remember:

1. *Number of digits:* Limit the number of digits in both integer values and in decimal values to seven. For decimal numbers this includes both the whole part of the number, and the decimal part, if any. In other words, in a floating point number the seven digits can all be to the left of the decimal point, like this:

1234567.

Or they can all be to the right of the decimal point, like this:

.1234567

Or they can be divided, with the decimal point somewhere in the middle, like this:

1234.567

2. *Magnitude of number, using exponents:* Limit a floating point value to approximately ten to the fortieth power (10^{40}). If this value is written out on a sheet of paper it consists of the digit 1 followed by 40 zeroes and then the decimal point. This would be a rather large number.

Limit an integer value to approximately two to the thirtieth power (2^{30}). Since this turns out to be something in the neighborhood of the largest value that can be written using the recommended seven digits (i.e. 9999999) it is probably simplest at first to think of limiting an integer value to something under 10,000,000, regardless of how the value is written.

On the surface, this limit seems to present something of a problem: Population figures would logically be integer numbers, since people do not have fractional parts. But the population of one urban area could be larger than what we are taking here as the largest permissible integer value. As we will see later, in such a case it is possible to treat the figures as floating point, simply adding decimal points after them, thereby benefitting from the much larger values possible in the floating point form.

There is a comparable limitation on how small a floating point number can be. An integer number, of course, since it has no decimal part, can be no smaller than one. But because of their decimal parts, floating point numbers can represent very small values. Using the exponent again, but this time with a minus sign to indicate a number smaller than 1, the limit here might conservatively be placed at 10^{-40}. This would be written out as a decimal point followed by 39 zeroes and finally a 1.

The size limitations discussed here refer to *absolute* values. That is, an integer number may have seven digits, but this may represent either a positive or negative value. Similarly, a floating point number may be as large as 10^{40} or as small as 10^{-40}, and in either event can be either positive or negative. For any positive number, a plus sign is optional. But if a number is negative a minus sign must be used, regardless of whether the number is going into the computer as data or is coming out as an answer, or is written in the computer program itself.

It is important to remember these limitations on the size of numbers, because they apply not only to data values we give the computer, but also to the size of values created at steps during a calculation. For example, if we multiply two values, their product must also be stored in one of the locations in the computer's storage area, and is therefore also subject to the size limitations imposed by the physical limits of the computer. So it is quite possible that while the two original values might be under the size limits, their product might be too large to be stored in a location. Note, however, that if arithmetic with integer numbers might produce intermediate or final results too large for the limits on integer numbers, we can again use the device of converting them to floating point and proceed with the arithmetic, benefitting from the greater limits of the floating point form.

A computer may tell us when we exceed its limits on the size of numbers, but it is also possible that the computer will try to work with numbers that are too large or too small, in which case the results will be meaningless. The dangerous thing in the latter case is that we may not know these results are *garbage,* because we did not realize our values were too large or too small. So be very careful to keep values well within the recommended limits for your computer.

Social scientists would not usually work with numbers smaller than 10^{-40}. Too large numbers, on the other hand, can be a real danger for us. For example, the factorials of large numbers can quickly exceed the allowable size. Since social scientists use figures in the hundreds of thousands or higher (for example, population or voting figures) there is a danger of creating too large values in the course of certain statistics.

Fortran has a special kind of number designed to deal with large values, called an *E-number*, with the E standing for *exponent*. However, at the early stages of your programming you will probably not be concerned about extremely large numbers, and since E numbers are not vital for your learning, they can be left for later until you are skilled enough as a programmer to be interested in perhaps using the computer for large scale projects.

Some computers allow us to work with larger values than the ones suggested here. Others limit us to smaller values. But by taking the middle course recommended here, a programmer can adjust either upward or downward to the limits of a given computer without too much trouble. And remember that to find out about the limits of any particular computer, simply ask someone at that computing center.

COMMAS NOT USED

Another thing to keep in mind about numbers used on the computer is that commas are not used in writing them. Therefore, for integer numbers we would write:

1234567

We would not write:

1,234,567

Similarly, for floating point numbers we would write:

1234567.

We would not write:

1,234,567.

APPROXIMATING FRACTIONS

Finally, we should note that as far as fractions are concerned, some values can only be approximated by the computer. For example, the fraction 1/3 will be treated in floating point form as:

.3333333

It will be only an approximation of the value of 1/3. This should not be a real problem for social scientists; the reason for mentioning it here is that it can be startling at first to multiply 1./3. by 3. and not get 1.

EXAMPLES

1. The following are valid integer numbers:

0	18
—61	+2
5176	(Plus sign is optional)

2. The following are *not* valid integer numbers:

16,876   (has a comma)
87.3   (has a decimal point)
93849578473   (too large)

3. The following are valid floating point (decimal) numbers:

0.5	1.0
14.0	.8
176.03	0.0
1897.006	+73.
—82.6	(Plus sign is optional)

4. The following are *not* valid floating point (decimal) numbers:

83,004.8   (has a comma)
582   (has no decimal point)
894.8^{648} (too large)
384738509.3   (too many digits)

EXERCISES

See exercises 1–14 in Chapter Two of the accompanying *Workbook in Basic Computer Programming* (*Fortran IV*). It is strongly recommended that you work out this set of exercises, and all others referred to in this text, to make sure that you understand each point before going on to the next one.

Chapter Three

VARIABLES AND CONSTANTS

Each of the kinds of values discussed in the last chapter (integer and floating point) can be either a *constant* or a *variable.*

A constant is a value written out in its numerical form. Because it is written as a number, the value of this notation is the same, or *constant,* everywhere it appears in a program. For example, the number 2 has the same value everywhere it appears: therefore 2 is a constant. Because it has no decimal point, this is an integer constant. A floating point constant would look like this:

2.0   or   2.

The idea of variables is somewhat more complex, but we are helped by the fact that the term *variable* in programming means about what it does in social science, with a notable addition. Recall that in social science, when we speak of a *variable* we literally mean something that can vary. For example, if we have a group of people, *amount of education* can be a variable because the amount of education can vary from person to person. In studying a group of cities, we can take population size as a variable because the size of the population can vary from city to city.

In programming, the term *variable* includes this kind of thing. However, it also includes things the social scientist would not call variables: things like the very size of a group or sample we are studying. This is because when we go to the trouble of writing a program, we usually want to use it with more than one group; that is, with more than one set of data. To illustrate why this also means taking something like group size as a *variable,* say we write a program to find the average age of a group of 100 people. For this one group, its size is fixed. But if we want to use this same program to find the average age of another group, this one having 250 members, we find that as far as the computer program is concerned, *size of group* (or as we would say, *size of sample*) is also something which varies. Therefore, to use the program with different groups we also treat group size, or sample size, as a variable.

The same also is true of such values as average, or standard deviation. These would be fixed for one group on a given variable (as in average age of the members of a group) but would vary from group to group. Therefore to the computer these are also variables.

NAMING VARIABLES

The meaning of the term *variable* will become clearer as we work with different variables here. But before we can work with a variable, we must have a way of referring to it in a program. For this we use what we call a *variable name.*

To expain what a variable name is, and what it does, let us begin with a pair of questions. First, since even a small computer has many, many storage locations in its memory, if we give it an item of data, how does it know which location to put this figure in? Furthermore, if we later ask it to do something with this piece of data, how does the computer remember which of those many locations to go back to, to get just that particular item?

The answer to both questions is that we write a variable name in the program. This is any name we make up (according to certain rules we will see in a moment). When a variable name appears in a program, the computer goes to its storage area and assigns that name to one of the locations there. This name is then the *label* identifying that location for this particular running of the program. When we assign a value to that name in the program, the value is stored in the location bearing that name.

We will see in the next few chapters how we actually assign a value to a variable name; that is, how we arrange to have a particular value stored in the location to which the computer has assigned a particular name. Here the important thing to remember is that once a value has been stored in a particular location, then we can use this value in a program simply by writing the name of that location in an instruction. If we want the computer to use a particular value in some calculation, we write the name of the location containing that value, and the computer goes to that location, *pulls out* the value stored there, and does with that value what we have requested. So the variable name is the device which allows us to store a value in the computer in such a way that at any time in a program we can direct the computer back to just that value.

At the same time, a variable name also establishes a relationship between a variable we are studying and one or more of the locations in the computer's storage area. To illustrate this, say we have the number 24 which represents the age of a person in a survey we have done. In a program we write the variable name AGE. The computer then assigns this name to one of its storage locations. Next, by means we will study shortly, we tell the computer to place this value 24 in the location to which it has assigned the name AGE. Thus we can say that the location named AGE *represents* the variable *age* because we have placed a value for that variable in that location. Similarly, we can say the value of the variable name AGE is the value stored in the location the computer knows by that name; it is the contents of the particular storage location identified by that name. Finally, we can say the name AGE also *represents* the variable *age* because we have stored a value for the variable *age* in the location known as AGE.

If we draw a picture of what we are saying, it might look something like Figure 1.

The box in Figure 1 represents a storage location in which we have placed the value 24, meaning 24 years of age. Therefore, we can say that this storage location represents the variable *age*. The name AGE above the box is the variable name assigned to this storage location. The number 24 in the box can be viewed in several ways. It is the value for this variable (that is, a value of 24 for the variable *age*) because it is stored in the location *representing* this variable. It is also the value of the variable name AGE, because it is the value in the location to which the computer has assigned this name. Therefore, in programming terms we would say: *AGE has the value 24*, or *AGE is 24*.

AGE

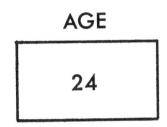

Figure 1. The storage location named AGE.

When we want to perform some operation using the value in this location (that is, a calculation involving this value of the variable *age*) we write the name AGE in the program. This tells the computer to go to this location, take the value stored there, and treat that value as we direct. For example, if we wanted the square of the value stored in the location known as AGE, we tell the computer: *Square AGE*. The computer obviously does not square the name AGE; it squares whatever value is stored, at that point in the program, in the location known as AGE. So here, if we told the computer, *square AGE*, it would go to the location it has labeled AGE, and would square the value 24 that it found there. The result, 576, would then be treated according to our further instructions.

When we use the name of a location this way, we say we are *symbolically manipulating* that name. This means we are using the name, in a sense, as a symbol which *stands for* the value in the location bearing that name. So when we tell the computer to *do something with a name* (as in saying *square AGE*) we are manipulating a symbol as a way of telling the computer to perform the indicated operation with the value that symbol represents (i.e. do that operation with the value in the location bearing that name).

As another example, we can tell the computer: *Add A and B*. Here the computer would go to the location named A, and also to the location named B, and would add the values it finds in those locations.

Basically, this is the same thing we do in working out an arithmetic formula by hand. If we see a notation like this:

$A + B$

we know there must be some value for A and some value for B, and that this notation tells us to add these two values. The only difference when using a computer is that the values for A and B would be in storage locations bearing these two names, rather than in our head, or on a sheet of paper.

The way the computer assigns names to locations is part of the inner workings of the computer. Here there are only several aspects of it that we need mention. One is that if we give the computer a value to be stored under the name AGE, it will store that value in the location carrying that name, not in some other location labeled INCOME, or in some location with no label (name) at all.

Secondly, once a name has been assigned to a location, that name remains with that location throughout the entire running of a program. Also, at the end of a program, all the labels (names) are taken off the storage locations, so that the next program which comes into the computer can assign its names to those same locations.

Finally, only one number can be stored at a time in any one location in the computer's storage area. If there is a number in a storage location, and if another number is then placed in that same location, the new number wipes out or replaces the previous number, so that this new number then becomes the value in that location. The reason for this is that if we could store two values at one time in one location, then when we used the name of that location in a program the computer would not know which of the two values to produce.

SIZE OF CONSTANTS AND VARIABLES

Since a constant is any value written out as an actual number, the rules for writing constants are the same as the rules for numbers discussed in the last chapter. Briefly, a constant may be either integer or with a decimal point. If it is negative, it will be preceded by a minus sign. If it is positive, the plus sign is optional. Also, no commas are used in writing constants.

The limits on the size of constants are the same as the limits on size of numbers described earlier. These limits apply both to the number of digits used in writing a constant, and to the magnitude of the constant. Remember that integer constants are subject to the limits on integer numbers, and floating point constants are subject to the limits on floating point numbers.

The same rules apply to the values assigned to variable names. That is, a variable name may have any value which could, if we chose, be legitimately written as a constant. For example, the value assigned to a variable name may be either integer or floating point. The value may be either positive or negative. If floating point, the value may be as large, but no larger, than the largest floating point constant we could write, and so on. (Remember that when we speak of the value assigned to a variable name, we mean the value placed in the location bearing that name.)

FORMING VARIABLE NAMES

A variable name may be from one to six letters or numbers long. However, each name must begin with a letter, although numbers can appear anywhere else in the name. F68 is an acceptable variable name; 68F is not, because it does not start with a letter. Where letters are used they are capital letters, because the computer has no provision for dealing with lower case letters in programming statements.

The reason each name must begin with a letter is that the computer looks at the first letter of a name to see whether an integer or a decimal value will be associated with this name. An integer variable name will have an integer value assigned to it: that is, a value without a decimal point. Similarly, the value associated with a floating point variable name will have a decimal point, and may have a decimal part.

To show that it is integer, a variable name begins with one of these six letters:

I   J   K   L   M   N

A floating point or decimal variable name begins with any other letter.

In short, the first letter of a variable name tells the computer the same thing that the presence or absence of a decimal point tells it when it looks at a constant value. And the computer must know whether a certain value (either variable or constant) is integer or floating point, because it treats the two kinds of values differently, and in different parts of the machine.

The rule that only letters and numbers may be used in variable name means that both integer and decimal names may *not* use such special characters as the period . or the parentheses ( ) or the percent sign % or the slash /. It also means that this is one of the few places where spaces are not permitted. A space is considered here as a special character, and is ruled out because if a space appeared in a variable name, the computer would see it as a space separating two variable names.

EXAMPLES

1. The following are valid names for *integer* variables:

M	NCASE
K	J2TEMP
NDATA3	ISTOR3
NARRAY	L1984

2. The following are *not* valid names for *integer* variables:

POP%	(Uses wrong character: could be written POPPCT)
INTERNAL	(Too long)
6MON	(Does not begin with a letter: could be written MON6)
TEMP	(Begins with wrong letter: T is a floating point letter. Could be written NTEMP to be integer)
MIN/NO	(Uses wrong character, the /)
MIN NO	(Spaces not allowed)

3. The following are valid names for *floating point* variables:

A	DATRAY
X	FNAME
DATAI	CASENO
ARRAY	TOT4

4. The following are *not* valid names for *floating point* variables:

VAL+F	(Uses wrong character, the +)
AMOUNTS	(Too long)
7DAYS	(Does not begin with a letter: could be written DAYS7)
NONTEM	(Begins with wrong letter: N is an integer letter. Could be written FNONTM to be floating point)
XVAL.	(Uses wrong character, the .)
PCT VAL	(Space is not allowed)

MODE

In talking about integer and floating point values, programmers may use the term *mode*, which is another way of saying *the nature of* a particular constant or variable. Both constants and variable values (that is, values assigned to variable names) which have decimal points and decimal parts are said to be in the floating point mode. While the value assigned to a variable name can vary, whereas a constant can not, both kinds of values share the fact that they are floating point values. This is their mode: the floating point mode. Thus we can speak of floating point variables and floating point constants.

Similarly, integer constants and integer variables have in common the fact that they are both in the integer mode. While one can vary and one can not, they both represent values having no decimal points, so they are both in the integer mode.

What we said about truncation with integer values also applies to the values assigned to integer variable names. For example, if we asked the computer to store the value 7.5 in the location having the integer name NVAR, the fractional part of the value would be dropped and the value actually stored in NVAR would be 7.

Table I sums up the relationship between decimal (or floating point) kinds of values and integer kinds of values, as well as the distinction between values which are constant and values which are variable. In the top part of the table are constants; in the bottom part of the table are variable names. *All* items in the left column (top and bottom) are integers; all items in the right column are floating point.

CHOOSING NAMES FOR VARIABLES

When variable names are used, the computer is concerned with only two things. One is whether the name is *legitimate.* That is, does the name consist of one to six letters (but beginning with a letter) and is it free of such characters as a blank space, a period, or a slash?

The other thing the computer is interested in is the first letter of the variable name. Since each name must begin with a letter, the computer looks at only this first letter to see whether that name refers to a floating point variable or to an integer variable. The other characters in the name (as long as they are *legal,* which is to say, as long as they are letters or numbers) are of no concern to the computer.

Therefore, as long as the first letter of a name properly shows whether it refers to an integer or to a floating point variable,

TABLE I
INTEGER AND FLOATING POINT MODES

Integer Mode		Floating Point Mode
	Constants	
7		7.2
6		6.0
12		12.
0		.001
	Variables	
NX		X
KASE		CASE
MAX		FMAX
JYSNO		SYSNO

and as long as the rest of the name is made up of letters or numbers, we can use any name we want to represent a variable.

In this choosing of a name, there are several things .to keep in mind. One is that when the letter X appears in a variable name, this does *not* mean multiplication. That is, the letters FXY do not mean *F times Y*, as they might in algebra. They merely mean the name FXY has been used as a variable name.

Another thing to remember is that every separate combination of letters or numbers is a different name. That is, FXY could be a name for one variable. The name FYX would not refer to that same variable, but would be an entirely new name for some other variable.

Given this freedom, how do we decide which name should be used to represent which variable? We could, of course, simply fall back on the old standbys X, Y, or Z. For integer variables we could use the names J, K, or N.

However, there are several reasons for being more sophisticated in choosing names for variables. One is the fact that if properly chosen, each name that appears in a program can indicate which variable it refers to. For example, if a variable is the income for a person in a survey, it makes sense to refer to this variable by the name FINCOM. Here we precede the name with the floating point letter F, to have a floating point variable name, because usually with income figures we do things like averages, which may produce fractions. Furthermore, if we used an integer name like INCOME, it would rule out the possibility of expressing cents as decimal places.

Another example of a name that shows what it refers to is the name NCASES to refer to the number of cases in a sample. The number of cases, of course, is a *counting* kind of value, since we can not have fractions of cases. Therefore it is logically expressed as an integer. But we may want to do floating point arithmetic with the value, as in finding the average income or education of members of a sample. Since this means dividing by the number of cases, it might produce a remainder. And in order not to lose this remainder through truncation, we could use a floating point name for this value, a name like FNCASE.

Giving each variable a name showing what that name represents offers several advantages. It helps us keep our variables straight as we get more and more variables in a program. Also, it refreshes our memory if we go back to modify or improve a program months or years after it was written.

Furthermore, variable names can show what each of the various steps in a program is doing. For example, if one part of a program adds up a list of figures, we can refer to the resulting total as just that: TOTAL, or SUM. If we are doing one of the statistics which uses a sum of squares, we could refer to this value as SUMSQ. Similarly, an intermediate value produced during the course of a statistic could be SUBTOT.

MEANING OF VALUES

A final note to keep in mind in connection with the numbers and names used in programming is this: The computer assigns no *meaning* to the number we give it to store in a location to which a name has been assigned. The name, as far as the computer is concerned, is merely a label for a storage location, and the value going into that location is merely a value. If we use the name FINCOM in a program (suggesting an income figure will be stored in that location) but then give the computer a figure representing years of education to store in that location, the computer will place that value in that location without the slightest question.

In short, the computer takes the figures we give it and does with those figures exactly what we ask. If so instructed, it will dutifully add one number to another, without knowing, or caring (or even wondering) whether it is adding dollars, or years, or pencils, or whatever. If we give it one figure representing dollars, and another figure representing the number of lamp posts on a city block and instruct it to multiply these two figures, it will do so. It is not up to the computer to say what the answer represents: whether it is the total cost of the lamp posts, or the number of dollars visible on a cloudy night, or the number of drunks with holes in their pockets, or anything else. So whatever *meaning* may be attached to the numbers going into the computer, this is meaning for the programmer alone. It is up to him to tell the computer how to handle these numbers in a way that makes sense, in view of their meaning for the programmer.

EXERCISES

See exercises 1–12 in Chapter Three of the *Workbook*.

Chapter Four

INPUT

In the work of social science, a computer program is usually a set of instructions telling the computer to perform one or more operations on a set of data. But before the computer can perform an operation, the figures making up the data must somehow be taken into the storage locations inside the computer. Usually, therefore, a program includes a set of instructions telling the computer to *read* certain data values, and telling it also where to find these values, and what form they are in.

Getting (or *reading*) data values into the computer is called the *input* process. We will devote a great deal of time to this, because input is one of the most vital, and yet most difficult, aspects of programming. Indeed, it is often suggested that most programming errors are involved either in getting data into the computer, or in getting figures back out (the *output* process discussed in the next chapter). Therefore, the beginning programmer can avoid many problems later by taking the time to thoroughly understand how input is handled. Remember that even the finest program in all other regards is useless, even dangerous (because its results can be misleading) if the computer does not have the right data at the right time.

For the sake of simplicity here, we will limit ourselves to input using data punched on cards. While it is also possible to take data from other sources, such as magnetic tapes or disks, the beginning social science programmer is probably more familiar with the way data appear on cards, so our discussion should be most meaningful if it is based on this form.

In simplest terms, in reading data the computer *takes* a data value from a punched card and places this value in a storage location. Actually, of course, the word *take* is figurative, be-

35

cause the data values on a punched card are represented by holes punched in certain positions, and after the computer has finished reading data from a card, the holes are still there. What actually happens is that the computer places in a storage location a value *equal* to the value indicated by the hole(s) punched in a card.

The mechanics of this operation are again part of the complex inner workings of the computer, and again we need not worry about this because we have a language like Fortran. For our purposes, recognize merely that if we handle the programming statements properly in telling the computer to read data, the effect is that a data value from a card is placed in one of the computer's storage locations where it is then available for whatever operation we want to perform on it.

In the last chapter we said that when we write a variable name in a program, the computer assigns that name to a storage location. We also said that when we assign a value to that variable name, that value is actually stored in the location bearing that name.

One way of getting a data value into a location is by having the computer read that value into the desired location. This means the input process must accomplish two things: It must get a data value into the computer (that is, into one of the storage locations) and it must get the value which is to be assigned to a particular variable name into the location bearing *that* name.

PARTS OF THE INPUT PROCESS

To accomplish this, the input process actually consists of three parts:

1. A READ statement, which:
   a. Instructs the computer to read one or more data values, and
   b. Shows which value is to be assigned to which variable name. In effect, this means telling the computer which location to put a particular value in.

2. The computer must be told where to find the data values. This is done by including in the READ statement a reference to some data input device.
3. The computer must be told what form the data are in: how many columns each data item takes on a data card, for example. This is done by including in the READ statement a reference to some other instruction in the program which gives this information: a FORMAT statement.

Since the READ statement is the core of this process, the statement which actually causes it to happen, we will begin with this statement.

READING INTEGER DATA

Integer and floating point numbers are handled in slightly different ways as they are read into the computer. Since the lack of a decimal point makes integer numbers somewhat simpler to deal with, we will start with them.

To instruct the computer to read a data value, we use what we call a *READ statement*. This statement begins with the word READ, followed by a variable name. It is this variable name that tells the computer where to place, or store, the data value it reads; that is, the data value is to be placed in the location bearing this variable name.

For example, say we want the computer to read a data value from a punched card, and assign that value to the name NVAR. To accomplish this, we literally tell the computer:

READ NVAR

This instruction tells the computer several things. First of all, it tells the computer that NVAR is a variable name, because one rule of the programming language is that a word appearing after the word READ is taken as a variable name. The fact that NVAR begins with N tells the computer that this is an integer variable name; that an integer value will be assigned to this name. Therefore, the computer assigns this name to a storage location in that part of the computer devoted to integer values.

Then, because of the word READ, the computer reads, from the punched card we have given it, a value and places this value in the location now bearing the name NVAR. Because this is an integer value, the computer recognizes that no decimal point will appear with the data value either on the card, or as it is placed in its storage location.

Therefore, the effect of this instruction:

READ NVAR

is to assign to the name NVAR (i.e. place in the location bearing the name NVAR) whatever value the computer finds on the punched card. This is the value NVAR will have in this particular running of the program (or until we do something to change that value).

To illustrate, say we give the computer a data card having the value 5 punched on it, and also give the computer this instruction:

READ NVAR

The result of this combination of data card and READ statement is that the computer would place the value 5 in the location bearing the name NVAR (which also means that the value 5 has been assigned to the name NVAR).

Reading Several Values

The computer can also read two or more data values from one data card. For the time being, to simplify our introduction to READ statements, we will assume that one READ statement reads the data from one punched card. Each value the computer reads must be stored in a location known by a separate variable name. Therefore, when a READ statement is reading several data values from a card, there must be one name in the READ statement for each value read from that card.

When the computer reads two or more data values from one data card, it goes from left to right, just as we read, and it also takes the variable names in the READ statement from left to right.

So the first or left-most value on a data card is assigned to the first or left-most variable name in a READ statement reading that card. The second value on the data card goes with the second variable name in the READ statement, and so on.

For example, say we have this READ statement:

READ NVAR1, NVAR2

This tells the computer to read from a data card two values. Both are to be considered integer; the first is to be placed in the location known as NVAR1 and the second in the location known as NVAR2.

Now say we give the computer a data card with the values 5 and 9 punched on it, like this:

5　　9

We instruct the computer:

READ NVAR1, NVAR2

The computer will read from that data card the value 5, which appears first (farthest to the left) on the card. This value will be assigned to the variable name NVAR1, because this name appears first in the READ statement. From then on, until we do something to change it, NVAR1 will have the value 5. Next the computer will read the figure 9 from that same data card, and will assign this value to NVAR2.

Punctuation and Spacing

When two or more variable names follow the word READ, these names are separated by commas. A comma is not used after the last name, however. This is part of a general rule that an instruction to the computer never ends with a comma or with a period. As we will see later, the only punctuation character which can end an instruction is a right parenthesis.

Related to punctuation is the question of blank spaces. In the list of variable names following the word READ, spaces may appear anywhere except within the variable names themselves.

The following READ statements would all be acceptable:

READ NVAR1,   NVAR2

READ NVAR1,NVAR2

READ   NVAR1   ,   NVAR2

The computer is so generous in its rules on blank spaces that it is much easier to learn those few cases (as in variable names) where spaces are not permitted, than to mention every place they can be used. So in the absence of words to the contrary, use spaces wherever you feel they would improve the neatness and readability of your instructions to the computer. This is with *your* reading in mind. You will be reading each program many times as you write it and hunt for errors in it, so anything which makes it easier on your eyes is to your benefit.

Matching Names and Data Values

We said earlier that when a READ statement is reading two or more values from a single data card, there must be one variable name in the READ statement for each data value to be read from that data card. This means that if there are more values on the data card than there are variable names in the READ statement, then some of those values will not be read from that card. The values omitted would be those farthest to the right on the card, since they are the last to be read.

To illustrate, consider this READ statement:

READ N, L, K, NF

Say that for this READ statement we give the computer a data card with these six data values on it:

3   7   5   8   4   2

Here only the first four values would be read into the computer. N would be given the value 3, L would become equal to 7, K would be 5, and NF would equal 8. The last (right-most) two values on the card, 4 and 2, would be ignored because there are no variable names in the READ statement to which they can be assigned.

To put this another way, these last two values would not be brought into the computer because the computer has not been given the variable names it needs as the labels for storage locations for these two values. Without these names, the computer can not designate storage locations for these values, and with no place to put the two values, the computer ignores them.

On the other hand, if a READ statement has *more* variable names than there are data values on a card the computer is reading, the computer will read zeroes until it has made up enough data values. For example, say we again give the computer this READ statement:

READ N, L, K, NF

Now, however, we give it a card containing only the data values 3 and 7, like this:

3   7

In this case the last two variable names, K and NF, would both be given the value 0. This is because the computer would continue reading columns on the data card until it had provided a value for each of the variable names in the READ statement.

Remember that each of the variable names in the READ statement is taken by the computer as an indication that it must assign that label to some storage location. Having done this, it then looks for some data value to store in each named location. But since the last columns it would read on the data card would in this example be blank, the last two variable names would be set equal to zero. That is, the value of zero would be stored in the last two named storage locations. The reason, a point to remember, is that *the computer reads blank data columns as zeroes.*

Placing of Data Cards

One confusing part of the READ process for a beginning programmer has to do with the physical placing of a READ statement and the data card supplying the value(s) for that READ statement. Very often, beginners assume that the logical place for a data card is right after the READ statement reading from that data card. This is *not* the case, however.

We will show later how data cards and the cards containing the statements in the program (including READ statements) are arranged as they are presented to the computer. Here we can say briefly that we give all the statements in a program to the computer in one package. Then after this package we put the data cards in a *separate* package.

When a computer gets a program, basically what it does is store all the statements in the program in a storage area in the computer. Then it begins *executing* (that is, obeying) these statements, or instructions, one by one. When it gets to a READ statement, the computer then turns to the package of data cards, and reads from a card there.

Reading Several Cards

Since we are saying here that one READ statement reads values from one data card, this means that for each READ statement in a program we must give the computer a data card to be read. When there are two or more cards to be read, the computer matches them with the READ statements in a program by moving in sequence. That is, the first READ statement in a program reads data from the first card in the package of data cards which follow the program. For the second READ statement in a program, the data is read from the second data card in the package, and so on.

If we give the computer too few data cards, so that it does *not* find a data card for each READ statement to be executed, it will stop a program. For example, if we have four READ statements in a program, but give the computer only three data cards for that program, the computer will read the first three data cards, but when it comes to the fourth READ statement, it would find no more data cards. In this situation the computer would have no way of knowing whether we gave it too many READ statements, or too few data cards. And because of this uncertainty, it would simply stop the program.

This is an important point, because frequently a program will simply stop, with no indication as to why. In this event, the first place to look is at the data cards, to make sure that for each READ statement to be executed in a program there is a data card to be read.

The opposite kind of error is giving the computer too many data cards; that is, more data cards than there are READ statements in the program. In this event the program will not stop; it will simply ignore the extra data cards. For example, say we give the computer a program which contains three READ statements, but give it four data cards for the program. The computer would read the data values from the first three cards, but it would ignore the fourth (last) data card, because there is no READ statement to read the data from that card.

The point here is not to assume that simply because we have given the computer a data card for a program, the data on that card will automatically get into the computer. Data will be read from a data card *only* if there is a READ statement to be executed for that card.

Matching Data Cards and READ Statements

In sum, the computer will not read data properly unless the data values to be read are precisely matched with the READ statements, both in terms of number of values on a single card, and the number of data cards themselves. If there are *fewer data values* on a card than there are variable names in the READ statement for that card, the computer will read zeroes to get the required number of values; in contrast, if there are *fewer data cards* than there are READ statements in a program, the computer will stop the program (in this event it can not again read zeroes, because there would not be enough cards). On the other hand, if there are *more* data values on a card than there are variable names in the READ statement for that card, the computer will ignore the last value(s), just as it will ignore the last card(s) if there are more data cards than there are READ statements in a program.

EXAMPLES

1. Values appearing in this order on a data card:
      4   16   17   18   2
   READ statement:
   READ NED1, NED2, NED3, NED4, NED5
   This combination of data card and READ statement would assign these values to the respective variable names:
   NED1 = 4   NED2 = 16
   NED3 = 17   NED4 = 18
   NED5 = 2

2. Values appearing on a data card:
      16   5   1   7   8   9
   READ statement:
   READ NDATA1, NDATA2, NDATA3, NDATA4
   This combination of data card and READ statement would assign these values to the respective variable names:
   NDATA1 = 16   NDATA2 = 5
   NDATA3 = 1   NDATA4 = 7
   Note that the last two data values on the card would not be assigned to any variable name, and therefore would be ignored by the computer.

3. Values appearing on a data card:
      2   4   5
   READ statement:
   READ NRESA, NRESB, NRESC, NRESD, NRESE
   This combination of data card and READ statement would assign these values to the respective variable names:
   NRESA = 2   NRESB = 4
   NRESC = 5   NRESD = 0
   NRESE = 0
   Note that the computer, in trying to find data values to assign to the last two variable names, would read blank columns on the data card, and therefore would supply the value 0 for the last two names.

4. Values appearing on *two* data cards:

| 1 | 7 | 3 | 2 | (card 1) |
| 4 | 5 | 0 | 1 | (card 2) |

READ statements:

READ NA, NB, NC, ND

READ NE, NF, NG, NH

Assuming the first READ statement reads the first data card and the second READ statement reads the second data card, this combination of data cards and READ statements would assign these values to the respective variable names:

NA = 1	NB = 7
NC = 3	ND = 2
NE = 4	NF = 5
NG = 0	NH = 1

READING FLOATING POINT DATA

The READ statement operates exactly the same for floating point variables as for integer variables, except that the decimal point in floating point numbers means the variable names appearing in the READ statement will be floating point names. This is determined by the first letter of each name. For example:

READ VAR1, VAR2

Since V is a *floating point letter*, this instruction would tell the computer to read two floating point data values, and assign the first of these values to VAR1 and the second to VAR2.

EXAMPLES

5. Values appearing on a data card:

| 4.0 | 15.6 | 28.9 | 17.2 | 8.5 | 17.8 |

READ statement:

READ SCOR1, SCOR2, SCOR3, SCOR4, SC5, SC6

This combination of data card and READ statement would assign these values to the respective variable names:

SCOR1 = 4.0	SCOR2 = 15.6
SCOR3 = 28.9	SCOR4 = 17.2
SC5 = 8.5	SC6 = 17.8

6. Values appearing on a data card:

    24.   67.   78.   58.   15.   90.

READ statement:

    READ DATA1, DATA2, DATA3, DATA4

This combination of data card and READ statement would assign these values to the respective variable names:

DATA1 = 24.	DATA2 = 67.
DATA3 = 78.	DATA4 = 58.

Note that the last two data values would not be assigned to any variable name and therefore would be ignored by the computer.

7. Values appearing on two data cards:

    4.0   3.0   6.0

    2.0   5.0   7.0

READ statements:

    READ RESA, RESB, RESC

    READ RESE, RESF, RESG

This combination of data cards and READ statements would assign these values to the respective variable names:

RESA = 4.	RESE = 2.
RESB = 3.	RESF = 5.
RESC = 6.	RESG = 7.

8. Values appearing on a data card:

    12.0   16.5   5.8

READ statement:

    READ RESA, RESB, RESC, RESD, RESE

This combination of data card and READ statement would assign these values to the respective variable names:

RESA = 12.0	RESB = 16.5
RESC = 5.8	RESD = 0.
RESE = 0.	

The last two variable names would end up with the value of zero because there were no data values to be assigned to them.

EXERCISES

See exercises 1–8 in Chapter Four of the *Workbook*.

WHERE TO FIND THE DATA

In its simplest form, then, the statement or instruction which tells the computer to read data looks like this:

READ A, B, C   (for floating point data)
READ NA, NB, NC   (for integer data)

A READ statement consists of the word READ and a list of one or more variable names. This list of names is called just that: a *list*. If there is a reference to the *list of a READ statement,* or *READ name list,* or simply *READ list,* this means the one or more variable names in a READ statement. For the first READ statement immediately above, the *list* would consist of the variable names A, B, and C. The *list* for the second READ statement would be NA, NB, and NC.

In this simple form, however, the READ statement does not tell the computer everything it must know to read a set of data. The computer must be told where to find the data. Also, it must be told whether each value on a data card takes one or two or three columns, whether there are blanks between the various numbers, and so on.

The first of these points, *where* to read the data, is handled by expanding the READ statement to this form:

READ (5,   ) A, B, C
READ (5,   ) NA, NB, NC

We add a pair of parentheses after the word READ, and in these parentheses we place the number 5. The 5 added to each READ statement tells the computer, in effect: Find the data item(s) you are to read on Input Device Number 5.

This reference to Input Device Number 5 requires a word of explanation. There is a physical limit to how fast computers can read punched data cards. Therefore, to save computer time, the instructions in a computer program itself, together with the associated data items, can be read from their original punched cards on to magnetic tape in some auxiliary reading device in the computing center. Then this tape is mounted on a tape drive, from which the computer reads the program instructions and the data much more rapidly than it could from the original punched cards. A number of programs and their associated data can be stored on one tape, so that this tape can be mounted on a tape drive and the computer can rapidly work its way through the programs on the tape one by one. Meanwhile, in another part of the computing center, one or more other tapes are being slowly built up out of the original punched cards containing yet other programs.

There are a number of these tape drives in a computing center, doing different jobs. The one used for feeding programs and data into the computer is often called Number 5. So when we give the computer an instruction like this:

READ (5,   ) NVARA, NVARB

we are really telling the computer: Go to tape drive Number 5, read from the tape there two values, and assign the first of these values to NVARA and the second to NVARB.

There is a very important point to remember in this connection. Even if data values are on magnetic tape when they go into the computer, we will continue to visualize these data values *as though* they were still on the original data cards. On tape, values are represented by tiny impulses, rather than by the relatively large holes punched in a data card, but these tiny impulses are arranged in such a way on the tape that the effect of reading data from the tape is the same *as though* the computer were reading from the original data cards. Indeed, it might be helpful to *imagine* the data cards being shrunk to a fraction of their original size, but reproduced one after the other on the tape in every detail, including any blank spaces.

FORMAT STATEMENT

So far we have seen how we tell the computer to read one or more data values, and how we tell it where to put these values: in the storage location(s) having the name(s) appearing in the READ statement. We have also seen how we tell the computer where to find the data it is to read. Now we must also tell the computer what kind of data to look for. That is, we must tell it what form the data will be in. We do this in another statement, called a *FORMAT statement*. A FORMAT statement is the kind of statement in a program that does not actually cause anything to happen, but gives the computer information.

Since a program consists of a series of statements, we need some way of telling the computer that for a particular READ statement it must be guided by the information in a particular FORMAT statement. This we do by giving the FORMAT statement a number, and then using this same number in the READ statement.

A FORMAT number goes inside the parentheses in the READ statement, following the 5 and separated from it by a comma. Therefore, a READ statement might look like this:

READ (5, 18) A, B, C

Here the 18 in the parentheses refers to the instruction numbered 18 in the program of which this READ statement is a part. In the instruction numbered 18 is information which describes how the data are arranged as they are presented to the computer. That is, it tells whether the data are in one column or two columns or three columns, whether the numbers on the data card are next to each other or are separated by blank columns, and so on.

This is an excellent example of how specific we must be in telling the computer *everything*, down to the tiniest detail. If we told the computer only that it should take three values off a data card, it would be helpless. Even if there were only three figures on the card, the computer still would not know whether they were three separate values, or whether all three figures made up one value (such as 279) and that the other two variable names should be assigned the zero values the computer would get from reading blank columns after these three figures. So we must use the FORMAT statement to tell the computer precisely where and in what form the data are.

Including a FORMAT statement number in the READ statement gives us the complete form for the READ statement. When we write:

READ (5, 18) A, B, C

we are actually telling the computer a number of things:

1. Read from Input Device Number 5 three data values.
2. Read these values according to the FORMAT information which is found in statement number 18 in the program.
3. Assign these values respectively to the variable names A, B, and C.

NUMBERING STATEMENTS

At this point we should discuss briefly this matter of numbering instructions or statements in a program. The numbers assigned to particular statements are arbitrary. They need not be in order, and they need not have lower numbers before higher numbers. For example, we could use only numbers which are multiples of 10, and use them in this order: 10, 50, 100, 20, 40, 30, 110. The only requirement is this: Any particular statement number can appear only once in a program. The reason for this is obvious. If we have two instructions with the same number, say 180, and from some other part of the program we tell the computer to refer to the instruction numbered 180, it would not know which of the two instructions we meant.

There is some variation in the range of numbers which can be used for this purpose, but it is common to find we can use numbers from 1 through 99999. Even with very large programs, there is no danger of running out of numbers, because not every instruction in a program needs a number. We need only number those instructions we want to refer to from somewhere else in the program.

In this sense, of course, these numbers are not really numbers at all; they are merely addresses or labels. They are akin to the numbers we assign to response categories, and which represent the nominal level of measurement. They say only that an instruction with one number is different from an instruction with another number. There is no implication that one instruction is *higher* or *lower* than another. We do not count these numbers, nor do arithmetic with them. This is why they need not be consecutive, nor even in order.

To illustrate a final point about the statement number as used with FORMAT statements, the two numbers inside the parentheses of the READ statement are completely independent of each other. The first number refers to an input device, the second refers to a FORMAT statement. So even the number 5 can be used in the second position, where it refers to a statement number, like this:

READ (5, 5) M, K

This tells the computer to read data from Input Device Number 5, and to read the data according to the information in the FORMAT statement numbered 5 in that program.

In short, the *only* requirement for a number to appear in the second position inside the ( ) of the READ statement is that there be a FORMAT instruction carrying that number somewhere in the program.

FORMAT SPECIFICATIONS FOR INTEGER DATA

In the FORMAT statement is where the difference between the treatment of integer values and floating point values is most marked. Since integer values do not have decimal parts, we need not consider decimal places in describing these values in a FORMAT statement. But since floating point values do have decimal parts, in a FORMAT statement we must not only tell the computer how many columns on a data card are occupied by a particular floating point number; we must also indicate how many of these columns make up the decimal part of the value.

We will take the easier topic first: the FORMAT statement for integer numbers. The word FORMAT here means the same as when we speak of the *format* of a book or magazine. It refers to the physical layout of certain material: in this case the data values we are asking the computer to read.

When the computer is instructed to read an integer number, we tell it two things about this data value. First, we tell it that the value is in fact integer. This we do by means of the letter I.

Then we tell it how many columns this value occupies on the data card. This we do by putting after the I a number which represents the number of columns the value occupies on the data card. Thus a one-column data value in the integer mode would be referred to as I1. An integer number occupying two columns on a data card would be described as I2. An integer number occupying three columns on a data card would be described, or specified, as I3.

This procedure is followed for any integer data value up to the maximum number of digits permitted. If a minus sign is present an extra column must be specified to include it. For example, the number −289 would be described as I4. If we specified only I3, this would cover only the first three columns, so the computer would read the number −28. In cases where a value may be negative sometimes, but positive other times, we provide an extra space for the minus sign in the FORMAT statement. Then if no sign is present, this column would be blank, and since the computer reads blank columns as zeroes, this blank would not change the data value in any way.

The location of each value on a data card is called the *field* of that value. This is a term we will be using repeatedly, so it is worth remembering. The first value on a data card occupies the first field, the second value occupies the second data field, and so on. The number of columns a given value occupies is called the *width* of that field. Consider the following values, appearing in this order on a data card:

85   166   241   6   1   81942

We would say the value 85 occupies the first field on the data card, and that field is two columns wide. The value 166 occupies the second data field, which has a field width of three columns. The value 81942 occupies the sixth field, which on this card happens to be the last data field because this is the last data item. This field has a width of five columns.

This idea of fields applies also to blank columns. A blank column on a data card can make up a field. In this case we would speak of a blank field. The width of any given blank field would be the number of empty columns appearing in one group.

In showing how the FORMAT statement actually works, let us begin with the simplest case of reading one data value from a card. Say we want to read the value 7 from a card, and assign this value to the variable name NA. Therefore we use this READ statement:

READ (5, 104) NA

The 104 inside the parentheses here means that before executing the READ statement the computer will look through the program for a FORMAT statement having the number 104, because in this statement will be information describing the value to be read into NA.

Therefore, we give the computer this FORMAT statement:

104 FORMAT (I1)

In form, the FORMAT statement begins with its number, here the number 104, showing the computer that this is the FORMAT statement associated with the above READ statement. After the statement number comes the word FORMAT, telling the computer that this statement does indeed contain a description of data to be read. It is useful to have the word FORMAT in this kind of statement, because other statements in a program may also be numbered, but do entirely different jobs.

The information which actually describes the data value is then enclosed in parentheses after the word FORMAT. Looking inside the parentheses, the first character, the I, refers to the fact that NA is an integer name, so that the value assigned to this name will be an integer value. The 1 following the I means the value for NA occupies one column on its data card.

The combination of I and 1 is called a *field specification*. This term reflects the fact that the notation I1 *specifies* the characteristics of a data field, telling the computer that it is a field which is one column wide and which contains an integer value.

There is one of these field specifications for each value read from a data card. To illustrate this, say we want to read three data values from a card, assigning these values to the names MO, MP, and MQ, respectively. Assume that each value occupies one column on the data card:

READ (5, 800) MO, MP, MQ
800 FORMAT (I1, I1, I1)

Here we see in the FORMAT statement three field specifications, one for each of the values to be read. Each I1 notation is a separate field specification, each describing, again, the nature (in this case *integer*) and the width (in this case *one column*) of a separate data field.

The field specifications inside the parentheses are separated from each other by commas. Spaces are allowed anywhere in a FORMAT statement, including between the number and letter which go to make up one field specification. Thus we could write:

800 FORMAT (I 1 , I 1 , I 1)

To sum up the relationships among data card, READ statement, and FORMAT statement, remember we said that for the moment we are assuming that the number of variable names in one READ statement matches the number of data values read from one data card. This means that one FORMAT statement shows how the data are arranged on one data card. This also means that for each variable name in a READ statement, there is a field specification in the associated FORMAT statement.

To illustrate, say we have this combination of READ and FORMAT statements:

READ (5, 483) KA, NZ, MONTH, NRATE
483 FORMAT (I1, I2, I2, I4)

Since there are four variable names in the READ statement, the computer would take four data values from the data card. Therefore, since each data value must be described for the computer, this means the FORMAT statement describing the data card must contain four field specifications. If only three field specifications were present, the computer would lack the necessary information about the last data value. Conversely, if five field specifications were present the computer would try to use the information in reading a fifth data value, whereas the READ statement has given it only four names which can be used in labeling storage locations, so there would be no place to put the fifth value described in the FORMAT statement. In either case the computer would be unhappy, and would probably ask us to try again, with the number of field specifications matching the number of variable names in the READ list.

The one or more field specifications in one FORMAT statement are sometimes collectively referred to as a FORMAT *code*. A FORMAT code, then, would contain all the information necessary for the reading of one data card.

Let us show another example of a READ statement. We will again change the number of the FORMAT statement, to show that this can vary at will, as long as it matches the number in the associated READ statement.

READ (5, 72) NCAS1, NCAS2, NCAS3

Assume that the data associated with this READ statement look like this on a data card, beginning in column one:

4215361

For our example here, consider that the first two numbers (the first two columns if this were a real data card) represent one value. The next value takes up three columns, and the final value occupies two columns. Thus we would use this FORMAT statement:

72 FORMAT (I2, I3, I2)

This combination of data card and READ and FORMAT statements would assign the value 42 to NCAS1, the value 153 to NCAS2, and the value 61 to NCAS3.

To emphasize again the physical relationship among the elements of the READ process, a READ statement and its associated FORMAT statement are in the package of statements making up the program. All these statements in a program are first taken into the computer and stored there. This means that when the computer comes to a READ statement in the program, the FORMAT statement (also part of the program) will be stored in the computer. The computer than searches through its storage until it finds the FORMAT statement with the number referred to in the particular READ statement being executed. And with the information in the FORMAT statement, the computer *then* goes to the separate package of data cards to use this information in reading the data value(s) from the next card in succession.

Let us illustrate this physical relationship with the READ statement we used just above:

READ (5, 72) NCAS1, NCAS2, NCAS3

This READ statement would be stored in the computer, along with this FORMAT statement:

72 FORMAT   (I2, I3, I2)

Also, of course, all the other statements in this program would be stored along with these two statements.

Say that this was the first READ statement in the program. Upon reaching this READ statement, the computer would then look for FORMAT statement number 72. Then it would go to the package of data cards submitted along with the program, and from the first card there it would read the values 42, 153, and 61.

Actually, of course, as we indicated earlier, the contents of the data cards would probably have been placed on magnetic tape behind, or after, the instructions making up the program. So in looking for the data card for this first READ statement the computer would go to the tape device holding this tape and would read the contents of the first data card from that tape. But remember that we said the effect of putting instructions and data on tape was *as though* the computer was reading directly from the original punched cards. This holds here, so that when we say the computer would read data from the first card in the package of data cards following the program, this in effect is exactly what happens, even though it may occur *via* a magnetic tape.

EXAMPLES

Each of the following examples is presented in two parts. In the first part, there is a READ statement, an associated FORMAT statement, and a line of figures which we will pretend are punched on a data card, beginning in column 1 of the card. Finally, there is a list of variable names showing which value would be assigned to each name by this combination of data card and READ and FORMAT statements. Go through *Part One* of each example in this manner: Look at the field specifications inside the parentheses of the FORMAT statement. See what field width is indicated there for the first data value, as indicated by the number following the first I. Then on a separate sheet of paper write this many of the digits from the *data card* in a group. Leave a space, and then write that group of digits which makes up the second data field, as many digits as the second field specification in the FORMAT statement indicates.

If you procede in this manner in the first example here, you will end up with a line of figures that looks like this:

22   112   09   4   620

This will help you match up the numbers on the data card with the variable names to which they will be assigned by the associated READ statement. It will also help you get used to looking at a long row of digits, and dividing them into their respective values through the use of the FORMAT statement, just as the computer does.

Then to aid in understanding each example, these same relationships between data values and READ and FORMAT statements are illustrated in a second and simpler way. *Part Two* of each example consists of three lines across the page. The first line contains the variable names for that particular example. In the second row the values on the data card are separated to show the individual data fields. Each data field is shown underneath the variable name to which it applies. Finally, in the third row, underneath each data field, is the field specification which applies to that field. Use the breakdown of the relationships in *Part Two* to make sure you understand the various relationships in the input process, *as these would appear in their natural form.*

9. *Part One:*

Values appearing on a data card:

22112094620

READ statement:

READ (5, 480) NCASE, IQ, NOOC, NCLAS, IREC

FORMAT statement:

480 FORMAT (I2, I3, I2, I1, I3)

This combination of data card and READ and FORMAT statements would assign these values to the respective variable names:

NCASE = 22	IQ = 112
NOOC = 09	NCLAS = 4
IREC = 620	

Part Two:

Variable names:	NCASE,	IQ,	NOOC,	NCLAS,	IREC
Data fields:	22	112	09	4	620
Field specs:	I2,	I3,	I2,	I1,	I3

10. *Part One:*

Values appearing on a data card:

01832482018015916

READ statement:

READ (5, 120) NCITNO, IPOP, NBLOCS, NPREC

FORMAT statement:

120 FORMAT (I3, I6, I5, I3)

This combination of data card and READ and FORMAT statements would assign these values to the respective variable names:

NCITNO = 18	IPOP = 324820
NBLOCS = 18015	NPREC = 916

Part Two:

Variable names:	NCITNO,	IPOP,	NBLOCS,	NPREC
Data fields:	018	324820	18015	916
Field specs:	I3,	I6,	I5,	I3

SKIPPING COLUMNS ON THE DATA CARD

At this point we can handle any combination of integer values, regardless of how values of different sizes are mixed together on a data card. But as yet we can only handle them if they appear directly next to each other, with no blank columns between them. Yet we know that data cards often contain blank columns interspersed among the data values, and also, that frequently we want to pick out only some of the values on a card for a particular calculation.

We can not just ignore columns which are blank or which contain data values unwanted for the moment. Somehow we must provide for them in a FORMAT statement, along with columns containing data to be read. The reason for this is that we must account for every column on a data card *up to the last column the computer reads*. Remember there are 80 columns on a data card. If we want data read only from the first 20 columns of a card, and nothing from the last 60 columns, then we can ignore those last 60 columns, but we must account, in our instructions to the computer, for every one of those first 20 columns.

We need not worry about any of the columns after the last column the computer reads because when the computer hits the closing parenthesis in a FORMAT statement it leaves the data card it is currently reading. We are saying for the moment that there is one FORMAT statement for each data card the computer is instructed to read. On this basis, we might say that the first parenthesis in a FORMAT statement is a sign the computer is to begin reading from a data card, and the closing parenthesis is a sign the computer is to stop reading from that card. Thus if we have this FORMAT statement:

FORMAT (I3)

the computer is thereby instructed to read only the first three columns from that data card and to ignore the rest of it.

But since we must account in the FORMAT statement for every column up to the last column the computer reads on a data card, and since some of these columns might be blank, or might contain data values not needed in a particular program, we need a way to tell the computer to skip some columns as it moves along a data card.

We do this with the letter X in the FORMAT statement. Placed inside the parentheses of the FORMAT statement, an X tells the computer to skip columns on the data card, with a number before the X showing exactly how many columns to skip at one time. By writing 1X, we instruct the computer to skip one column, for example. By writing 6X, we tell the computer to skip six adjoining columns. Remember that the *number of columns* goes *before* an X, although in describing an integer data field, *number of columns* involved there goes *after* the letter I.

The columns skipped by an X notation may be blank, or they may contain figures we do not want the computer to read. For example, say that on a data card the first three columns contain an ID number we do not want in the computer. Since the computer reads a card from left to right, and since the three columns to be skipped in this example are farthest to the left (that is, columns 1, 2, and 3) they are the first thing the computer will encounter on reading this card. Thus the first item in the FORMAT statement for this card would be an instruction to skip three columns: the notation 3X.

To continue this example, say that after skipping the three columns, we want the computer to read an integer value which occupies columns 4 and 5, and to assign this value to the name NPLACE. We could use this READ statement:

READ (5, 66) NPLACE

The FORMAT statement to accomplish the skipping of the first three columns and the reading of the value in the next two columns would be:

66 FORMAT (3X, I2)

Now let us further complicate the example. Say that after reading the value from columns 4 and 5, the computer is to skip the next column (column 6) which is blank. Then it is to read a four-column value located in columns 7 through 10, and assign this value to the name NDIS. Now the FORMAT statement, skipping the first three columns, reading a two-column value, skipping a column, and reading a four-column value, would look like this:

66 FORMAT (3X, I2, 1X, I4)

The associated READ statement would look this:

READ (5, 66) NPLACE, NDIS

A refinement, sometimes useful, on skipping columns, is that if we have a set of adjoining columns to be skipped, we can use several X notations, each skipping some of the columns. For example, if there is a set of six adjoining columns to be skipped, it can be done by 6X, or by 3X,3X, or by 2X,4X, and so on.

REPEATING FIELD SPECIFICATIONS

When reading a series of integer values, if the values are next to each other, and all occupy the same number of columns on the data card, we can simplify the FORMAT statement by using one notation to cover all the values. For example, say we want to read from a data card four integer numbers, each value occupying one column, and all located in adjoining columns. In this case we need not write out a field specification for each value. like this:

(I1, I1, I1, I1)

Rather, we can indicate before the I the number of times that a particular field specification is repeated: that is, the number of consecutive data values to which this particular field specification applies. So with four integer values, each taking one column, and with no columns between them, we can write simply:

(4I1)

This device is particularly useful with something like questionnaire data, which often consists of whole sets of one-column responses. But this kind of *repetition notation* or *collective* field specification is not limited to one-column data. If we have six data values, all next to each other, and with each value occupying three card columns, the field specification could refer to them collectively as 6I3. Or say we had a set of ten items of census data, each with six digits. Then we could write 10I6. The only criteria for using this kind of shortcut are these:

1. All the data values included in one collective field specification must be directly next to each other on the data card.
2. All must occupy the same number of columns on the data card.
3. All must be of the same mode; in our examples here, all are integers.

We need not use this repetition device if we do not want to. If we have six values, each occupying two columns, and all six values right next to each other, we can write 6I2. We can also write a separate I2 field specification for each of the values. Finally, we can divide the collective field specification into several groups, like 3I2,3I2, or 2I2,2I2,2I2, or I2,5I2, and so on.

EXAMPLES

These examples are arranged like the ones in the last set. Each example shows the relationship between a series of values on a data card and the READ and FORMAT statements that would tell the computer about the form of each data value, and which variable name it is to be assigned to. These relationships will again be illustrated in two ways, with each example presented in two parts.

NOTE: In these examples, a blank column on a data card is indicated by the # character.

11. (Repeating field specifications)

Part One:
Data card:
130143526
READ statement:
READ (5, 68) ID, NQI, NQ2, NQ3, NQ4, NAGE
FORMAT statement:
68 FORMAT (I3, 4I1, I2)

This combination of data card and READ and FORMAT statements would assign these values to the respective variable names:

ID = 130   NQI = 1
NQ2 = 4   NQ3 = 3
NQ4 = 5   NAGE = 26

Part Two:

Variable Names:	ID,	NQ1,	NQ2,	NQ3,	NQ4,	NAGE
Data fields:	130	1	4	3	5	26

Field specs: I3,   4I1,   I2

12. (Repeating field specifications and skipping blank card columns)

Part One:

Data card (blank columns indicated by #):
    107##73-5
READ statement:
    READ (5, 16) ID, NRES1, NRES2, NRES3
FORMAT statement:
    16 FORMAT(I3, 2X, 2I1, I2)

This combination of data card and READ and FORMAT statements would assign these values to the respective variable names:

ID = 107   NRES1 = 7
NRES2 = 3   NRES3 = —5

Part Two

Variable Names:	ID,		NRES1,	NRES2,	NRES3
Data fields:	107	##	7	3	—5

Field specs: I3, 2X,   2I1   I2

13. (Repeating field specifications and skipping columns which contain numbers)

Part One:
Data card:
    2653040212

READ statement:
     READ (5, 27) NRES1, NRES2, NRES3, NED
FORMAT statement:
     27 FORMAT (3X, 3I1, 2X, I2)
This combination of data card and READ and FORMAT statements would assign these values to the respective variable names:

NRES1 = 3	NRES2 = 0
NRES3 = 4	NED = 12

Part Two:

Variable names:		NRES1,	NRES2,	NRES3,		NED
Data fields:	265	3	0	4	02	12
		- - - - - - - - - - -				
Fields specs:	3X,		3I1,		2X,	I2

14. (Repeating field specifications and skipping both blank columns and columns containing numbers)

Part One:
Data card:
     223###710717507-2
READ statement:
     READ (5, 3010) IND, NSIZE, NED, MARST
FORMAT statement:
     3010 FORMAT (I3, 3X, 2I2, 5X, I2)
This combination of data card and READ and FORMAT statements would assign these values to the respective variable names:

IND = 223	NSIZE = 71
NED = 7	MARST = −2

Part Two:

Variable names:	IND,		NSIZE,	NED,		MARST
Data fields:	223	###	71	07	17507	−2
			- - - - -			
Field specs:	I3,	3X,	2I2,		5X,	I2

EXERCISES

See exercises 9–24 in Chapter Four of the *Workbook.*

FIELD SPECIFICATIONS FOR FLOATING POINT DATA

The FORMAT procedure for floating point values is essentially the same as for integer values. However, we begin a floating point field specification with the letter F, rather than the letter I, to show that the data value referred to is floating point rather than integer.

After this initial F, we place a number showing how wide the data field is. Thus we would use the notation F6 to refer to a floating point value which occupies six columns on a data card, just as we would use I6 to refer to an integer number which occupied six columns.

But we have one additional problem with floating point data that we do not have with integer data: We must also show how many columns of a floating point data field are to be considered as representing decimal places. This we handle by adding a decimal point to the field specification, and then follow this decimal point with a second number to show how many, if any, of the columns in the field are to be taken as decimal places. Thus a number which takes up six columns on a data card, and which has two decimal places, would be referred to as F6.2.

In general, the form of the specification used to describe floating point numbers is:

Fw.d

The F tells the computer that the value referred to by this field specification is floating point. The number in the position indicated by the small w shows how wide the field is—how many columns it occupies on the data card. This must include the column occupied by the decimal point if one is actually punched on the data card, and it must also include a column for the minus sign if the data can be negative. Then the number appearing in the position indicated by the small d shows how many of the columns in that total field are to be taken as representing decimal places.

To illustrate, the positive value 85.76 would be referred to this way:

F5.2   (If a decimal point appeared on the data card, so that a total of five card columns are involved)

F4.2   (If no decimal point appeared on the data card, so that only four card columns are involved)

Note that whether or not a decimal point actually appears in the data, when we speak of decimal *places*, we are referring to decimal *digits*—the decimal point itself does not count as part of the decimal portion of the number.

PRESENCE OR ABSENCE OF DECIMAL POINTS IN DATA

We should pause to consider the fact that the decimal point in floating point values may or may not appear on the data card. If it does appear, the computer reads it as a decimal point and stores the value as the decimal point directs.

There are several things to remember about a data value where the decimal point actually appears on the data card. One is that the total field width (the number immediately following the F in the field specification) must be wide enough to include the column occupied by the decimal point, as well as the columns occupied by all the digits that make up the value. For example, in Table II below, each value in the left-hand column would be described by the field specification appearing opposite that value. Assume that each value in the left column appears on a data card, and that the decimal point is punched into the card along with the digits. Note that in each case the number immediately following the F in the field specification is one more than the number of digits in the corresponding value on that line. The *one more* is to allow for the decimal point.

The second thing to remember about a data value with the

TABLE II

FIELD SPECIFICATIONS FOR VALUES HAVING DECIMAL POINTS
PUNCHED WITH THEM

Data Value	Field Specification
14.5	F4.1
5739.59	F7.2
.2	F2.1
2.2	F3.2
22.	F3.0

decimal point actually punched on the data card is that if the decimal point in the data does not match the decimal point indicated in the field specification, the decimal point in the data is the controlling one. For example, say we have this number, including decimal point, punched on a data card:

522.61

Now say this field specification was used to refer to that value:

F6.1

As long as the entire width of the data field is properly indicated in the field specification (in this case it is, by the 6 following the F) then the computer would ignore the 1 following the decimal point in the field specification. Instead, after reading the data value, the computer would store it with the two decimal places indicated by the decimal point in the data.

In such a case we say the decimal point in the data *over-rides* the decimal point in the field specification.

In Table III below are several more examples of a decimal point punched in the data card over-riding the decimal indication in a field specification, where the two do not match.

Remember, however, that this over-riding of the decimal point in the field specification is *only* possible if the total width of the data field is accurately described in the field specification by the number immediately following the F. If not, the actual value read into the computer will be useless.

The fact that we might have something in a program that does not match the data might seem odd, particularly in view of our emphasis on the fact that we must be absolutely precise in the instructions we give the computer. However, this is one

TABLE III
DECIMAL POINTS PUNCHED IN DATA OVER-RIDING DECIMAL
INDICATIONS IN FIELD SPECIFICATIONS

Data Value	Field Specification	Value Read Into Computer
.05	F3.0	.05
512.213	F7.5	512.213
4.2	F3.2	4.2
18.	F3.2	18.

place where we have a bit of latitude. It is important in advanced programming because it gives us more flexibility in reading data values. It is also important for you to be alerted to this feature here, so you will not be puzzled if someone says that a decimal point in the data card need not match the decimal indication in the field specification.

In practice, this circumstance is not likely to arise often enough to be bothersome because it is probably more common that decimal data values do not actually have decimal points punched in them on the data cards. There are several reasons for this. One is that the decimal points occupy card columns, so that if each value has a decimal point punched in it, fewer data items can go on each card. This in turn means more data cards to keep track of, to carry, to store, and so on. Also, it takes longer to punch data values with the decimal point in them. So we often punch decimal values on a card without decimal points, and use the field specifications in the FORMAT statement to tell the computer what portion of each value, if any, should be considered its decimal part.

EXAMPLES

15. (Decimal points punched in the data values match field specifications)

Part One:
Data card:
    417.09.-57.88160.9
READ statement:
    READ (5, 50) FID, CASENO, SCORE, TOTAVE
FORMAT statement:
    50 FORMAT (F4.0, F3.0, F6.2, F5.1)
This combination of data card and READ and FORMAT statements would assign these values to the respective variable names:

FID = 417.	CASENO = 9.
SCORE = −57.88	TOTAVE = 160.9

Part Two:

Variable names:	FID,	CASENO,	SCORE,	TOTAVE
Data fields:	417.	09.	−57.88	160.9
Field specs:	F4.0,	F3.0,	F6.2,	F5.1

16. (Decimal points punched in the data values do *not* match the field specifications)

Part One:
Data card:
16.0287.01-2.75882.60
READ statement:
READ (5, 81) OUTSC, FINSC, AVEAGE, AVINC
FORMAT statement:
81 FORMAT (F5.0, F5.4, F4.2, F7.0)
Since the widths of the respective data fields are properly indicated in the field specifications, this combination of data and card READ and FORMAT statements would assign these values to the respective variable names:

OUTSC = 16.02	FINSC = 87.01
AVEAGE = −2.7	AVINC = 5882.6

Part Two:

Variable names:	OUTSC,	FINSC,	AVEAGE,	AVINC
Data fields:	16.02	87.01	−2.7	5882.60
Field specs:	F5.0,	F5.4,	F4.2,	F7.0

17. (Decimal points are not punched in the data values)

Part One:
Data card:
99-169241-51217519
READ statement:
READ (5,99) CASE, RAD, FRE, DATA1, DATA2
FORMAT statement:
99 FORMAT (F2.0, F3.2, F4.2, F4.1, F5.3)
This combination of data card and READ and FORMAT statements would assign these values to the respective variable names:

CASE = 99.	RAD = −.16

DATA2 = 17.519   FRE = 92.41
DATA1 = −51.2

Part Two:

Variable names:	CASE,	RAD,	FRE,	DATA1,	DATA2
Data fields:	99	−16	9241	−512	17519
Field specs:	F2.0,	F3.2,	F4.2,	F4.1,	F5.3

18. (Decimal points punched in some floating point values, but not in others)

Part One:
Data card:
-0516.3222459495.268150.042
READ statement:
    READ (5. 87) SIG, GPAVE, XVAL, XSQ, YSQ, Q
FORMAT statement:
    87 FORMAT (F3.2, F5.2, F5.3, F5.1, F4.1, F5.3)
This combination of data card and READ and FORMAT statements would assign these values to the respective variable names:

SIG = −.05   GPAVE = 16.32
XVAL = 22.459   XSQ = 495.2
YSQ = 681.5   Q = .042

Part Two:

Variable names:	SIG,	GPAVE,	XVAL,	XSQ,	YSQ,	Q
Data fields:	−05	16.32	22459	495.2	6815	0.042
Field specs:	F3.2,	F5.2,	F5.3,	F5.1,	F4.1,	F5.3

SKIPPING AND REPEATING DATA FIELDS

When dealing with floating point data, we can skip columns just as we did with integer data. An X is used, preceded by a number which shows how many columns are to be skipped. If columns containing data are being skipped, it makes no difference whether those data items are floating point or integer, or whether they have decimal points or not. The important thing is how many columns are to be skipped, not what is in those columns.

We can also repeat field specifications with floating point data, just as we did with integer data. The data fields to be repeated must all be of the same mode: here, floating point. The fields must all be next to each other, and they must all occupy exactly the same number of columns on the data card. But floating point numbers have an additional requirement for using the repetition notation; the number of decimal places in each field must also be the same. For example, if we have a series of percentages, each with two decimal places, we could write something like this:

10F5.2

This would mean ten values on the data card, each value a floating point number, each occupying five columns on the data card, and each value having two decimal places. Of course, there could be no spaces between the values if they are to be covered in this collective field specification.

As in the case of the single floating point field specification, the critical thing is the total width of each data field. Here too, if a decimal point in the data does not match the specified number of decimal places in the FORMAT statement, then the decimal point in the data is the controlling one. However, as a practical matter it will be easier to use this repetition device if any decimal points punched in the data *do* match those in the field specifications. Also, it will be easier if the values to be grouped together this way either all have decimal points punched in them on the data cards, or all do not have decimal points physically present.

EXAMPLES

19. (Field specifications repeated, with decimal points punched in the data)

Part One:
Data card:
    613.013.0016.1285.036.991
READ statement:
    READ (5, 66) TOTAL, CASE1, CASE2, CASE3, S

FORMAT statement:

66 FORMAT (F5.1, 3F5.2, F5.3)

This combination of data card and READ and FORMAT statements would assign the following values to the respective variable names:

TOTAL = 613.0	CASE1 = 13.0
CASE2 = 16.12	CASE3 = 85.03
S = 6.991	

Part Two:

Variable names:	TOTAL,	CASE1,	CASE2,	CASE3,	S
Data fields:	613.0	13.00	16.12	85.03	6.991

- - - - - - - - - - - - -

Field specs:	F5.1,	3F5.2,	F5.3

20. (Field specifications repeated, with decimal points not punched in the data)

Part One:

Data card:

40164250719962044190561

READ statement:

READ (5,6204) PROJ, CAT1, CAT2, CAT3, CATTOT

FORMAT statement:

6204 FORMAT (F3.0, 3F5.3, F6.2)

This combination of data card and READ and FORMAT statements would assign the following values to the respective variable names:

PROJ = 401.	CAT1 = 64.250
CAT2 = 71.996	CAT3 = 20.441
CATTOT = 9056.17	

Part Two:

Variable names:	PROJ.	CAT1,	CAT2,	CAT3,	CATTOT
Data fields:	401	64250	71996	20441	905617

- - - - - - - - - - - - -

Field specs:	F3.0,	3F5.3,	F6.2

21. (Field specifications repeated, with decimal points punched in some data values but not in others)

Part One:

Data card:

56.0532.911350112517.5

READ statement:

READ (5, 16) AVAG, AVA, EDM, EDW, PCT

FORMAT statement:

16 FORMAT (2F5.2, 2F4.2, F4.1)

This combination of data card and READ and FORMAT statements would assign the following values to the respective variable names:

AVAG = 56.05   AVA = 32.91

EDM = 13.50   EDW = 11.25

PCT = 17.5

Part Two:

Variable names:	AVAG,	AVA,	EDM,	EDW,	PCT
Data fields:	56.05	32.91	1350	1125	17.5
Field specs:		2F5.2,		2F4.2,	F4.1

22. (Skipping columns, with decimal points punched in some data values but not in others)

Part One:

Data card:

###421##05#185762.07

READ statement:

READ (5, 94) CLASS, STU, GRA, AVE

FORMAT statement:

94 FORMAT (3X, F3.0, 5X, F2.0, F2.0, F5.2)

This combination of data card and READ and FORMAT statements would assign the following values to the respective variable names:

CLASS = 421.   STU = 18.

GRA = 57.   AVE = 62.07

Part Two:

Variable names:	CLASS,		STU,	GRA,	AVE
Data fields:	### 421	##05#	18	57	62.07
Field Specs:	3X, F3.0,	5X,	F2.0	F2.0	F5.2

23. (Skipping columns and repeating field specifications; decimal points punched in data values)

Part One:
Data card:
    18.016.05205.##17.0309.52
READ statement:
    READ (5, 5783) PNO, FN, FMX, FMN
FORMAT statement:
    5783 FORMAT (F4.1, 5X, F4.0, 2X, 2F5.2)
This combination of data card and READ and FORMAT statement would assign the following values to the respective variable names:

PNO = 18.   FN = 205.
FMX = 17.03   FMN = 9.52

Part Two:

Variable names:	PNO,		FN,		FMX,	FMN
Data fields:	18.0	16.05	205.	##	17.03	09.52
Field specs:	F4.1,	5X,	F4.0,	2X,	2F5.2	

24. (Skipping columns and repeating field specifications; decimal points not punched in data values)

Part One:
Data card:
    10850002160218196407
READ statement:
    READ (5, 2784) GP, CITY, PCTA, PCTB, PCTC
FORMAT statement:
    2784 FORMAT (F2.0, 3X, F3.0, 3F4.2)
This combination of data card and READ and FORMAT statements would assign the following values to the respective variable names:

GP = 10.   CITY = 2.
PCTA = 16.02   PCTB = 18.19
PCTC = 64.07

Part Two:

Variable names:GP		CITY,	PCTA,	PCTB,	PCTC
Data fields:	10	850	002	1602	1819	6407

- - - - - - - - - - - - - - -

Field specs:	F2.0,	3X,	F3.0,		3F4.2

25. (Skipping columns and repeating field specifications; decimal points punched in some data values but not in others)

Part One:
Data card:
  18208##201.2981.0
READ statement:
  READ (5,2974) COMM, REG, PCI, PCP
FORMAT statement:
  2974 FORMAT (F3.0, F2.0, 2X, 2F5.1)
This combination of data card and READ and FORMAT statements would assign the following values to the respective variable names:

COMM = 182.	REG = 8.
PCI = 201.2	PCP = 981.0

Part Two:

Variable names:	COMM,	REG,	PCI,	PCP
Data fields:	182	08	## 201.2	981.0

- - - - - - - -

Field specs:	F3.0,	F2.0,	2X,	2F5.2

EXERCISES

See exercises 25–40 in Chapter Four of the *Workbook*.

ORDER OF FIELD SPECIFICATIONS

When writing a FORMAT statement, field specifications for floating point values and for integer values may be mixed in any order. This is the same as saying that integer and floating point values may appear in any combination on a data card. Similarly, floating point and integer names may appear in any order in the list of variable names in a READ statement.

The only requirement in this regard is that the names, the field specifications, and the data values all match. That is, the first data value on a data card is assigned to the first variable name in the READ list, and this value is described by the first field specification in the FORMAT statement. If this first data value is integer, the first variable name must be integer as well, and the first item in the FORMAT statement must be an integer field specification. The second data value on a card is assigned to the second name in the READ statement, and this value is described by the second field specification in the FORMAT statement, and so on.

In short, for each name in the READ statement, there is a data value in the accompanying position on the data card, and in the corresponding position in the FORMAT statement there is a field specification which describes that data value in terms of mode (which must match the mode of the corresponding variable name), in numbers of columns involved, and for floating point values, in number of decimal places.

It should be emphasized that the ultimate arrangement of the list of names in a READ statement is determined by which variable names we want to assign to which data values. And this in turn is influenced by what each data item represents: which variable it pertains to. For example, say a series of values is to be read from a data card, and the third of these values is a figure for years of education. If we want to refer to this data item by a meaningful name (YEARED, say) then this name must come third in the list of variable names. Similarly, the field specification describing that value comes third among the field specifications in the FORMAT statement.

This care in matching the parts of the input process is necessary because we can *not* simply include a list of variable names in a READ statement, and then expect that since the third data item on the card is the figure for years of education, the computer will assign this value to the name YEARED. The computer will not do this because the third data item means nothing to it. *We* know this third item pertains to years of education, but the computer does not know this. The name YEARED has meaning for us; it is a way of letting us know what a particular data item represents. Therefore it is up to us to see that this name ends up with the appropriate value from the data card, by making sure that the position of that variable name in the list of names in the READ statement is the same as the position of that particular data value in the series of data items on the card the READ statement will read.

To further illustrate this point, say we have three data items on a card. The first is average education of members of a group, the second is their average income, and the third is average years of membership in that group. We want to refer to these values, respectively, by the names AVGED, AVGINC, and AVGYR. On the data cards the respective values look like this:

13.2   5246.82   1.9

The first of these values is for education, the second for income, and the third for average years of membership. Thus our READ statement should list the variable names in this order:

READ (5, 82) AVGED, AVGINC, AVGYR

This would result in AVGED being set equal to 13.2, AVGINC being set equal to 5246.82, and AVGYR being set equal to 1.9.

Now say that somehow we get the variable names in a different order, while the arrangement of items on the data card remains the same. Say our READ statement now looked like this:

READ (5, 82) AVGYR, AVGED, AVGINC

If there was *not* a corresponding change in the order of the data values, this READ statement would assign these values to the respective variable names:

AVGYR = 13.2   AVGED = 5246.82   AVGINC = 1.9

Note that we could still get the desired results from our program if we knew these names in this second example did not refer to the variables they suggest. The computer does not care if we assign a value of 5246.82 to a name which suggests years of education. As long as we remember this name refers now to an income figure and treat it accordingly, despite what the name itself suggests, we can do what we want with it. But the chances of misleading ourselves as we look at the program, and thereby getting ridiculous results, are obvious. In short, the only way to get a value on the data card assigned to the desired variable name is to arrange the list of names in the READ statement so that they are in an order that matches the order of the data items to which these names are to refer.

EXAMPLES

26. (Skipping columns; decimal points punched in floating point values)

Part One:
Data card:
    117##0217#2042.02
READ statement:
    READ (5, 689) ID, IRESPA, IRESPB, PCTYES
FORMAT statement:
    689 FORMAT (I3, 2X, I2, I2, 3X, F5.2)
This combination of data card and READ and FORMAT statements would assign the following values to the respective variable names:

ID = 117	IRESPA = 2
IRESPB = 17	PCTYES = 42.02

Part Two:

Variable names	ID,		IRESPA,	IRESPB,		PCTYES
Data fields:	117	##	02	17	#20	42.02
Field specs:	I3,	2X,	I2,	I2,	3X,	F5.2

27. (Repeating field specifications; decimal points punched in floating point values)

Part One:
Data card:
    07214.7216.000507
READ statement:
    READ (5, 420) KAS, RES1, RES2, IR3, IR4
FORMAT statement:
    420 FORMAT (I3, 2F5.2, 2I2)

This combination of data card and READ and FORMAT statements would assign the following values to the respective variable names:

KAS = 72	RES1 = 14.72
IR4 = 7	IR3 = 5
RES2 = 16.	

Part Two:

Variable names:	KAS,	RES1,	RES2,	IR3,	IR4
Data fields:	072	14.72	16.00	05	07
		- - - - - - - -		- - - - - -	
Field specs:	I3,	2F5.2,		2I2	

28. (Skipping columns and repeating field specifications; decimal points punched in floating point values)

Part One:
Data card:
  19680722##4047.2942.77
READ statement:
  READ (5, 5397) IELECT, ICITY, PCTIR, PCTID
FORMAT statement:
  5397 FORMAT (2I4, 4X, 2F5.2)
This combination of data card and READ and FORMAT statements would assign the following values to the respective variable names:

IELECT = 1968	ICITY = 722
PCTIR = 47.29	PCTID = 42.77

Part Two:

Variable names:	IELECT,	ICITY,		PCTIR,	PCTID
Data fields:	1968	0722	##40	47.29	42.77
		- - - - - - - -		- - - - - - - -	
Field specs:	2I4,		4X,	2F5.2	

29. (Skipping columns and repeating field specifications; decimal points not punched in floating point values)

Part One:
Data card:
8702###4879##1649
READ statement:
READ (5, 47) PCT, IA, IB, XSQ, YSQ
FORMAT statement:
47 FORMAT (F4.2, 3X, 2I2, 2X, 2F2.0)
This combination of data card and READ and FORMAT
statements would assign the following values to the respective
variable names:

PCT = 87.02   IA = 48
IB = 79   XSQ = 16.
YSQ = 49.

Part Two:

Variable names:	PCT,		IA, IB,		XSQ, YSQ	
Data fields:	8702	###	48 79	##	16	49
	- - - -		- - -		- - - - -	
Field specs:	F4.2,	3X,	2I2,	2X,	2F2.0	

30. (Repeating field specifications; decimal points not punched
    in floating point values)

Part One:
Data card:
    2537461409
READ statement:
    READ (5, 789) IA1, IA2, IA3, DIS, PRE
FORMAT statement:
    789 FORMAT (3I2, 2F2.0)

This combination of data card and READ and FORMAT
statements would assign the following values to the respective
variable names:

IA1 = 25   IA2 = 37
IA3 = 46   DIS = 14.
PRE = 9.

Part Two:

Variable names:	IA1,	IA2,	IA3,	DIS,	PRE
Data fields:	25	37	46	14	09
		- - - - - - - -		- - - - - -	
Field specs:		3I2,		2F2.0	

SUPPLEMENTARY IDEAS

The FORMAT statement described in this chapter illustrates several things which should be remembered about the computer. One is its flexibility. Any conceivable arrangement of data values can be handled in a FORMAT statement, regardless of how thoroughly integer and floating point values are mixed, regardless of how many different sizes of numbers appear, regardless of whether decimal points do or do not physically appear in floating point values, and so on. This means the computer can be instructed to read any data we would ever want to give it.

However, most FORMAT problems will probably not be as complicated as some of those demonstrated here. This is particularly true if we have a say when the data are arranged and punched on data cards, so we can tailor the data to make it easier to handle in a FORMAT statement. For example, it might be possible to group integer data values together, to make them appear in data fields all of the same width, and so on. Remember that the computer is, after all, merely a machine, so it is much easier to use when there are regularities or patterns in the material we give it.

However, we occasionally encounter data already punched on cards in a way that has no pattern or regularity. If we have mastered the material here, we can still find a way to get the data into the computer. It might take a very complicated FORMAT statement, but writing even the most complicated FORMAT statement is easier and quicker than repunching a whole set of data.

These FORMAT statements also illustrate the common observation that there is no one way to do things with a computer. There are certain rules which must be followed, to be sure. But within these rules, there are many different ways to approach a given problem. With FORMAT statements, for example, if there is a series of data items to be described, it is often possible to decide between grouping some of them together, or describing each of them in an individual field specification. Here, as in all else about the computer, the more complex a problem is, the more ways it can be approached.

Thus while we are limited by certain rules of procedure in programming, we have great freedom in deciding how we combine these rules to solve a given problem. The more capable we become with a computer and the more complicated the tasks we approach with it, the less it will limit or dominate our thinking. It is a demanding tool, yet paradoxically, the more its demands are met, the less it appears as that which machines are so often accused of being: a device which stifles thought and limits creativity.

In this connection, however, there should be a word of caution offered the beginning programmer. Do not let the prospect of creativity go right to your head. Rather, work up to it slowly, step by step. For example, if a series of floating point values are not absolutely identical, do not try to devise a fancy field specification which will cover all of them, simply for the sake of using the collective field specification. Rather, take them one at a time, tailoring each field specification to the data item it applies to. Here, as in many other areas of programming, it is wise to take at first the slow, but at the same time safest, approach. There are shortcuts which can greatly reduce programming time, and the beginning programmer should learn that they exist and how they operate, but should work up to them slowly. This will minimize errors, and therefore make the early programming more pleasurable.

Another point has to do with the difference between Fortran II and Fortran IV. This bears on our earlier discussion of whether programming languages change so rapidly and extensively that it is a waste of time to learn one.

The READ statement discussed in this chapter illustrates the way the two versions of the Fortran language differ. We have seen that to read from a data card three floating point values, and to assign them to three floating point variable names, we would use something like this:

READ (5. 18) AVAL, BVAL, CVAL
18 FORMAT (F3.0, F5.2, F4.1)

This is the way it would be done in Fortran IV. The equivalent form for Fortran II would be:

READ INPUT TAPE 5, 18, AVAL, BVAL, CVAL
18 FORMAT (F3.0, F5.2, F4.1)

In both cases the FORMAT statements operate exactly the same way. In the READ statement, however, the words INPUT TAPE no longer appear in Fortran IV. On the other hand, in the newer version parentheses have been added around the input tape number and the FORMAT reference number in the READ statement. This is not a substantial difference, and READ statements can be converted from Fortran II to the Fortran IV form with little trouble.

Furthermore, this, together with a comparable change in the output statement we will study next, is the only change which must be made for earlier Fortran II programs to run on a computer which uses Fortran IV. So with this slight modification of READ and output statements, it would be possible to use Fortran II programs even while learning the new features added in Fortran IV.

We should also note in connection with FORMAT statements that there are features we have not discussed here. For example, one has to do with a data item expressed with an exponent: the *E number* discussed earlier. But since such specialized FORMAT features are not nearly as important for the beginning social science programmer as the things stressed in this chapter, we will leave them for later discussion.

A WARNING

Since input is the source of so many errors, we will close this chapter with a warning about a common problem in reading data. Because a field specification describes a data value, when there is a mismatch between a field specification and a data value, the computer has no way of knowing where the fault lies. Therefore, where there is a problem in reading data, it is common to find the computer indicating an error in terms something like this: Either illegal character in data or faulty field specification.

Often the problem will be that someone erroneously punched a decimal point in a column where only digits should be. If the computer has been told in a field specification to read a digit in this column on the data card, it has no way of knowing whether the punching in that column was wrong, or whether the field specification was wrong.

In short, when there is a problem in reading data, consider *both* the READ segment of a program, *and* the data card(s). Since the relationship among these elements is so close, an error in any one part can throw the whole process off. In such a case, the computer may be reduced to a rather plaintive comment, to this effect: There is something wrong here, but I can't tell exactly what. Then it is up to the programmer to look for the error, and he must look everywhere—the READ statement, the FORMAT statement, *and* the data.

EXERCISES

See exercises 41–75 in Chapter Four of the *Workbook*.

Chapter Five

OUTPUT

U sually in social science programming we want the computer to read a set of data, perform one or more operations on the data, and then give to us one or more figures representing answers or results. When a figure comes to us from inside the the computer, this is known as *output*, or *print-out*, because the computer literally *puts*, or prints, the figure out in a form we can use. We also say the computer *writes* out a figure, and speak of it *writing out* its results.

In this chapter we will again use a great number of examples, to provide an understanding of how the basic output process works. Since input and output combined are often said to be responsible for most errors in programs, time spent at this point can save the beginning programmer many problems later on. As motive for spending this time, remember that even if a program is perfect in every other regard, it is still useless unless it can bring out to you the results it produces.

The principles involved in getting values out of the computer are almost identical to those involved in reading data into it. This is because both operations represent the same basic process: the transfer of numbers between some external device and storage locations inside the computer.

Yet there are differences between input and output statements stemming from the fact that they are moving in opposite directions. While the input statement moves a number from outside the computer to a storage location inside it, the output statement moves a number *out* of a storage location to some external destination.

In the same way that we limited ourselves to reading data from punched cards, although it is also possible to read data from other sources such as magnetic disk or tape, we will simplify our discussion of the output process here by concentrating on the form of output where the computer gives us figures on paper, although it is also possible to have figures printed out in other forms, such as on magnetic disk or tape.

In simplest terms, in writing out a figure, the computer goes to a designated storage location, sees what value is stored there, and writes this value on a sheet of paper. Note that in this process the computer does not actually *take* anything from that location; it merely writes out the equivalent of the value in that location so that the value itself remains in that location. Through the output, or writing, process we simply have a way of seeing what that value is.

The actual internal operations involved in this process are again something we need not worry about because if we use the Fortran language in the way described in this chapter, we can ask the computer to write out a particular data value (the value assigned to a particular variable name) and we will get a print-out of that value and no other.

PARTS OF THE OUTPUT PROCESS

Since it, too, is concerned with transferring numbers, the output process consists of the same kind of elements that are involved in the input process. For output, the three elements are these:

1. A WRITE statement, which:
   a. Instructs the computer to write out data values, and
   b. Shows which values are to be brought out of the computer.
2. The computer must be told what to do with the data values it brings out: where to put them. This is done by including in the WRITE statement a reference to the number of some data output device.
3. The computer must be told what form to write the data in; how many spaces to allot to each value on a printed page, for example. This is done by including a reference to some other instruction in the program which gives this kind of information. Again we use a FORMAT statement for this,

although we are now concerned with an *output FORMAT* rather than the input FORMAT statement we considered in the last chapter.

Since the WRITE statement is the core of the output process, we will consider it first.

WRITING INTEGER DATA

Since the lack of a decimal point makes integer values easier to handle here, as well, we will again begin with them.

There are two fundamental things to keep in mind about the writing out of figures on a computer. One is that when we ask the computer to write out a figure, it is usually because we want to see the value assigned to a variable name: that is, the value stored in the location bearing a particular variable name. The other point is one mentioned earlier: When we want to do something with a particular value, we put in an instruction the name of the location containing that value. When the computer sees that name, it goes to the designated location and does with the value there whatever we have requested.

Taking these two points together means that when we want the computer to write out a particular value, we must tell the computer two things: (1) the name of the location containing that value, and (2) what to do with that value, namely, write it out. We do this in a statement which begins with the word WRITE, followed by the name of the location containing the value we want written out. So at its simplest, the instruction telling the computer to write out an integer value could look like this:

WRITE NVAL

This instruction tells the computer several things, beginning with the fact that NVAL is a variable name. Just as a word following the word READ is automatically taken as a variable name, so too is it a rule of the programming language that a word following the word WRITE is a variable name.

The fact that NVAL begins with N tells the computer that

it will be dealing with an integer value. Then, because of the word WRITE, the computer goes to the location bearing the name NVAL and prints out the value it finds there, printing the value without a decimal point on the paper because it is an integer value.

Therefore, the effect of this statement:

WRITE NVAL

is to produce on paper whatever value the computer finds in the location it knows as NVAL.

To illustrate, say the value 5 is stored in NVAL. Given the instruction:

WRITE NVAL

the computer goes to that location, sees the value 5 stored there, and therefore writes out the figure 5 on a sheet of paper. This tells us what value NVAL has at this point in the program containing this WRITE statement. NVAL will continue to have that value until such time as we do something to place a new value in that location.

Note that it makes no difference to the computer whether the value it prints out is one which was originally read into the computer from outside, or whether that value was stored in that location as the result of some calculation in the program.

Writing Several Values

For the time being, to simplify our introduction to WRITE statements, we will assume that one WRITE statement prints out the value(s) on one line of printing. This means that if we want more than one value printed on a single line, we must have more than one variable name in the WRITE statement. In other words, for each value to be printed on a line, the WRITE statement must include the name of the location containing that value, so there will be just as many data values on one line of printed output as there are variable names in the WRITE statement which produced that line.

To illustrate this, say that in the computer the value 12 is stored in the location known as NVAL1 and the value 18 is stored in NVAL2. We tell the computer:

WRITE NVAL1, NVAL2

The computer goes to the location known as NVAL1 and prints out the value it finds there. Then it goes to the location known as NVAL2 and prints out the value it finds there. Both values appear on the same line of printing, because both variable names appear in the same WRITE statement.

The names under which these two values are stored are integer variable names because they begin with the letter N. This means the values stored in the locations known by these names must also be integer values. Therefore they would appear on the output paper without decimal points. Thus the result of this WRITE statement, given these values stored in the indicated locations, would be this line of printing:

12   18

After this line has been printed, of course, these values remain in NVAL1 and NVAL2, respectively, for whatever further use we want to make of them, or until we change these values.

Punctuation and Spelling

The rules for punctuation and the use of blank spaces are exactly the same for a WRITE statement as for a READ statement. The variable names are separated from each other by commas, but no comma appears before the first name or after the last name.

Matching Names and Data Values

As in the case of the READ statement, the order of the variable names in the WRITE statement is related to the order in which the respective data values appear. We have seen that the computer reads a data card from left to right. Similarly, when printing two or more values on a line, the computer moves, in effect, from left to right, just as we write. So the first or left-most value appearing on a line is the contents of the storage location known by the first variable name in the WRITE statement. The second value on a line comes from the location bearing the second variable name in the WRITE statement, and so on.

Here, however, is one reflection of the fact that while the READ and WRITE statements are both concerned with the same basic process, they carry it in different directions. In the READ statement, the order of the data items determines the way the variable names, under which we want to store the respective data items, are arranged in the READ list. In the WRITE statement the direction of this influence is reversed. That is, the order of the variable names in the WRITE list determines the order in which the data items referred to by those names will appear.

If we want a particular data value to appear first in a row of printed figures, then the variable name for this data item must appear first in the WRITE statement. If we want another data item to appear second in this row of printing, the second name in the WRITE statement must be the variable name associated with that value, and so on.

If we use too few variable names in a WRITE statement, some of the values we want will not be brought out of the computer. This is comparable to making the same mistake in the READ statement, in which case some of the values we want would not be brought into the computer. In either case, we might consider that we have not called for these values by name; thus they do not *move*.

In the case of the WRITE statement, say we have three integer values in the computer:

4   12   17

These values are stored respectively in the locations known as J, K, and L. If we instruct the computer:

WRITE J, K

only two values will be written out, because only two variable names appeared in the WRITE statement. Since those two names are J and K, the line of printing resulting from this statement would be:

4   12

The last value, 17, would not appear on the paper because the name of that storage location did not appear in the WRITE statement. Even though we want to know what value is stored under the name K, we will not see that value unless we include the name K in the WRITE statement.

Here is another example of how explicit we must be in giving the computer instructions. To a person we might say something like this: Let me see all the data values involved in this calculation. He would know which values these are, and would write them down for us. With the computer, however, we must know which values we want to see, and then must specifically call for each one of them *by name*.

Undefined Names

The opposite kind of error is that of including *too many* variable names in the WRITE list; that is, including the name of a location without having a value stored in that location. We have said that when a variable name appears in a WRITE statement, the computer goes to the location it knows by that variable name and prints out the value it finds there. But what happens if we have not previously placed a value in that location?

When a value is assigned to a location, the name associated with that location is said to be *defined*. This means that variable name now has a value assigned to it. There are several ways of *defining* a variable name; that is, there are several ways to give a value to a variable name, or to get a value into the storage location which carries that name. One is to read a data value into that location through the use of a READ statement. Another way is to place in that location a value which is the result of some calculation in the program (a matter we will speak about later). Here the point is merely that if a variable name has not been defined in one of these ways, there will be no value stored in the location known by that name. If such a variable name should show up in a WRITE statement, the computer would look in that location for a value, and since we have put nothing there, it is hard to tell what the computer would find. If the computer zeroes out (empties) all storage locations prior to the running of each different program, then the value stored in an undefined location will be zero. If not, we may get some value left over from someone else's program, or even something like a string of X's, some kind of what is called *garbage*. (It may be that a computer will protect against using an undefined name. That is, if it is told to do something with the value in a location, but has not placed anything *in* that location previously in a program, the computer may stop the program and indicate, in an *error message* of the kind discussed in Chapter Eight, that the name associated with that location is undefined. This would obviously protect the programmer against accepting a wrong figure written out; however, do not get in the habit of relying completely on this kind of protection from the computer: your computer may not offer it, or if it does offer such protection, the computer may slip up occasionally. The safest course is to make as sure as possible, *yourself*, that a program is correct, that all variable names have values when they are used, etc.)

Printing Several Lines

Since we are saying for the moment that the variable names in one WRITE statement produce the figures on one line of paper, if we want some data values to appear on one line, and others on a second line, then we must use two WRITE statements. To illustrate, say we have the value 72 stored in the computer under the variable name NSIZE, and the value 84 stored in the location known as NWT. If we want both values to appear on one line on a sheet of paper, we put these variable names in the same WRITE statement:

    WRITE NSIZE, NWT

This would give us a line of figures on the output paper that looks like this:

72   84

However, if we wanted each value on a separate line, we would use two WRITE statements, like this:

WRITE NSIZE
WRITE NWT

This would produce two lines of output, looking like this:

72
84

EXAMPLES

In the first examples here, ignore the spaces which appear between the data values shown. Just consider that the values appear on a single line of printing, in the order shown. Later we will take up the question of blank spaces between numbers, and the general physical arrangement of data values on a sheet of paper.

In all these examples, the equal sign is used to show that a particular value is stored in a location carrying a particular variable name. That is, the notation NED1 = 14 means the integer value 14 is stored in the location known as NED1.

1. Values stored in locations known by these variable names:

   NED1 = 14   NED4 = 8
   NED2 = 6   NED5 = 12
   NED3 = 7

   WRITE statement:

   WRITE NED1, NED2, NED3, NED4, NED5

   This combination of data values and WRITE statement would result in this line of figures being printed on a sheet of paper:

   14   6   7   8   12

2. Values stored in locations known by these variable names:

   ID1 = 4   ID4 = 7
   ID2 = 15   ID5 = 5
   ID3 = 22   ID6 = 1

WRITE statement:

WRITE ID1, ID2, ID3, ID4, ID5, ID6

This combination of data values and WRITE statement would result in this line of figures being printed on a sheet of paper:

4   15   22   7   5   1

3. Values stored in locations known by these variable names:

NDATA1 = 16   NDATA4 = 7
NDATA2 = 5   NDATA5 = 8
NDATA3 = 1   NDATA6 = 9

WRITE statement:

WRITE NDATA1, NDATA2, NDATA3, NDATA4

This combination of data values and WRITE statement would result in this line of figures being printed on a sheet of paper:

16   5   1   7

Note that two data values would not be printed out, because the names under which they are stored did not appear in the WRITE statement.

4. Values stored in locations known by these variable names:

NRESA = 2   NRESC = 5
NRESB = 4

WRITE statement:

WRITE NRESA, NRESB, NRESC, NRESD, NRESE

This combination of data values and WRITE statment would result in this line of figures being printed on a sheet of paper:

2   4   5   X   X

Note that the computer, in trying to find data values to print out for the last two variable names in the WRITE list, would produce *garbage*.

5. Values stored in locations known by these variable names:

NH = 1   NG = 6
NF = 5   NE = 4
ND = 2   NC = 3
NB = 7   NA = 9

WRITE statements:

WRITE NA, NB, NC, ND
WRITE NE, NF, NG, NH

This combination of data values and WRITE statements would result in these lines of figures being printed on a sheet of paper:

9   7   3   2

4   5   6   1

WRITING FLOATING POINT DATA

The WRITE statement works the same for floating point variables as for integer variables, except that if a floating point value is involved, the variable name begins with a floating point letter. For example, the WRITE statement to print the floating point value stored in a location named VARA would look like this:

WRITE   VARA

A very important point, however, is that a value written in the floating point mode will *always* have a decimal point appearing with it on the paper. This contrasts with the reading of floating point values, where a decimal point may or may not appear in a value on a data card. With the WRITE statement there is not this option. Decimal points will appear in *all* values written out in the floating point mode. Even if there is no decimal part to a particular value, it will still appear with its decimal point, like this:

26.

EXAMPLES

6. Values stored in locations known by these variable names:

ED1 = 14.   ED4 = 8.

ED2 = 6.   ED5 = 12.

ED3 = 7.

WRITE statement:

WRITE ED1, ED2, ED3, ED4, ED5

This combination of data values and WRITE statement would result in this line of figures being printed on a sheet of paper:

14.   6.   7.   8.   12.

7. Values stored in locations known by these variable names:

SCORE1 = 4.0   SCORE3 = 28.9

SCORE4 = 17.2   SCORE 2= 15.6

WRITE statement:

WRITE SCORE1, SCORE2, SCORE3, SCORE4

This combination of data values and WRITE statement would result in this line of figures being printed on a sheet of paper:

4.0   15.6   28.9   17.2

8. Values stored in locations known by these variable names:

DATA4 = 58.   DATA1 = 24.
DATA2 = 67.   DATA3 = 78.
DATA5 = 15.

WRITE statement:

WRITE DATA1, DATA2, DATA3, DATA4

This combination of data values and WRITE statement would result in this line of figures being printed on a sheet of paper:

24.   67.   78.   58.

Note again that a data value would not be printed out, because the name under which it was stored did not appear in the WRITE statement.

9. Values stored in locations known by these variable names:

RESA = 12.   RESB = 16.5
RESC = 5.8

WRITE statement:

WRITE RESA, RESB, RESC, RESD, RESE

This combination of data values and WRITE statement would result in this line of figures being printed on a sheet of paper:

12.   16.5   5.8   X   X

Note again what might happen when the computer is asked to write out values which *do not exist.*

10. Values stored in locations known by these variable names:

RESE = 2.   RESF = 4.
RESG = 7.   RESA = 5.
RESC = 6.   RESB = 3.

Write statements:

WRITE RESE, RESF, RESG
WRITE RESC, RESB, RESA

This combination of data values and WRITE statements would result in these lines of figures being printed on a sheet of paper:

2.   4.   7.
6.   3.   5.

EXERCISES

See exercises 1–12 in Chapter Five of the *Workbook.*

WHERE TO PRINT THE DATA

In its simplest form, the instruction or statement which tells the computer to write out data values looks like this:

WRITE A, B, C,   (for floating point data)
WRITE NA, NB, NC   (for integer data)

There is the word WRITE and a list of one or more variable names. Again these names are called a *list*—in this case, a *WRITE list.*

In this simple form, however, the WRITE statement does not tell the computer everything it must know if it is to write out the figures we want. We must tell the computer where to put the figures it is bringing out of its storage locations. Also, we must tell the computer whether a figure should take one or two or three spaces on paper, whether two or more figures printed on the same line should be spaced close together, or widely separated across the paper, and so on.

The first of these points, where to put the data, is comparable to a question raised in connection with the READ statement. There we asked: Where does the computer find the data it is to read? That earlier question was answered by telling the computer to look at the magnetic tape mounted on an input device, often referred to as Device Number 5.

Similarly, for the WRITE statement we tell the computer to go to another tape unit, often known as number 6. There it puts on tape the data values we have asked it to write out. This tape then controls a printer something like a typewriter. A continuous band of paper moves through this printer and the figures the computer put on the magnetic tape are thus printed on the paper in a form we can read.

This band of paper consists of separate pages joined together at serrated edges, something like paper towels on a roll, except that these pages lie flat against each other. When we get the stack of paper that represents the output from a program, tearing it at each of these edges gives individual pages we can put in a large notebook.

The reason for using an auxilliary device like this for output is the same as in the case of input. Just as the computer can do calculations much faster than data cards can be physically moved, so can it do those calculations much faster than keys can be physically moved to print characters on a sheet of paper. So auxilliary tape units are used to save time in both the input and output processes, thereby allowing the computer to spend more of its time on what it does best, figuring. Then somewhere else in the computing center the tapes can be filled or emptied, as the case may be, rather slowly in comparison with the speed of the computer's calculations.

In arranging the output from the computer, do the same thing we suggested doing with the READ statement: that is, forget about the magnetic tape. We know the data values to be written out will probably go from the computer on to magnetic tape, rather than directly to the printer. But for our purposes here, think only about organizing the output on the paper. We can do this because each line of figures put on tape by the computer exactly represents the corresponding line of printing on a sheet of paper. On tape the figures will be in the form of tiny impulses, rather than ink, but the number of figures on one line, the number of spaces between figures, all these things will be a miniaturized version on tape of the way they will appear on paper. So the *effect* of the WRITE statement we are studying here is *as though* values were going directly on to the paper in the printer, just as the effect of the READ statement discussed earlier is *as though* the data were going directly from cards into the computer: even though magnetic tape may be used as an intermediary in both processes.

In the WRITE statement we put the output device number 6 in parentheses after the word WRITE, giving us something like this:

WRITE (6,   ) NA, NB, NC

The 6 added to the WRITE statement thus tells the computer, in effect: When you write out the values called for in the list of the WRITE statement, go to auxiliary tape device number 6 and put the values on the tape there.

FORMAT STATEMENT

So far we have learned to tell the computer to write out one or more values, and to tell it which value(s) we want to see— the value(s) stored in the location(s) known by the name(s) in the WRITE statement. By means of the 6 in the WRITE statement we tell the computer to write the value(s) on a magnetic tape, from which a printer will convert them to characters on a sheet of paper.

Now we must tell the computer *how* to write out these figures. This point also has its parallel in connection with the READ statement. There the question was: How do we tell the computer what form the data values are in on the data card? The corresponding question with the WRITE statement here is: How do we tell the computer what form to print the data values in, on the output paper?

In both cases we use a FORMAT statement. Here again we give the FORMAT statement a number, so the computer can find this particular statement in the program. We put this number inside the parentheses of the WRITE statement, after the 6 and separated from it by a comma. When we add this feature to our WRITE statement, we end up with this complete form:

WRITE (6, 28) NA, NB, NC

The 28 here refers to some other instruction numbered 28 in the program of which this WRITE statement is a part. So the relationship between a WRITE statement and its FORMAT statement is the same as the relationship between a READ statement and its FORMAT statement.

Everything said in the last chapter about numbering instructions in a program holds for the output FORMAT numbers. That is, the numbers need not be consecutive, nor in order. Also, there can not be duplicate numbers. If a FORMAT statement used with a READ statement has the number 50, for example, then no other input FORMAT and no output FORMAT, no other instruction in the whole program, may have this number.

Again the FORMAT number is independent of the number of the output device. Thus we could write this instruction:

WRITE (6, 6) NA, NB, NC

The first 6 in the parentheses refers to the output device, the second 6 refers to a FORMAT statement numbered 6 in the program.

In the output FORMAT statement we tell the computer such things as whether data values occupy one or two or three spaces, how many spaces to allot to the decimal part of a floating point value, how many spaces to leave between data values, and so on.

To summarize, when we include a FORMAT number in the WRITE statement, and write the complete form of the statement:

WRITE (6, 28) NA, NB, NC

we are really telling the computer a number of things:

1. Go to the locations named NA, NB, and NC, and see what values are stored in those locations, respectively.
2. Print these values on output device number 6.
3. Print these values according to the FORMAT information in statement number 28 in the program.

One major difference between the use of the FORMAT statement for input and for output is this: When we are reading data we take the values as they are and use the FORMAT statement to tell the computer what to look for and where to find the values. We may have had some say over how the data items were arranged on the data card, but when the time comes to read them in a program, we are still guided in writing the input FORMAT statement by the way the data items appear on the card. In output, however, we have complete say as to how the data values appear on paper. The information we give the computer in the output FORMAT statement determines how many spaces on the printed page each data item will occupy, how widely items are separated, and so on.

Despite this difference, however, it will become apparent in

the following pages that input and output FORMAT statements look very similar and are constructed in similar ways.
Therefore, you might wonder how the computer distinguishes
between the two kinds of FORMAT statements. The answer is
that it uses the FORMAT numbers. If a FORMAT statement
number appears in the parentheses of a READ statement, the
computer uses that FORMAT statement in reading data, and
if a FORMAT statement number appears in a WRITE statement, the computer uses that FORMAT statement in writing
data. Since no two FORMAT statements may have the same
number, the computer will not confuse the two kinds of FOR-
MAT statements.

FORMAT SPECIFICATION FOR INTEGER VALUES

In showing the computer how we want a given data value
written out on paper, we again use a *field specification*. In
output, too, integers are easier to handle because of the lack
of a decimal part, so we will again begin with them.

When we tell the computer to print out an integer value, we
tell it two things about that value. First, we tell it the value is
integer. In output, as in input, we use the letter I for this. Then
we tell the computer how many spaces on a line of printing
this value is to occupy. Again, we do this with a number after
the letter I. Remember, however, that in the output FORMAT
this number refers to spaces on a sheet of paper, rather than
to columns on a data card. For example, in an output FOR-
MAT the integer number 47 would again be described as I2.
In output, however, the 2 means two spaces on a sheet of
paper.

If a value is being written out with a minus sign, then an
extra space must be provided for the sign. Thus the output
field specification for the value −47 would be I3. When a
value may be negative sometimes but positive other times, we
can provide an extra space for the minus sign. Then if no sign
is present, the computer leaves this space blank.

In output, the number of spaces on a line of printing occupied by a value is known as the *field* of that number. Thus the

figure −47 would occupy a data field three spaces wide on a sheet of paper. Blank spaces may also make up a field, with the width of a blank field being the number of blank spaces appearing in one group.

In showing how the output FORMAT actually works, let us begin with the simplest case of printing out one value. Say that in a program there is the variable name NSAMP, and we want to see what value this name has; that is, see what value is stored in the location bearing this name.

Note that we seem to have something of a problem here. We do not know the value of NSAMP, otherwise we would not be asking to see this value. Yet we have said we must tell the computer how many spaces to use in writing out a value, which means we must already know something about the size of the value. We will soon see a way out of this paradox; for the moment simply say that we know, because of the way we use this variable name in the program, that its value can only be between zero and nine, meaning that whatever the actual value of NSAMP, it can be written with one digit. For the sake of our example, say the value actually stored in NSAMP is 7.

To write out the contents of NSAMP, we use this WRITE statement:

WRITE (6, 204) NSAMP

Before executing this statement, the computer would look through the program for the statement bearing the number 204, because in this statement will be the information showing how the value of NSAMP is to be placed on paper. Therefore we give the computer this FORMAT statement:

204 FORMAT (I1)

In form, the output FORMAT statement begins with its statement number (here, 204) showing the computer that this is the FORMAT statement associated with this WRITE statement. Again the word FORMAT follows this number, showing the nature of the statement.

The information actually showing how the data value is to be written is enclosed in parentheses after the word FOR-

MAT. Looking inside the parentheses, the first character here, the I, refers to the fact that NSAMP is an integer name, so that the value stored in that location is an integer, which means it will be written without a decimal point. Then following the I is a 1, meaning the value for NSAMP is to occupy one space on a line of printing.

Here again is the combination of WRITE and FORMAT statements:

WRITE (6, 204) NSAMP
204 FORMAT (I1)

Because of the WRITE statement, the computer would go to NSAMP and print out the value it finds in that location. Because of the FORMAT statement, this value would be printed in one space, like this:

7

The combination of I and 1 in 204 FORMAT above is again called a *field specification*, in this case specifying a data field one space wide and containing an integer value. There is one field specification for each value printed on a line. To illustrate this, say we wanted to print out the contents of three storage locations, and wanted all three of these values to appear on the same line. Say the three locations are named MA, MB, and MC, respectively, and that each of the values in these locations can be expressed with one digit:

WRITE (6, 801) MA, MB, MC
801 FORMAT (I1, I1, I1)

Here the FORMAT statement contains three field specifications, one for each of the values to be written. Each I1 notation is a separate field specification, each describing the nature (in this case *integer*) and the width (in this case *one space*) of a separate data field.

The rules for punctuation inside the parentheses are the same as in the case of the input FORMAT statement; that is, field specifications are separated by commas, spaces are permitted anywhere, and so on.

The one or more field specifications in an output FORMAT can again be referred to collectively as a FORMAT code. An output FORMAT code, then contains all the information necessary to describe the arrangement of a whole line of printed values.

To sum up the relationship between WRITE statement, output FORMAT statement, and a line of printing, remember we said that for the moment we are assuming that the number of variable names in one WRITE statement matches the number of data values printed on one line by that WRITE statement. This means that for each variable name in a WRITE statement there is a field specification in the associated FORMAT statement.

To illustrate, say we have these values stored in the indicated locations:

$$NA = 84 \qquad\qquad NDAY = 3$$
$$NZ = 197 \qquad\qquad NSIZE = 26$$

To have these values printed out, we use this combination of WRITE and FORMAT statements:

WRITE (6, 584) NA, NZ, NDAY, NSIZE
584 FORMAT (I2, I3, I1, I2)

Since there are four variable names in the WRITE statement, the computer would print four values on one line. Since the computer must be told how to print each value, the FORMAT statement describing this line of printing must contain four field specifications. If only three field specifications were present, the computer would not know how to write out the last value. Similarly, if five field specifications were present, the computer would try to use the information in the fifth field specification in printing out a fifth value. But the WRITE statement gave it only four variable names, meaning the computer has been sent to get data values out of only four storage locations. Thus there would be no value to write out in the field described by the fifth field specification. In such a case the computer might go to any other location at random and print out what it finds there, producing garbage. Or it might ask us to try again, with the number of field specifications matching the number of names in the WRITE statement.

For another example of a WRITE statement, say we have these values stored in these locations:

NCASA = 14   NCASB = 726
NCASC = 58

We use this WRITE statement and FORMAT statement:

WRITE (6, 87) NCASC, NCASA, NCASB
87 FORMAT (I2, I2, I3)

This would produce these values written out on one line:

58   14   726

SKIPPING SPACES

At this point we can ask the computer to write out on one line the contents of one or more storage locations, regardless of how values of different sizes are mixed together. But as yet we have no provision for separating the values on a line of printing. We saw in the input FORMAT that if field specifications appear next to each other in a FORMAT statement, this means the data values those specifications refer to are also right next to each other. The same is true of field specifications in the output FORMAT. For example, say we had these values stored in these locations:

M = 106   N = 57

We use this combination of WRITE and FORMAT statements:

WRITE (6, 88) M, N
88 FORMAT (I3, I2)

The result would be this line of printing, beginning at the left margin of the output paper:

10657

These figures illustrate two things about the way the computer actually arranges a line of output. First, the movement is from left to right, beginning at the left margin on the output paper (which we are representing here by the left-most digit in the line). Therefore, unless there is something in the FORMAT statement to tell it otherwise, the computer begins printing on a line at the left margin. In the above example, the first thing appearing in the FORMAT statement is a field specification for a field three spaces wide. Therefore, the first three spaces on the line are used for the digits making up the value of M, which is the first name appearing in the WRITE statement.

The second thing demonstrated by this example is the fact that unless otherwise instructed, the computer will print data values immediately next to each other. Previously in this chapter when we showed two or more figures on a line of output, we had these figures separated by several spaces. This was done purely for the sake of clarity here; in reality, when the computer prints two or more values on a line it puts them right next to each other *unless we tell it to do otherwise.*

In 88 FORMAT used in our example above, there is nothing between the two field specifications; therefore, there would be nothing between the two values printed out according to this FORMAT statement. It is obviously much easier for us to read a set of figures if they are separated by spaces, but the computer will *not* automatically space the values apart for us. Again, the computer does only what we tell it to do. If we tell it to print two data values on a line, it will. And if we do not tell it to separate these values, it will not.

In short, the computer requires an instruction as to what to do with each space on a line *up to the last space in which it prints something.* Note here the comparison with what we said in discussing input: about having to account, in our instructions to the computer, for every column on a card up to the last column read. Similarly, in output if we want the computer to use only the first twenty spaces on a line, we can ignore all the other spaces on that line, but we must account in our instructions to the computer for every one of those first 20 spaces.

As far as the maximum number of spaces available on one line of output is concerned, it is common to find the figure is 120. That is, up to 120 characters and/or spaces may be placed on one line of the output paper. This contrasts with the 80 columns available on a data card.

Despite the fact that we have 120 spaces available on one line of printing, however, for any one line we need worry about only those spaces up to the last one in which the computer prints a character. The reason for this is exactly the same as in the corresponding situation in reading data: that is, the effect of the closing parenthesis in the FORMAT statement. When the computer hits the closing parenthesis in the output FORMAT, it leaves the line on which it is currently printing, and moves on to a new line. Remember that we are saying for the moment that there is one FORMAT statement for each line the computer prints. On this basis we might say that the opening parenthesis in an output FORMAT is a sign to the computer that it is to begin printing on a line, and the closing parenthesis is a sign that it is to leave that line, and move to a new line. Thus if we have this FORMAT statement:

68 FORMAT (I2)

the computer is thereby instructed to print only in the first two spaces of a line, and to ignore the rest of that line: that is, ignore the other 118 spaces available on that line.

Yet if we want to separate data values by spaces, for easier reading, and if at the same time we must account for every space up to the last one used on a line, then we need some way of telling the computer to leave some spaces blank as it moves along a line. There are two ways to do this. One is to instruct the computer to skip certain spaces on a line of printing. This we do with X, just as we used X to tell the computer to skip columns in reading a data card. In output, an X means skip a space, with a number before the X showing how many spaces are to be skipped at one time. The notation 1X would instruct the computer to leave one blank space between two data items it prints. The notation 2X would call for two blank spaces, and so on.

To illustrate the skipping of spaces, say we had these values stored in these locations:

NVAL = 821   NRANGE = 1643

NPR = 59

We could use this WRITE statement to put all these values on the same line:

WRITE (6, 417) NVAL, NRANGE, NPR

Now say that as far as the spacing of these values on that line is concerned, we want the first value indented five spaces from the left margin of the output paper; that is, we want the computer to skip five spaces on the line before printing the first of these values. Since the computer moves from left to right along a line, just as we would if we were typing a line on a typewriter, if we want the computer to skip the first five spaces on a line, the first thing that must appear in the FOR-MAT statement governing the arrangement of that line is the notation 5X. Then, since the value stored in NVAL, the first name appearing in the WRITE statement, has three digits (821) we next put the field specification I3. So in the FOR-MAT statement, to tell the computer to skip the first five spaces on this line, and then write a three-digit integer value, we write:

417 FORMAT (5X, I3   )

The line of printing produced by this would be:

#####821

(The # sign indicates blank spaces on the output paper, beginning at the left margin.)

Now say we want to skip ten spaces on the paper before printing the next value, which would be the contents of NRANGE, the four-digit value 1643. This would bring our FORMAT statement to this:

417 FORMAT (5X, I3, 10X, I4   )

This would tell the computer to skip five spaces, print the three-digit value which is the contents of NVAL, then skip ten spaces, then print the four-digit contents of NRANGE. The line of printing resulting from using this FORMAT statement would be:

#####821###########1643

Now say that to complete this line of printing we want another ten spaces to separate the third and last value from the second one. This would make the complete FORMAT statement look like this:

417 FORMAT (5X, I3, 10X, I4, 10X, I2)

The result would be this line of printing:

#####821###########1643###########59

(The # shows blank spaces before and between the printed values; everything on this line after the 59 would also be blank, because upon hitting the closing parenthesis in 417 FORMAT, the computer would leave this line.)

Again, we can break up a set of blank spaces into several parts. For example, if we want to skip ten spaces, we can do this by 5X,5X, or by 7X,3X, or by 9X,1X, and so on.

EXAMPLES

The examples here proceed in this manner: At the beginning of each example is a series of data values. Each of these values is considered to be stored in some location in the computer, and each data value is identified with its variable name by the use of an equal sign.

Next are shown WRITE and FORMAT statements which are used to get these data values out on to the output paper. Then at the bottom of each example the data values are shown as they would be printed by the combination of WRITE and FORMAT statements used in that particular example.

To illustrate the spacing in a line of output, *we will pretend each line begins at the left margin of the output paper.* Any blank spaces at the beginning of a line or among the values on a line are denoted by #. Remember that after the last character printed on a line, the rest of that line would be blank.

11. (Numbers equally spaced on the output paper)
Values stored in locations known by these variable names:

NCASE = 22   NCLAS = 4
IQ = 112   IREC = 620
NOOC = 92

WRITE statement:
WRITE (6, 480) NCASE, IQ, NOOC, NCLAS, IREC
FORMAT statement:
480 FORMAT (I2, 3X, I3, 3X, I2, 3X, I1, 3X, I3)
This combination of data values and WRITE and FORMAT statements would result in this line of figures being printed out:

22###112###92###4###620

12. (Numbers unequally spaced on the output paper)
Values stored in locations known by these variable names:

NBLOCS = 18015   N = 916
NCITNO = 318   IN = 4250
IPOP = 324830

WRITE statement:
WRITE (6, 120) NCITNO, IPOP, NBLOCS, N, IN
FORMAT statement:
120 FORMAT (I3, 6X, I6, 3X, I5, 4X, I3, 5X, I4)
This combination of data values and WRITE and FORMAT statements would result in this line of figures being printed out:

318######324830###18015####916#####4250

SKIPPING SPACES WITH OVER-WIDE
FIELD SPECIFICATIONS

We can use X, therefore, whenever we want a certain number of spaces between any two values printed on a single line. But this means using an X notation between each two field specifications. To avoid putting this many additional elements into a FORMAT statement, there is another way to leave spaces between any two values on a line.

This approach makes use of the fact that if we tell the computer to write out a data field larger than the data value itself, the digits will appear at the right edge of the data field, and all other spaces in the data field are left blank. The reason for this has to do with what are called *leading zeroes.* Leading zeroes are those which appear to the left of the first significant digit in a value. For example, under an I6 field specification, the number 95 might be represented this way:

000095

But the leading zeroes add nothing to the value of the number. Therefore, the computer leaves them off when it writes the value out, just as we would if we were writing that value by hand. We say the computer *prints leading zeroes as blanks,* or that it *suppresses* leading zeroes; that is, keeps them from appearing on the output paper. Thus if we have the value 95, and tell the computer to write it out under the field specification I6, the result would be:

####95

(The # again shows blank spaces in the data field.)

This means, among other things, that we can write field specifications for much larger values than the computer can actually handle, with all the extra spaces left blank. For example, we can write I10 in an output FORMAT, even though we are conservatively saying here that the most digits for an integer value is seven. This would simply produce a data field with the left-most three or more spaces blank, depending on the actual size of the value being printed in that field. For example, if we printed out each of the following values under an I10 field specification, they would appear as shown below, with each value *right-justified* in its data field; that is, each value is located at the right-hand edge of its data field. (The # shows the spaces in each data field that would be left blank.) If the value of a data item is zero, one zero will be printed to show this. The zero will appear in the right-most space in its data field, and all other spaces in that field will be left blank.

####### 422

#########5

######## 17

7896897

#########0

The fact that we can specify a field larger than needed to print a particular value has several advantages. For one thing, this is how we resolve the seeming paradox of having to write a field specification without knowing the size of the value to be printed in that field. With the field specification we merely provide a field larger than any conceivable value to be printed in that field. The computer uses the number of spaces necessary to print the value, and leaves the other spaces in the field blank. This is why it is common to find I8 or I10 or I12 for output integer field specifications.

Another advantage of the over-wide field specification is that it gives us a second and more convenient way to separate values on a line of printing. To illustrate, say we have these values to be printed out, in this order, on one line: 84, 197, 46. These values could be written under this FORMAT statement:

862 FORMAT (I12, I13, I12)

Since each field specification was deliberately made ten spaces wider than the value which would appear in it, and since the leading zeroes in each field would be suppressed, this would leave ten blank spaces between each two values on the line, and between the margin and the first item, like this:

###########84############197##########46

We have, in other words, great freedom in manipulating field specifications in output FORMAT statements, a freedom we do not have in input FORMAT statements because for input each field specification has to be directly tailored to the value it is describing on the data card. As far as output is concerned, we can use field specifications not only to get the data values out of the computer and to describe the mode and size of each data value, we can also use them to spread the values across a line of printing to improve the readability of the figures the computer gives us. X's and over-wide field specifications may be combined in one FORMAT statement, to get the desired spacing on a line.

Remember, however, that X produces blank spaces *between* data fields, whereas the over-wide field specification produces blank spaces *in* a data field. With X we can call for an exact number of blank spaces between values. If we use an over-wide field specification to get blank spaces between two values, however, the number of spaces actually provided depends on the size of the value printed in the second of the two fields. To illustrate this, say we wanted to print on a single line these two values, in this order: 42, 875. Say we used an over-wide field specification for the second value to get blank spaces between it and the first value. If we used the field specification I8, this would provide five blank spaces between the two values, because the value 875 uses only the three right-most spaces in its field, leaving five blank spaces to the left in that field, like this:

42#####875

Now, however, say we wanted to write these two values on a line: 42, 123875. Say that again we use the I8 field specification for the second value. This would give us this line of output:

42##123875

Using the same field specification of I8 for the second value here means there would be only two blank spaces left to separate the two values, because only the two left-most spaces would be blank when a six-digit value is printed in an eight-space field.

REPEATING FIELD SPECIFICATIONS

There is another advantage to using over-wide field specifications. Consider the last FORMAT statement we wrote:

862 FORMAT (I12, I13, I12)

This would provide ten blank spaces between these figures printed on a line, like this:

##########84###########197##########46

But say we did not insist on exactly ten spaces between each pair of values, but rather, would be satisfied if we had at least five or six spaces between them, which would set the values far enough apart to be easily read. In this case, we could write out each of these values under an I10 field specification. This would give us, in this example, a maximum of eight and a minimum of seven spaces between any two figures. The FORMAT statement for doing this would be:

862 FORMAT (I10, I10, I10)

Under this FORMAT, the figures would print out this way, with the first data field beginning at the left margin of the output paper:

84   197   46

(Each of the underlines here shows a separate data field. That is, the line under the figure 84 shows the data field occupied by that value. The line under the 197 shows the field for that value, and so on. We will be using this device frequently from here on for showing the extent of separate data fields, so understand that underlining like this would *not* show up with figures actually printed out by the computer; it is simply a device we are using here for explanation.)

In the line of output above we have a series of data fields which are all integer and which are all the same size. Also, they are all next to each other. The blank spaces between the numbers are actually *part of the respective data fields* here. The fields themselves are next to each other (as shown by the underlines) as indicated by the fact that in the FORMAT statement there are no X's, which would be required to skip spaces *between* data fields.

If we have this situation, then we can use the same kind of repetition notation, or collective field specification, we used in the input FORMAT statement. In discussing input, we saw that if data fields were of the same width and same mode, and had no blank columns between them, we could use a number before a field specification to show how many times that field was repeated. In our example of output here, we have three fields, each ten spaces wide (with those spaces filled either with digits or with blanks) and the fields are all integer. Furthermore, there are no spaces between the data fields themselves. Therefore, we can use for all three data values the collective field specification 3I10. Putting this in the FORMAT statement would give us:

862 FORMAT (3I10)

As in the case of the input FORMAT, we can break down a set of fields into several separate groups. In this example, for instance, to show three ten-space fields, we could also write 2I10,I10, or I10,2I10, and so on.

In actual programming this repetition notation, or collective field specification, makes it very simple to write out a whole line of figures. We simply decide on a field width wider than the largest figure to be written out, and ask to have this field repeated for each figure. If the figures vary in size, they will obviously be separated by different size intervals, but we avoid having to write out a separate field specification for each figure.

The criteria for using this shortcut in output are the same as for using it in input: Briefly, fields of the same size, same mode, and adjoining. Remember that when we speak of *fields* here we include any blank spaces produced at the left side of an over-wide field.

EXAMPLES

These examples are organized like the ones in the last set, except that here we use underlines to show the different data fields involved in a line of output. In Example 13 here, for example, the first underline shows the data field for the value 130, the second underline shows the data field for the value 1, and so on. (Again, remember these underlines would not be part of the values as actually printed out by the computer.)

13. (Repeated field specification)

   Values stored in locations known by these variable names:

NQ2 = 4   NQ1 = 1
NQ4 = 5   NQ3 = 3
ID = 130

WRITE statement:

   WRITE (6, 68,) ID, NQ1, NQ2, NQ3, NQ4

FORMAT statement:

   68 FORMAT (5I8)

This combination of data values and WRITE and FORMAT statements would result in this line of figures being printed:

#130#######1########4########3#######5
- - - - - - - -   - - - - - - - -   - - - - - - - - -
                 - - - - - - - -   - - - - - - - -

14. (Same size data fields, not repeated)
Values stored in locations known by these variable names:

ID = 107   NRES3 = —5
NRES1 = 7   NAGE = 58
NRES2 = 3
WRITE statement:
WRITE (6, 16) ID, NRES1, NRES2, NRES3, NAGE
FORMAT statement:
16 FORMAT (I9, I9, I7, I7, I7)
This combination of data values and WRITE and FORMAT statements would result in this line of figures being printed:

######107#########7#######3#####— 5#####58
- - - - - - - - -   - - - - - -   - - - - - -
                 - - - - - - - - -   - - - - - - -

15. (Different size data fields)
Values stored in locations known by these variable names:

NRES1 = 3   NRES2 = 0
NRES3 = 4   NED = 12
NCITY = 5
WRITE statement:
WRITE (6, 27) NRES1, NRES2, NRES3, NED, NCITY
FORMAT statement:
27 FORMAT (I6, I6, I6, I8, I10)
This combination of data values and WRITE and FORMAT statements would result in this line of figures being printed:

#####3#####0#####4######12#########5
- - - - - -   - - - - - -   - - - - - - - - - -
                 - - - - - -   - - - - - - - -

16. (Skipping spaces with X's and with over-wide fields)
Values stored in locations known by these variable names:

IND = 223   KAGE = 38

INCOM = 6275   INT = 7

IRACE = 2

WRITE statement:

WRITE (6, 3010) IND, IRACE, INT, INCOM, KAGE

FORMAT statement:

3010 FORMAT (I5, 5X, 2I6, I8, 3X, I6)

This combination of data values and WRITE and FORMAT statements would result in this line of figures being printed out:

##223############2#####7####6275#######38
- ----   - - - - --   - - - - --
            - - - - --   - - - ----

Note that the five blank spaces after the value 223 and the three blank spaces after the 6275 are provided by X's. All the other blank spaces in this line are provided by over-wide data fields.

EXERCISES

See exercises 13–30 in Chapter Five of the *Workbook.*

FIELD SPECIFICATIONS FOR FLOATING POINT VALUES

In writing out floating point data values, we use the same kind of field specification we used in reading floating point data. Again, the general form of the field specification is:

Fw.d

The F shows a floating point value is involved. Then a number shows how wide the total field is; in output, this refers to the number of spaces the value occupies on the output paper. Next there is a decimal point in the field specification, followed by a number showing how many spaces in that data field are occupied by the decimal part of the value. Thus, in output, the field specification F6.2 refers to or describes a value using six spaces on the paper, with the two right-most spaces representing decimal places.

One important difference from the input process is the fact that when values are printed out in the floating point mode, they *always* appear on the paper with a decimal point, even if there is no decimal part involved in a value itself. Remember we said that when a floating point data is *read*, it may or may not have a decimal point physically present on the data card with it. In output, however, the decimal point will *always* appear, so that when a floating point value is written out, its field specification must always include a space for the decimal point; that is, the field specification must always provide at least one more space than the total number of digits involved in a value. Otherwise the fact that the decimal point must appear means losing a digit. For example, if we have a three-digit value with no decimal part (say 169.) we can not use an F3.0 field specification to provide for three digits and no decimal point, as we might in the input FORMAT. Rather, in writing out this number, we must use an F4.0 field specification, providing for the three digits and the decimal point, like this:

169.

If we tried to write a field specification of F3.0 for this value, ignoring the space required for the decimal point, one of several things may happen. The computer might try to print out the value anyway, but not having room for all the digits, would give us this value printed out on a page:

69.

The reason we would lose the left-most digit, of course, is that when printing out a data value, the computer aligns the value with respect to the right edge of the data field. So here it would put the decimal point in the right-most space in that field, then print as many other characters (to the left of the decimal point) as the data field provides room for.

Note that if we write an improper field specification which does not allow the computer to write out all the digits that make up a value, nothing is lost from that value as it exists in its storage location in the computer. The only effect is that we do not see what that value really is. But this is no small effect. We want to know what that value is, or we would not be asking the computer to write it out. Furthermore, when we take a value produced by an incorrect output field specification and use it for any purpose, we are using an incorrect value. So note this point well: *The effect of an incorrect field specification in the output FORMAT can be the same as though a mistake in arithmetic were made in the program.*

On the other hand, the computer may refuse to write out a value when the field specification for that value is incorrect. Some computers are arranged so that if they are told to print a value in a field too small for that value, they indicate this by putting something like a row of asterisks in that data field. On this kind of computer, for example, if we asked to have the value 169. printed out under and F3.0 field specification, the computer might print this in that data field:

* * *

On this kind of computer, you could also expect a comparable indication if an integer field specification provides too few spaces for the integer value to be printed in that field. For example, if we asked to have the integer value 169 printed out under an I2 field specification, the computer might print this in that data field:

* *

So if you see a line of output with some non-numerical characters in what is intended as a data field, this may indicate that the value to be printed in that field is larger than the field specification provides for. The solution for this is to go back to the FORMAT statement and change that field specification to provide more spaces in that data field (for a floating point value, more spaces to the left of the decimal point).

(To find out how your computer will react when given a field specification too small for the data value to be printed in that field, ask someone at the computing center.)

SKIPPING SPACES WITH X'S

With floating point field specifications we again have the problem of separating values to make them easier to read. To illustrate, say we have these values in the computer's storage, and want them written out on one line in this order: 42.007, 16.9, 18.25, 38. The FORMAT code for this set of values could look like this:

(F6.3, F4.1, F5.2, F3.0)

This FORMAT statement, when combined with the appropriate WRITE statement, would produce this line of figures on a page, beginning at the left margin:

42.00716.918.2538.

Again, there are two ways to separate such a series of figures into the individual values they represent. One is to use X's to skip spaces. If we want the four values we are dealing with here separated by equal distances on a sheet of paper, we could simply insert some value of X between each two field specifications. Say we wanted each value separated from the next one by nine blank spaces. Then the FORMAT code would be:

(F6.3, 9X, F4.1, 9X, F5.2, 9X, F3.0)

This would produce a line of figures looking like this:

42.007##########16.9##########18.25##########38.

(Again # indicates a blank space.)

EXAMPLES

17. (Equal spaces between values)
    Values stored in locations known by these variable names:
    FID = 417.   CASENO = 9.
    SCORE = −57.88   TOTAVE = 160.9
    WRITE statement:
    WRITE (6,50) FID, CASENO, SCORE, TOTAVE

FORMAT statement:

50 FORMAT (F4.0,7X, F3.1,7X,F6.2,7X,F5.1)

This combination of data values and WRITE and FORMAT statements would result in this line of figures being printed:

417.#######9.0#######—57.88#######160.9

18. (Unequal spaces between values)

Values stored in locations known by these variable names:

AVINC = 5882.6   OUTSC = 16.02

AVEAGE = —2.7   FINSC = 87.01

WRITE statement:

WRITE (6, 81) OUTSC, FINSC, AVEAGE, AVINC

FORMAT statement:

81 FORMAT(F5.2,4X,F5.2,6X,F5.2,5X,F7.2)

This combination of data values and WRITE and FORMAT statements would result in this line of figures being printed:

16.02####87.01######—2.70#####5582.60

SKIPPING SPACES WITH OVER-WIDE FIELD SPECIFICATIONS

We saw earlier that a second way to get blank spaces between the data values on a line is to write field specifications providing for more spaces than the values themselves will need. We can do this for floating point values, too, because again the computer puts all the characters used in writing a value at the right side of a data field. For example, if we used an F8.0 field specification for the value 483., we could *think* of the value being printed this way:

0000483.

But the leading zeroes would be suppressed, so the actual figure appearing on paper would be:

483.

When a value has a decimal part, the computer prints the desired number of decimal places at the right edge of the data field, even if this means filling in one or two decimal places with zeroes. In other words, if we call, in a field specification, for more decimal places than there are significant digits in the decimal part of a value, the remaining spaces in the decimal part of the field will not be left blank, but rather, will be filled out with zeroes. For example, say we have this value, 87.5, for which we write the output field specification F6.3. The value would then be printed out as:

87.500

The two *trailing zeroes* would be supplied by the computer to get the three decimal places called for in the field specification.

The fact that the computer supplies zeroes, if need be, to get the required number of *decimal* places in a data field means several things for us. First, it means that when we use over-wide field specifications to separate values on a line, all the blank spaces intended for spacing purposes should be allotted to the left side of the decimal point. There they will indeed produce blank spaces, whereas any extra spaces allotted to the right side of the decimal point would be filled with zeroes.

Second, the fact that the computer prints the desired number of decimal places in a data field means that the position of the decimal point in a field is determined by the number of decimal places specified for that field. In other words, the computer does not automatically line up the decimal points in a column of figures. To illustrate this, consider the following column of figures. The data fields are aligned, or lined up, vertically, but notice what happens to the decimal points, because of the fact that the number of decimal places in each value is different.

4.28
16.00127
314.
.013

If we want these values lined up on the decimal points, we

have to write field specifications which will give each value the same number of decimal places, so that each decimal point would be the same number of spaces from the right-hand edge of its data field. We could write out each of these values under an F12.5 field specification, which would cope with the value with the largest number of decimal places. This would give us a column of values like this (assuming the WRITE statements were arranged to print each value on a separate line, with the data fields lined up vertically):

```
    4.28000
   16.00127
  314.00000
     .01300
```

Again the over-wide field specification lets us provide an adequate field for a value whose size we are not sure of. With floating point values, there is the added feature that if we are not sure what might turn up in the decimal portion, we can provide for one or two extra decimal places, and if they are not needed for significant decimal digits the computer will fill the space or spaces with zeroes.

Since the computer supplies zeroes if needed to get enough decimal places, one way to get a series of values all with the same number of decimal places is to add trailing zeroes to the decimal parts of those values with the fewest number of significant decimal digits (as we did in the last column of figures above).

Another way to get a series of values all with the same number of decimal places goes in the opposite direction: reducing the number of decimal places in each value to match that value with the fewest significant decimal digits. We reduce the number of decimal digits printed out simply by writing field specifications calling for fewer decimal positions. The decimal digits thereby eliminated are those on the right end of the value. To illustrate, say we have the value 392.637. This would be described by an F7.3 field specification. But if we wanted only one decimal place in that value as it was written out, we could use this field specification: F5.1. This would print out the value as:

392.6

To show how we use this feature, consider these values again: 4.28, 16.00127, 314., .013 Each value has a different number of decimal places. If we did not need the degree of exactness represented by the last two decimal places in the second number, we could cut that number down to three decimal places simply by writing an F6.3 field specification for it. This same field specification could also be used for each of the other three values, and if this was done, with each value printed on a separate line and with the data fields aligned vertically, the result would be this column of figures printed out:

4.280
16.001
314.000
.013

Reducing the number of decimal places like this obviously raises the question of *rounding off*. To avoid any question about exactly how this is done in the machine, and to get the desired degree of precision in a decimal portion, simply ask the computer to write out one more decimal digit than needed in an answer, and do the rounding off by hand.

REPEATING FIELD SPECIFICATIONS

The fact that we can get a series of values each with the same number of decimal digits means we can again use the device of grouping field specifications in one collective field specification. To illustrate, consider this set of figures: 47.91, 165.3, 14. Each of these values could be written under an F12.2 field specification, with the computer supplying an additional decimal zero for the second value and supplying two zeroes to the right of the decimal point for the last value.

This would give us a series of values all in the floating point mode, and all with the same number of decimal places. Also, while the number of digits to the left of the decimal point would differ from value to value, all the fields (including blank spaces) would be the same size because the field specifications made them the same.

So here, as in similar circumstances in the input FORMAT, we could repeat a single field specification, like this:

3F12.2

This would print out the above values in this form (assume the first data field begins at the left margin of the output paper):

    47.91   165.30   14.00
- - - - - - - - - - -   - - - - - - - - - - -
               - - - - - - - - - - -

(Again the underlines show the separate data fields.)

Here there would be seven blank spaces to the left of the first value (that is, between the first value and the left margin). There would be six blank spaces at the left of the second data field—between the first and second values. There would be seven blank spaces at the left of the third data field—between the second and third values. As with integer numbers, this kind of repeated field specification would not give equal spacing between numbers which are of different sizes, but it would give a neat appearing and readable series of figures.

The criteria for using this repetition notation, or collective field specification, are the same as in the comparable situation in input. That is, the data fields affected must all be of the same mode: here, floating point. All the fields must be the same size, including any blank spaces appearing at the left edge of a field. All the fields must have the same number of decimal places, which in output we can arrange simply by writing the field specification accordingly.

In general, this requirement for the same number of decimal places means the collective field specification works best for a series of values all of the same kind, so they would probably be of the same size and with about the same number of decimal places. Therefore this device is most useful for something like writing out a series of percentages, a series of scores on a test, a series of census figures, etc.

To illustrate, say we had these percentages to be printed on one line, in this order: 14.3, 17.92, 16., 55.48. These could all be handled under an F10.2 field specification, so that the whole line could be described with the collective field specification 4F10.2. With the appropriate WRITE statement, the results would be this line of printing:

14.30 ##### 17.92 ##### 16.00 ##### 55.48

Again, such a collective specification can be broken into parts, so that instead of writing 4F10.2 we could also write 2F10.2,2F10.2, or 3F10.2,F10.2, and so on

The fact that we can manipulate the number of decimal places by the way we write a field specification raises the general question of how many decimal places we should provide for when writing out a given value. Several things are involved here. One is the limit on the maximum number of digits in a value: a total which includes digits on both sides of the decimal point. Thus the more decimal digits in a value, the fewer digits we can have on the left side of the decimal point.

Related to this is the question of how many decimal places are meaningful in a particular value. This decision is based on the kind of number it is: a significance level, a percentage, a census figure, or whatever.

Note that we are talking here about the number of decimal places in the values written out in a program. Inside the computer any decimal part of a number is carried out to the maximum number of decimal places the computer can keep track of through exponents. Nothing we do with decimal places in writing out a number changes this fact. This is part of the general rule that writing out a number does not in any way change that value as it is stored in its location. Note that this means we can try to avoid cumulative rounding errors by getting into one program as many stages of a calculation as possible.

EXAMPLES

In these exercises # is again used to show blank spaces among the values printed on a line, and blank spaces between the left margin of the output paper and the first value on a line. Those spaces on a line after the last character printed would of course also be blank. Again we use underlines to show the separate data fields on a line of output.

19. (Skipping equal spaces with over-wide field specifications)
    Values stored in locations known by these variable names:
    TOTAL = 613.   CASE1 = 13.
    CASE2 = 16.12   CASE3 = 85.03
    WRITE statement:
    WRITE (6, 166) TOTAL, CASE1, CASE2, CASE3
    FORMAT statement:
    166 FORMAT (F4.0,F9.0,F11.2,F11.2)
    This combination of data values and WRITE and FORMAT statements would result in this line of figures being printed:

    613.######13.######16.12######85.03
    ----   -----------
         ---------   -----------

20. (Skipping unequal spaces with over-wide field specifications)
    Values stored in locations known by these variable names:
    PROJ = 401.   CATTOT = 9056.17
    CAT3 = 20.441   CAT2 = 71.996
    CAT1 = 64.25
    WRITE statement:
    WRITE (6,6304) PROJ, CAT1, CAT2, CAT3, CATTOT
    FORMAT statement:
    6304 FORMAT(F4.0, F11.2, F9.3, F11.3, F14.2)
    Resulting line of output:
    401.######64.25###71.996#####20.441#######9056.17
    ----   ---------   --------------
         ----------   -----------

21. (Skipping equal spaces using both X's and oved-wide field specifications)

Values stored in locations known by these variable names:

AVA = 56.05	AVW = 32.91
EDM = 13.5	EDW = 11.25
PCT = 17.5	

WRITE statement:

WRITE (6,116) AVA, AVW, EDM, EDW, PCT

FORMAT statement:

116 FORMAT (F5.2, 5X, F5.2, F9.1, F10.2, 5X, F4.1)

Resulting line of output:

56.05#####32.91######13.5######11.25######17.5

Here the spaces not underlined are not part of data fields, but rather, are provided by the X notations.

22. (Skipping unequal spaces using X's and over-wide field specifications)

Values stored in locations known by these variable names:

REP = 2.053	FMAX = 12.
FMIN = 2.0	AVESCR = 9.17
ATT = .017	

WRITE statement:

WRITE (6, 1590) FMAX, FMIN, AVESCR, ATT, REP

FORMAT statement:

1590 FORMAT (3X, F3.0, F9.0, F7.2, 5X, F4.3, F9.3)

Resulting line of output:

###12.########2.###9.17######.017#####2.053

23. (Repeated field specification)

Values stored in locations known by these variable names:

CODNUM = 52.	DAY = 17.
G = 12.	CT = 2.
FM = 7.	Y = 66.

WRITE statement:

WRITE (6, 118) CODNUM, DAY, FM, Y, G, CT

FORMAT statement:
118 FORMAT (6F8.0)
Resulting line of output:

#####52.#####17.######7.#####66.#####12.######2.
- - - - - - - -　　　　　- - - - - - - -　　　　　- - - - - - - -
　　　- - - - - - - -　　　　　- - - - - - - -　　　　　- - - - - - - -

24. (Repeated field specification)
Values stored in locations known by these variable names:
　　CLASS = 421.　　　　STU = 18.
　　GRAD = 57.　　　　CUMGRD = 262.
　　AVE = 62.07
WRITE statement:
　　WRITE (6, 294) CLASS, STU, GRAD, CUMGRD, AVE
FORMAT statement:
　　294 FORMAT (3F8.0, 2F12.2)
Resulting line of output:

####421.#####18.#####57.######262.00#######62.07
- - - - - - - -　　　　- - - - - - - -　　　　- - - - - - - - - - - -
　　　- - - - - - - -　　　　- - - - - - - - - - - -

25. (Dropping decimal places and skipping equal spaces with X's)
Values stored in locations known by these variable names:
　　FMAX = 17.03　　　　FNVAR = 16.
　　FN = 205.　　　　PNO = 18.
　　FMIN = 9.52
WRITE statement:
　　WRITE (6, 6783) PNO, FN, FNVAR, FMAX. FMIN
FORMAT statement:
　　6783 FORMAT (F3.0,4X,F4.0,4X,F3.0,4X,F3.0,4X,F3.1)
Resulting line of output:

18.####205.####16.####17.####9.5
- - -　　　　　- - -　　　　　- - -
　　- - - -　　　　　- - -

26. (Dropping decimal places and skipping unequal spaces with X's)
Values stored in locations known by these variable names:

PCTC = 64.07   PCTB = 18.19
PCTA = 16.02   CITY = 2.
GP = 10.

WRITE statement:
WRITE (6, 3784) GP, CITY, PCTA, PCTB, PCTC
FORMAT statement:
3784 FORMAT (F3.0,6X,F2.0,2X,F3.0,4X,F3.0,4X,F3.0)
Resulting line of output:

10.######2.##16.####18.####64.
- - -   - - -   - - -
          - -   - - -

27. (Dropping decimal places and skipping equal spaces with over-wide field specifications)
Values stored in locations known by these variable names:

COM = 182.   REG = 8.
PC = 4201.25   P = 1981.07
POP = 24.2   S = 65.1

WRITE statement:
WRITE (6,1974) COM, REG, PC, P, POP, S
FORMAT statement:
1974 FORMAT (F4.0,F6.0,F11.2,F9.0,F7.0,F7.0)
Resulting line of output:

182.####8.####4201.25####1981.####24.####65.
- - - -   - - - - - - - - - - -   - - - - - - -
     - - - - - -   - - - - - - - -   - - - - - - -

EXERCISES

See exercises 31-48 in Chapter Five of the *Workbook*.

ORDER OF FIELD SPECIFICATIONS

In an output FORMAT statement, field specifications for integer and floating point values may be mixed in any order. This is the same as saying that integer and floating point values may be arranged in any order on a line of printing. This in turn means that integer and floating point names may appear in any order in the WRITE statement.

The only requirement here is the same as in the case of matching the input FORMAT to the data and to the READ statement; here again, the variable names, the field specifications, and the data values (in this case printed, rather than read) must all match, in terms of mode, and for floating point values, in the number of decimal places. That is, the first value printed on a line relates to the first name in the WRITE list, and this value is described by the first field specification in the FORMAT statement. If the first name is a floating point name, the first value printed out will be floating point, and the first field specification must therefore be a floating point specification describing the field width and number of decimal places in that value. If the second variable name in the WRITE statement is integer, the second value printed on that line will be integer, described by the second field specification in the FORMAT statement, and so on.

In short, for each variable name in a WRITE statement, the value of that name appears in the corresponding position in the line of output produced by that statement, and the field specification for that value must be in the corresponding position in the FORMAT statement.

Remember the basic different between input and output in this regard. In input, the order of names in a READ statement is determined by the order in which the data values, being assigned to these names, appear on the data card. In output, however, we are free to arrange the names in the WRITE list as we choose, with this order determining the order in which the data values appear in the line of printing produced by this WRITE statement.

VERTICAL SPACING OF LINES OF OUTPUT

We have seen how values are spaced on a single line of output. But most programs produce more than one line of output. This raises the following question: How are these lines to be spaced relative to each other?

To put this question another way, if we are printing lines of information on a sheet of paper, we need to be able to tell the printer whether to start any given line at the top of a page, or to put it below the last line printed earlier on a page. In the latter event, is the newest line to be separated from the line immediately above it by single-spacing or by double-spacing? This is the same thing we would have to decide if we were using a typewriter to print lines on a page.

Remember that when we speak of *page* in connection with computer output, we are referring to the fact that while the paper goes through the printer in a continuous band, this band has serrations which make it possible to tear the paper into separate pages. Thus when we speak of a line of output beginning a new page, we mean the printer will skip down to the next serration and begin printing on the first line after this serration. Then when the paper is torn at that serration, producing a separate page, this line is the first thing appearing on that page.

Analogous to the spacing lever on a typewriter, we have a device for telling the computer how we want lines spaced on a printed page. This is a *print control character*. In a FORMAT statement we use one of these print control characters to show whether the line written out according to that FORMAT statement is to come immediately after the line above it, or whether the printer is to skip a line before printing this line of figures, which would be the equivalent of double-spacing. Or it might be that the line in question is to start a new page of printing.

The print control character appears immediately inside the left parenthesis in the FORMAT statement. There are two ways to use the print control character. One way uses the notation 1H followed by either a 1, a zero, or a blank space. If the digit 1 follows the 1H, like this:

1H1,

this tells the computer that the line printed out according to the FORMAT statement in which this notation appears is to be put at the top of a new page

But obviously it could be quite expensive in terms of paper if each line of output was placed on a separate page. Therefore, we can also write:

1H0,

The *zero* (not the letter O) following the H instructs the computer to print this line on the same page it has been using, but to skip a vertical space before printing this line. The line involved here is to be double-spaced, in other words.

Finally, if we use a blank space after the 1H, like this:

1H ,

we are telling the computer to single-space a line. That is, the line involved here is to be printed immediately after the line preceding it.

Regardless of which character we have placed after the 1H, the whole notation is separated from the rest of the FORMAT statement by a comma.

As an example of print control characters in operation, say we have these values in the computer: 12.0, 15.1, 7.9. We want these figures printed out in a column. Each of the figures can be written according to this FORMAT statement:

542 FORMAT (1H , F4.1)

(Here we are not using over-wide field specifications, but the effect of this print control character is always the same in spacing lines vertically, regardless of how data values are spaced horizontally along any one line.)

Using a blank space after the 1H for print control in 542 FORMAT above would give us the three values printed out on three successive lines on the paper. They would be single-spaced, like this:

12.0
15.1
7.9

But now say we would like a blank line between each two values to make them easier to read. The FORMAT statement for this can be the same in every respect except that in the print control character we use a zero now after the 1H:

542 FORMAT (1H0, F4.1)

This would give us the same column of figures, but now double-spaced; that is, with a blank line between each two lines of printing:

12.0

15.1

7.9

Whether we use single-spacing or double-spacing depends mainly on how many values we want to get on one page of output. Double-spacing is obviously easier to read, but if there are many lines of printing, we may want to single-space to get as many figures as possible on one page. Figures on one page would be a little harder to read, but we would not have to flip back and forth through as many pages to study the output.

If we used a 1H1 as our print control character, we would get each of the above three figures printed at the top of a separate page. The printer would put the value 12.0 at the top of one page. Then it would go to the top of the next page and print the value 15.1. Then it would go to the top of the third page and print there the value 7.9.

The second form of the print control character also uses 1,0, and blank space to indicate new page, or double-spacing or single-spacing, respectively. However, rather than using the 1H notation, it simply uses an apostrophe on each side of the 1, or 0, or blank space. For example, instead of using 1H0 to ask for double-spacing, we can use '0', like this:

542 FORMAT ('0' , F4.1)

EXAMPLES

28. (Dropping decimal places; skipping equal spaces with over-wide field specifications)

Values stored in locations known by these variable names:

IA = 2   IB = 17
PY = 42.02   PN = 16.27
ID = 117   SCORE = .07

WRITE statement:

WRITE (6, 1689) ID, IA, IB, PY, PN, SCORE

FORMAT statement:

1689 FORMAT (1H1, 13,15,16,F7.0,F7.0,F7.2)

Resulting line of output, appearing at the top of a new page:

117####2####17####42.####16.####.07
- - -   - - - - - -   - - - - - - -
    - - - - -   - - - - - - -   - - - - - - -

(The underlines again show separate data fields.)

29. (Dropping decimal places; skipping unequal spaces with over-wide field specifications)

Values stored in locations known by these variable names:

PCT = 13.027   IT = 19
I4 = 7   I3 = 5
RES2 = 16.   RES1 = 14.72

WRITE statement:

WRITE (6, 1420) RES1,RES2, I3, I4, IT, PCT

FORMAT statement:

1420 FORMAT (1H , F10.1, F6.1, I5, I3, I6, F12.1)

Resulting line of output, single-spaced:

######14.7##16.0####5 ##7## ##19#########13.0
- - - - - - - - - -   - - - - -   - - - - - -
        - - - - - -   - - -   - - - - - - - - - - - -

30. (Dropping decimal places; skipping equal spaces with X's and over-wide field specifications)

Values stored in locations known by these variable names:

IELECT = 1968   ICITY = 722
P1R = 42.32   P1D = 42.74
P2R = 43.42   P2D = 49.02

WRITE statement:

WRITE (6,6397)IELECT,ICITY,P1R, P1D, P2R, P2D

FORMAT statement:

6397 FORMAT (1H0,I4,I7,4X,F4.1,F8.1,4X,F3.0.F7.0)

Resulting line of output, double-spaced:

1968####722####42.3####42.7####43.####49.
- - - -   - - - -   - - -
- - - - - - -   - - - - - - -   - - - - - -

(Again, spaces not underlined are not part of a data field, but are provided by X.)

31. (Skipping unequal spaces with X's and over-wide field specifications)

Values stored in locations known by these variable names:

DIF = —.02   YS = .02
XS = .001   NYSQ = 49
XSQ = 16.421   IB = 79

WRITE statement:

WRITE (6, 147) IB, XSQ, NYSQ, XS, YS, DIF

FORMAT statement:

147 FORMAT (' ', I6,F9.0,3X,I2,F9.3,2X,F3.2,F8.2)

Resulting line of output, single-spaced:

####79######16.###49#####.001##.02####—.02
- - - - - -   - -   - - -
- - - - - - - - -   - - - - - - - -   - - - - - - - -

32. (Skipping equal spaces with repeated field specifications)

Values stored in locations known by these variable names:

P = 91.   IATT1 = 25
IATT3 = 46   ISUBJ = 14
IATT2 = 37   D = 14.

WRITE statement:

WRITE (6, 1789) ISUBJ, IATT1,IATT2,IATT3, D, P

FORMAT statement:

1789 FORMAT (1H , I2, 3I6, 2F7.0)

Resulting line of output, single-spaced:

14####25####37####46####14.####91.
- -   - - - - - -   - - - - - - -
- - - - - -   - - - - - -   - - - - - - -

33. (Skipping unequal spaces with repeated field specifications)
Values stored in locations known by these variable names:

NC = 124   NB = 99

NA= 4   NRANKS = 12

CB = —.8   CA = 62.0924

WRITE statement:

WRITE (6, 19) NRANKS, NA, NB, NC, CA, CB

FORMAT statement:

19 FORMAT ('1', 2I5, 2I6, 2F9.2)

Resulting line of output, beginning a new page:

```
###12####4#####99###124######62.09######—.80
- - - - -          - - - - - -     - - - - - - - - -
          - - - - -          - - - - - -      - - - - - - - - -
```

34. (Adding decimal places to use repeated field specifications)
Values stored in locations known by these variable names:

PLACE = 17.   ISIZE = 19

L = 22   S = 22.47

XS = 32.   YS = 17.

WRITE statement:

WRITE (6,7666) PLACE, ISIZE, L, S, XS, YS

FORMAT statement:

7666 FORMA (1H0, F3.0, 2I6, 3F9.2)

Resulting line of output, double-spaced:

```
17.####19####22####22.47####32.00####17.00
- - -          - - - - - -     - - - - - - - - -
     - - - - - -          - - - - - - - - -     - - - - - - - - -
```

35. (Adding and dropping decimal places to use repeated field specifications)
Values stored in locations known by these variable names:

PRO = 42.8317   S = 16.3

E = 13.1   R = 142.

SER = 23.04   PR = 16.432

WRITE statement:

WRITE (6, 186) PR, SER, PRO, S, E, R

FORMAT statement:
186 FORMAT ('0', 6F8.1)
Resulting line of output, double-spaced:

####16.4 ####23.0 ####42.8 ####16.3 ####13.1 ###142.0

- - - - - - - -   - - - - - - - -   - - - - - - - -

          - - - - - - - -   - - - - - - - -   - - - - - - - -

INTEGER VALUES IN OUTPUT

One other point in connection with output bears on one use of integer numbers in the kind of work social scientists do. As indicated, the printed page on which data values or answers will be written out is often 120 spaces wide. If we write out 20 items of data, and if a decimal point is printed with each number, then 20 of the 120 total spaces would be used for decimal places, leaving only 100 spaces for digits and for the spaces between values. Often the figures printed out are a kind which really do not need decimal points: for example, straight frequency distributions. If such values are written in the floating point mode, the spaces occupied by the decimal points are for all practical purposes wasted. Also, they can make the data look odd to the social scientist who is used to seeing such values appear without decimal points. The decimal point implies a fractional part to the value it appears with, but for a frequency distribution this would imply something like part of a person. Therefore, when dealing with data which do not inherently need decimal points, refer to them by integer names as far as possible. Then when the figures are printed out they will neither confuse, nor waste spaces with decimal points.

LOCATING FORMAT STATEMENTS

FORMAT statements for both input and output may appear anywhere in a program. The computer reads in all the instructions in a program, translates them into its machine language, and stores them before it begins reading the first item of data. Thus when a READ or WRITE statement refers to the number of a FORMAT statement, the computer simply goes into its storage area, finds the instruction carrying that number, and obeys it. So it makes no difference to the computer where the

FORMAT statements are physically located in the program we give it.

Some programmers prefer to group all their FORMAT statements either at the beginning or at the end of a program. Then when they want to look at a FORMAT statement they know exactly where to find it. Other programmers prefer to put each FORMAT statement with the READ or WRITE statement which refers to it. Then when they see a READ or WRITE statement they do not have to turn the several pages a large program might cover in order to find the appropriate FORMAT statement.

COMPARISON OF FORTRAN II AND FORTRAN IV

We saw in the last chapter that the form of the READ statement differs from Fortran II to Fortran IV. There is a similar difference in the form of the WRITE statement between the two versions of the language. A WRITE statement in Fortran II might look like this:

WRITE OUTPUT TAPE 6, 49, X

The same WRITE statement would look like this in the Fortran IV version we are using here:

WRITE (6, 49) X

Again the differences are slight. In the current version we do not use the words OUTPUT TAPE, but we do use the parentheses. In either case the FORMAT statement works exactly the same way.

Changing the input/output statements from the one form to the other is all that is necessary to make Fortran II programs suitable for a computer using Fortran IV. If a programmer also chooses to learn the additional features in the new version of the language, his original programming knowledge remains valid, and he merely adds to it his knowledge of the new features available. This illustrates something of the meaning of our earlier statement that programming languages change gradually enough so that with little effort a programmer can

keep up with the changes; it is not a matter of change so drastic as to suddenly make all his past knowledge useless.

A WARNING

We will close this chapter with a warning: If you find, by
asking someone at your computing center, that your computer is
the kind that will try to print out a value in a data field even
though the field specification for that field does not provide
enough spaces for that value, then try to make sure that an
output field specification is at least one space larger than the
data value which will be printed in that field. This is to be sure
that the computer has actually printed out all the digits that
make up a value (in floating point, all the digits to the left of
the decimal point).

If a value uses every space in a data field, we have no way
of knowing whether the value might not have one or two more
left-most digits that do not appear because the field specification
was too small. And this in turn means we can not be sure we are
not taking an error and using it as though it were an accurate
result.

On the other hand, if there is at least one blank space at the
left of a data field, we know the computer did not need all the
spaces in that field to print out that value, which in turn means
that we see all the digits (in floating point, all the digits to
the left of the decimal point) in that value.

So if a value uses up every space in a data field (even if the
value *looks* all right) try to rerun the program with a larger
field specification for that value, until there is at least one
blank space left in the data field.

(If your computer shows, by means of a row of asterisks or
something comparable, that a data field is too small for the
value to be printed in that field, then there is obviously not this
danger of accepting an incorrect value. But this still requires
that the program be run again with a larger field specification
for that data field.)

EXERCISES

See exercises 49–81 in Chapter Five of the *Workbook*.

Chapter Six

LABELING OUTPUT

Most programs produce so much output that we need some way of telling which value is which as we study the figures the computer has written out for us.

H FIELDS

For this, we use a technique which causes the computer to label, or identify, each value as it prints out that value. This was saved for a separate chapter because it uses something different from anything we have seen so far. This is the idea of the *Hollerith field*. The word *Hollerith* is a bit misleading here; it does not directly describe the characteristics of a particular kind of field, as the words *integer* and *floating point* do. Rather, it is a man's name, used as a kind of acknowledgement of an early contribution to data processing.

Yet what we call a Hollerith field does have two special characteristics. One is that in a Hollerith field all characters (letters, numbers, and signs like the plus sign or equal sign or slash) are considered *only characters to be printed out*. Thus when we put a number in a Hollerith field (also known as an *H field*) the computer does not see this number as a constant to use in the program. Similarly, a letter in an H field is not taken as a variable name. Finally, the computer takes no instructions from the contents of an H field. In short, the contents of an H field are not used for any purpose in a program except to be printed as part of the output.

The second characteristic of an H field is that anything appearing in it will go through the computer and come back out to us in exactly the same form in which we wrote it.

141

LABELING OUTPUT

Because of these two characteristics, we can use an H field to label output. Basically, the way we do this is to put a message in an H field in a FORMAT statement. Then when the computer executes the WRITE statement associated with that FORMAT statement, it also writes out the message in the H field exactly as we arranged that message in the FORMAT statement.

There are fundamentally two ways of setting up an H field. The first one we will consider uses the letter H, followed by whatever we want in an H field: that is, whatever we want written out as a message on the output paper. Then before the letter H we put a number showing how many characters long the field is (including blank spaces).

To illustrate, say that in a program there is a location named SUM, and that in this location is the result of some calculation. To see what this result is, we must of course put the variable name SUM in a WRITE statement. But to be sure we know, when we read the output that this value is really the contents of the location named SUM, we want to arrange our output so that when this value appears on the paper, it will be accompanied by a *message* telling us this is indeed the value of SUM. Thus we might use this simple *message* in an H field:

SUM=

To get this message on the output paper means identifying it in the program as an H field, like this:

4HSUM=

The H indicates this is an H field, and the 4 before the H tells the computer this field is four characters long. When the computer sees the 4H, it knows that the four characters *after the H* are to be printed on the output paper. The H and the number preceding the H are *not* themselves printed out. In the output we will see only the stipulated number of characters which follow the H.

To have this message printed out, along with the value of SUM, we put the H field in that FORMAT statement which governs the printing of the value of SUM. Where the H field goes in the FORMAT statement depends on where we want the message to appear on paper, relative to any other item appearing on the line of printing governed by that FORMAT statement.

For example, if we want the characters SUM= to appear *before* the value of SUM on a line of output, then in the FORMAT statement the H field with these four characters goes before the field specification for the value of SUM. To illustrate, say the value of SUM is 14.23. To get this value printed out, we put the name SUM in a WRITE statement:

WRITE (6, 407) SUM

The FORMAT statement to provide the characters SUM= followed by the *value* of the name SUM would be (assuming double-spacing):

407 FORMAT (1H0, 4HSUM=,F5.2)

This combination of WRITE and FORMAT statements would result in this line of output:

SUM=14.23

The message appears before the number because the H field comes before the field specification for the value of SUM in the FORMAT statement. This line would begin at the left margin of the output paper because the H field is the first element (aside from the print control character) in the FORMAT statement. That is, there is nothing in the FORMAT statement that would tell the computer to skip any spaces before printing the characters SUM= .

Errors in H Fields

As this example indicates, an H field is one element in a FORMAT statement, and is separated from the other elements by the standard comma. Note that the comma following the H field in 407 FORMAT above would not appear on the output paper because the comma is not in the H field. The reason it is not is because the 4 before the H shows that only the four characters following the H make up the field. A common error with an H field is to miscount (overcount) the number of characters involved, and perhaps include in the H field itself the comma which is meant to be part of the punctuation of the FORMAT statement. To illustrate, consider again the FORMAT statement shown above, but now with a 5 instead of a 4 inadvertently placed before the H:

407 FORMAT (1H0, 5HSUM==, F5.2)

Here the 5 before the H means the computer would include the comma in the H field, whereas the comma is really intended as part of the FORMAT punctuation. And with the comma included in the H field, the computer would see no comma coming in the expected position between this FORMAT element and the following one. This would be treated as an error in punctuation in the program, merely because the value before the H was *more* than the number of characters in the H field.

Another kind of error is to undercount the number of characters in the H field. In this error, the number before the H is *less* than the number of characters in the field, which means part of the H field is left out in the FORMAT statement where it does not belong. To illustrate, take again our example of writing out the value of SUM, but this time with a 3 inadvertently placed before the H in the FORMAT statement:

407 FORMAT (1H0, 3HSUM==, F5.2)

Here the equal sign would not be included in the H field because the 3 before the H limits the field to three characters. Thus the == sign would appear to exist independently in the FORMAT statement. Since there is no provision for the == sign in a FORMAT statement outside an H field, this character would be taken as an illegal character in the FORMAT statement. Also, of course, there would be an error in punctuation, in that the comma does not come after the H field here; the H field in this case contains only the name SUM, because the 3 before the H tells the computer the field here is only three characters long, and the equal sign, not included in the H field, seems to separate the H field from the comma that should follow it.

As the last few paragraphs suggest, H fields are a fertile source of errors in FORMAT statements, and these errors can be particularly frustrating, because they are so hard to find. The reason for this is that often they do not look like the errors they really are, and this may confuse the computer. For example, in the H field above where the number before the H was too small (3) so that the = sign would be left outside the H field, the computer might decide this was an error in punctuation because the H field was not immediately followed by the required comma; that is, there was a character between the H field and the comma. This would be due to the equal sign being left out of the H field, and this error would therefore really be a matter of the wrong number before the H. But with the computer indicating an error in punctuation, one is likely to search for an error in the punctuation in the FORMAT statement, rather than looking at something to do with the H field.

We will see shortly a way of writing H fields which minimizes, though it does not eliminate, chances of making this kind of error. So here we might offer a word of advice: Whenever there is something wrong with a FORMAT statement, look first at any H field. Then after making sure that everything in H fields is right, go on to check other parts of the FORMAT statement.

Spacing Between H Field and Number

Here again is the same FORMAT statement used in writing out the value of SUM, but this time written correctly to show the length of the H field:

407 FORMAT (1H0, 4HSUM=, F5.2)

Printed according to this FORMAT statement, the output for the value of SUM and its label would appear with no blank spaces, because we have provided for none in the FORMAT statement. If we want spaces in this kind of output, we can get them in one of several ways, depending on where we want the spaces. If the spaces are to come *between* the message in the H field and the value this message identifies, we can use either X or an over-wide field specification. For example, we could use this FORMAT statement:

407 FORMAT (1H0, 4HSUM=, 5X, F5.2)

In combination with the WRITE statement for SUM, the result would be this line of output:

SUM=#####14.23

(Again # indicates blank spaces on the output paper.)

Here the 5X in the FORMAT statement would produce five blank spaces between the message and the data field. Note that the location of the blank spaces is determined by the position of the X notation in the FORMAT statement. Since the notation 5X appears between the H field and the field specification, the blank spaces appear between the H field and the data field in the output.

Another way of getting spaces in this position is to use an over-wide field specification for the value. For example, we might use this FORMAT statement in writing out the value of SUM:

407 FORMAT (1H0, 4HSUM=, F10.2)

This would again produce this line of output:

SUM=#####14.23

Here, however, *the data field comes immediately after the H field,* and the five blank spaces between the message and the data value are due to the fact that the left-most five spaces in the data field are not needed for this value. Remember that when we use an over-wide field specification to get spacing, the exact number of spaces left blank depends on the size of the value actually printed in that data field. Here, therefore, if the value of SUM used more digits, there would be fewer blank spaces left between that value and the equal sign.

Spacing Within An H Field

To get blank spaces within the message itself, we merely put them in the H field by leaving blank spaces as we write the field in the FORMAT statement. The blanks are then taken as *characters* (this is one of the few places, as in the print control character, where the computer does keep track of blank spaces). Thus we could write this H field:

6HSUM = ,

This would produce on the output paper the name SUM, followed by a blank space, then the equal sign, then another blank space, before the computer printed whatever came next.

Providing for spaces within the H field, and again using the value of SUM for illustration, the FORMAT statement might look like this:

407 FORMAT (1H0, 6HSUM = , F5.2)

With the same WRITE statement for SUM, the result would be this line of output, again beginning at the left margin of the output paper:

SUM = 14.23

Remember that the space after the equal sign on the output paper is due to the fact that we have provided for one in the FORMAT statement by putting the 6 before the H. Six characters after the H includes the blank space after the equal sign. (As this indicates, the H field ends not with the comma which follows it as part of the FORMAT punctuation, but rather, ends with the last of the characters provided for by the number before the H. Then the comma comes after the last character in the H field, and even may be separated from the H field by blank spaces. Blank spaces are ignored *unless* they are specifically included in the H field by the number before the H.)

Changing Position of the H Field

If we want an H field to follow the value it is identifying on the output paper, we simply place the H field *after* the field specification for that value. To illustrate again with the value of SUM, say we use the same WRITE statement for SUM, and this FORMAT statement:

407 FORMAT (1H0, F5.2,20H IS THE VALUE OF SUM)

The result would be this line of output, beginning at the left margin:

14.23 IS THE VALUE OF SUM

The blank space after the H and before the IS in the FORMAT statement provides the blank space on the output paper separating the value 14.23 from the words following it. The 20 before the H shows that the H field here is twenty spaces (characters) long, including blank spaces. In this FORMAT statement the H field is of course not followed by a comma because it is the last notation in the FORMAT statement.

Remember that in all the above examples the reason the value of SUM shows up on the output paper is because this name appears in the WRITE statement. The relationship between variable name and field specification here is exactly the same as discussed in the last chapter. The only new thing here is that by including an H field in the FORMAT statement, we can get the contents of the H field printed on the output paper. The position of such a message, relative to anything else printed on the same line, is determined by the arrangement of elements in the FORMAT statement. If the H field appears before a data field specification, then the message will appear before the value printed according to that field specification, and vice versa.

Note that in all our examples here, the message and the data value were both printed on the same line because the H field and the field specification both appear in the same FORMAT statement, and we are saying for the moment here that one FORMAT statement governs the printing of one line.

EXAMPLES

1. WRITE and FORMAT statements:
   WRITE (6, 27) X
   27 FORMAT (1H ,17HTHE VALUE OF X IS, 3X, F7.3)
   Value stored in this location:
   X = .437
   This combination of WRITE and FORMAT statements would produce this line of output (single-spaced):
   THE VALUE OF X IS######.437

Here the first three spaces after the word IS are produced by the 3X in the FORMAT statement; the second three spaces prior to the number .437 are provided by the fact that the field specification calls for three more spaces than the number uses.

(Again assume a line of output shown in examples here actually begins at the left margin of the output paper. In this chapter we will use the # sign to indicate blank spaces where this seems useful: for example, where there are a number of consecutive blank spaces, and the # will help to more accurately count the number of spaces involved. On the other hand, where only one or two spaces are involved, they may simply be left blank. Also, of course, the spaces after the last character printed on a line are assumed to be blank. So remember that here we will be showing blank spaces either as really blank, or by #, whichever seems most helpful in understanding how a line of output is arranged.)

2. WRITE and FORMAT statements:
WRITE (6, 98) N
98 FORMAT (1H0,I10,19H##IS THE VALUE OF N)
Value stored in this location:
N = 32856
This combination of WRITE and FORMAT statements would produce this line of output, double-spaced:
#####32856##IS THE VALUE OF N
Here the field specification comes first in the FORMAT statement, so the number 32856 is printed before the message contained in the H field. The two spaces between the number and the first word are produced by the two spaces beginning the H field. Note that the same two spaces could have been provided by using 2X after the field specification, and then beginning the H field with its first letter.

EXERCISES

See exercises 1–8 in Chapter Six of the *Workbook*.

COMBINATIONS OF H FIELDS

A message written in an H field can be of considerable length. Remember, however, that commonly a line of output is 120 spaces, and if, for the moment, we are saying that one FORMAT statement governs the arrangement of one line of output, then the total number of spaces provided for in field specifications, H fields, and X fields in one FORMAT statement should not total more than 120.

Subject to this limitation, however, we can get great flexibility with H fields. For example, a message can be broken into two or more parts, with a value printed in between. To illustrate this, say we want a line of output looking like this:

SUM IS####14.23 HERE

This is accomplished by breaking the message into two separate H fields, one printed before the number, and the other after it. Assuming we are still using the WRITE statement for SUM, the FORMAT statement to produce the above line of output might look like this:

407   FORMAT(1H0,7HSUM   IS ,F8.2,5H   HERE)

The first blank space after the IS in the line of output is produced by the blank space ending the first H field in the FORMAT statement. The other three spaces before the number are produced by the over-wide field specification for that value.

The same flexibility allows us to print several values and/or several messages on one line. For example, say we have two variable names, A being equal to 14.2, and B equal to 7.5. In one line of output we want to print the values of A and B, identifying both. We use this WRITE statement:

WRITE (6, 47) A, B

We could use a FORMAT statement like this:

47 FORMAT (1H0, 6HA IS##, F8.1, 8H   B IS##, F8.1)

The resulting line of output would be:

A IS######14.2, B IS#######7.5

Note here that we can use a comma as part of a message in an H field, with the comma beginning the second H field so that it comes after the 2. The computer will not mistake this comma for the comma used as punctuation in the FORMAT statement, because when a comma is placed within an H field it is treated there like any other character in an H field.

In the first part of the line of output above, after the words A IS, the first two spaces are provided by the two spaces at the end of the first H field, and the remaining four spaces before the 14.2 are due to the fact that the field specification provides four spaces more than the value of A requires. After the words B IS, the first two spaces are provided by the two spaces at the end of the second H field, and the remaining five spaces before the 7.5 are due to the fact that this data field is five spaces wider than the value of B requires.

EXERCISES

See exercises 9–20 in Chapter Six of the *Workbook*.

HEADINGS FOR OUTPUT

An H field can also be used to write a message on output paper *without* a data field being involved. We have seen that to get a message printed, we put it in a FORMAT statement. Now what if we were to use a combination of WRITE and FORMAT statements like this:

WRITE (6, 512)
512 FORMAT(1H1,10HCHI-SQUARE)

This WRITE statement does not contain a variable name, which means there is no instruction to the computer to go to a location and write out the value it finds there. Yet there *is* a WRITE statement which must be executed, and there *is* a FORMAT statement governing that WRITE statement. So the computer would write something, according to 512 FORMAT. The only element in 512 FORMAT (other than the print control character) is the H field containing a message, and it is this message which would be printed by the WRITE statement.

So the above combination of WRITE and FORMAT statements would produce this line of output, beginning at the left margin:

CHI-SQUARE

In sum, the contents of an H field in a FORMAT statement are printed, regardless of what else may or may not appear in that FORMAT statement.

The above message would appear on a line by itself, since the FORMAT statement contains no other element to be printed on that line. Therefore, the main use of a line printed this way is to put on the output paper headings or titles for a set of output, or for portions of output.

This is illustrated by the above example. We assumed, in writing it, that we wanted the message in the H field above to be the heading for all the output from the program containing these two statements. This is why we used the print control character 1 in 512 FORMAT. This directs the computer to skip to a new page before executing the WRITE statement, so that the message would appear at the top (on the first line) of a page. If this WRITE statement were the first one in the program, this would be the first line of output printed by the program, thus serving as a heading to identify the output, answers and/or data, following it. This is useful when working on several programs at once, because it offers a quick way to identify the output from each program.

This device can also be used to write messages to ourselves within the output; for example, to provide subheadings for various kinds of output. To illustrate, say a program reads in raw data and produces a frequency distribution, then from this calculates a percentage distribution. The first output statement, to put a message at the head of the first page of output, thus providing a title for all that follows, might be:

WRITE (6, 1001)
1001 FORMAT (1H1,20HDISTRIBUTION PROGRAM)

Following this message, and double-spaced down from it, we

identify the first set of figures printed out as making up the frequency distribution:

WRITE (6, 1002)
1002 FORMAT (1H0,22HFREQUENCY DISTRIBUTION)

Then would come the output statements printing out the frequency distribution figures. Each of these, of course, could have its own label on the line with it, indicating which part of the frequency distribution it represented.

Next we want a message to serve as the subheading for the percentage distribution figures:

WRITE (6, 1003)
1003 FORMAT(1H0,23HPERCENTAGE DISTRIBUTION)

Next would come statements writing out the figures making up the percentage distribution, with each of these figures having its own label if desired.

Note in this set of examples that the FORMAT statement numbers are all as similar as possible. This was done to show that these statements all do a similar job—in this case, presenting messages to be printed in the output. This is one example of how we can choose statement numbers to show that certain statements are related in their function in a program.

SPECIAL LINES IN UNDERLINING

Finally, say that in our example above, after printing out the frequency and percentage distribution figures, we want some distinctive marking to show the end of the program's output. Since the characters in an H field go into the computer and come back out in the same form, and are otherwise ignored by the computer, we can use special characters in an H field to do special jobs, such as printing a row of asterisks at the end of a set of output. This row of asterisks will both *dress up* the output (a matter of some pride among many programmers) and simultaneously assure us we have gotten all the output from a program.

We can accomplish this by using this combination of WRITE

and FORMAT statements as the last bit of output from the program:

WRITE (6, 1004)

1004 FORMAT(1H0,50X,21H* * * * * * * * * * *)

This would fill 21 spaces on the output paper with alternate asterisks and blank spaces. The reason for separating the asterisks by blanks is that the computer's printer may hit the paper with such force that with a solid row of asterisks the paper may be cut at that line (though this danger is of course greater with a line all the way across the paper than with a short line like the one here).

This last FORMAT statement indicates something else we can do with H fields: namely, center them on the output paper. This is the reason for using 50X in the FORMAT statement before the H field. This means the computer will skip 50 spaces before printing the row of asterisks. Assuming 120 spaces on the line, if we subtract the 21 characters in the H field, this leaves 99 spaces on the line. To center the H field on that line, therefore, we merely use the 50X to skip the first 50 spaces, which leaves 49 blank spaces at the end of the line, after the row of asterisks. By using the desired value for X in a FORMAT statement before an H field, we can center the heading of a program, indent headings or subheadings five or ten or more spaces from the margin, and so on.

Note also that while we used a row of asterisks here, the same kind of effect can be produced with an H field made up of any of the characters available on the computer: dashes, plus signs, slashes, a letter, etc. The length and makeup of a set of characters like this depends on how we write the H field in the appropriate FORMAT statement. Remember to show the length of the field, including blank spaces, before the H. Then the position of the characters on a line depends on the use of X to indicate the number of spaces skipped before the field.

This technique can be used for a variety of purposes. One is to draw lines in the body of a set of output, to separate different portions of it. Another is to underline a message, using for this purpose an H field made up of dashes.

To illustrate underlining, say that in a program we have this heading, beginning at the left margin:

CHI-SQUARE

To underline this message in the output means moving the computer down a single space to print a row of dashes. The heading uses ten characters, so to underline it we need an H field ten characters long. Therefore, after the WRITE statement producing the above heading, the next WRITE/FORMAT combination could be something like this:

WRITE (6, 802)
802 FORMAT(1H ,10H- - - - -)

The reason for skipping spaces between dashes is again to protect against the force of the printer tearing the output paper. Note that the H field ends with a space here to get the required ten characters.

The result of using this H field to underline the message would be:

CHI- SQUARE
— — — — —

If we want this heading centered, which means also centering the underlining beneath the heading, we accomplish this by placing the necessary X field before both H messages: both in the FORMAT statement containing the heading, and in the FORMAT statement containing the field of dashes. Since the message is ten spaces long, this leaves 110 blank spaces on a line (assuming 120 spaces available on the line). Thus before the H field in both FORMAT statements we place the notation 55X, like this:

801 FORMAT(1H1,55X,10HCHI-SQUARE)
802 FORMAT(1H ,55X,10H- - - - -)

With appropriate WRITE statements, the computer would move to a new page, skip 55 spaces on the first line, and print the ten characters in the heading. It would then leave the last 55 spaces on that line blank (because hitting the closing parenthesis in

801 FORMAT tells the computer to go to a new line). On the next line (single-spaced) the computer would again skip 55 spaces, then print the ten characters of underlining (including the blank space ending the H field) and then leave 55 spaces at the end of that line.

The point to remember here is that this kind of similar spacing on successive lines does not happen automatically; the spacing of each line must be directed through the makeup of the FORMAT statement controlling the printing of that line.

A similar technique can be used to draw lines under columns of figures to show sums are being calculated, or to underline the headings over columns of figures, or to draw horizontal lines through the body of a table, and so on.

MESSAGES USING SEVERAL LINES

So far we have concentrated on messages which can be contained in one FORMAT statement. What if we want a longer message? For the time being we can handle this by putting part of the message in one FORMAT statement, part in a second FORMAT statement, if necessary a third part in another FORMAT statement, and so on. The portion of the message in each FORMAT statement will then be printed on a separate line.

To illustrate, say we had these three WRITE/FORMAT combinations:

WRITE (6,91)
91 FORMAT(1H1,15HCORRELATIONS ON)
WRITE (6,92)
92 FORMAT(1H ,22HSELECTED VARIABLES FOR)
WRITE (6,93)
93 FORMAT(1H ,18HMAJOR CENSUS AREAS)

The result would be this set of output, all lines beginning at the left margin, and the first line appearing at the top of a new page:

CORRELATIONS ON
SELECTED VARIABLES FOR
MAJOR CENSUS AREAS

SKIPPING LINES AND PAGES

Another use of H fields in arranging output is to make a WRITE statement which does nothing but skip a line or two on paper. To illustrate, say we had this combination of WRITE and FORMAT statements:

WRITE (6, 37)
37 FORMAT (1H0, 1H)

The WRITE statement would be executed, and would *print* the H field in the FORMAT statement. But since the H field provides for only a blank space, this WRITE statement would not actually put anything on paper. The computer would, however, have double-spaced before *printing* this line. The effect of this, therefore, would be to provide an extra double space between the prior line and the line to follow. Assuming that the next line was also double-spaced, this would be analogous to flipping twice, rather than once, the shift lever of a typewriter set for double-spacing.

The amount of extra spacing produced this way can be precisely controlled. If we use single-spacing with a blank H field, one line is skipped. So the effect of putting a blank line before a printed line which itself is double-spaced is to leave two blank lines between this line of printing and the preceding one, rather than the one blank line produced by regular double-spacing. By the same token, if we use a point control character of 0 and a blank H field between lines of output which are themselves double-spaced, the result is three blank lines, rather than the one produced by regular double spacing.

In short, by using the 0 and/or blank print control characters with a blank H field, we can get any desired interval between two lines of output.

Furthermore, if we use the print control character 1 the same way, and follow it with a line of output which also uses 1 for the print control character, we can make the computer skip a whole page in the middle of a set of output. To illustrate this, say we have this WRITE/FORMAT combination:

WRITE (6, 302) Z
302 FORMAT(1H0, 17HTHE VALUE OF Z IS, F8.1)

The next WRITE/FORMAT combination is:

    WRITE (6, 500)
    500 FORMAT(1H1, 1H)

Next comes:

    WRITE (6, 600)
    600 FORMAT(1H1,18HDATA FOR EDUCATION)

Here the computer would first print the value of Z, with its message. The next WRITE statement, because of the print control character 1, would direct the computer to the first line of a new page, where the computer would *print* the blank in the H field. The next (third) WRITE statement would again direct the computer to a new page, where it would print the message in that H field. The effect thus would be a blank page between the page ending with the value of Z and the page beginning with the heading for the data on education.

REPEATED USE OF A FORMAT STATEMENT

In this connection we might mention another useful feature of FORMAT statements. Say we want to write some statements that will skip a series of blank lines. We use this set:

    WRITE (6, 42)
    42 FORMAT (1H , 1H)
    WRITE (6, 43)
    43 FORMAT (1H , 1H)
    WRITE (6, 44)
    44 FORMAT (1H ,   1H)

Notice, however, that the FORMAT statements are the same, except for their numbers. (Remember that the computer ignores blank spaces outside H fields.) In a case like this we can, in effect, use a single FORMAT statement over and over again. So the same effect could be produced by these statements:

    WRITE (6, 42)
    42 FORMAT (1H , 1H)
    WRITE (6, 42)
    WRITE (6, 42)

While all these WRITE statements use the same FORMAT statement, the relationship between any one WRITE statement and the single FORMAT statement is just what we learned that relationship must be. That is, any one of the WRITE statements refers to a FORMAT statement, which governs the execution of that WRITE statement. Furthermore, only one statement is actually numbered 42, even though that statement number is used in several different WRITE statements.

In sum, where two or more WRITE statements use FORMAT statements which are identical in every way inside the parentheses (including the print control character) then all those WRITE statements can use the same one FORMAT statement. Remember that when we say *identical* we mean the kind and sequence of elements in the FORMAT statements; variation in spacing between elements is ignored.

This rule also holds for FORMAT statements involved in reading or writing data, as we will illustrate when we come to appropriate examples. But since this means data arranged the same way on different sets of cards, or in different sets of output, it occurs less frequently than the situation pictured here: simply using one FORMAT statement to skip a number of lines in output.

EXAMPLES

3. This line of output, beginning at the left margin, is to be the last line on one page:

THE SUM IS####710.24

The next two pages are to be blank. After these two blank pages, the next page is to have, centered, at its top this notation:

***DATA FOR MALES

Next on this page are four blank lines, followed by this notation, beginning at the left margin:

THE NUMBER OF MALES IS###236

The output statements for this output could be:

WRITE (6, 433) SUM
433 FORMAT(1H0, 10HTHE SUM IS, F10.2)
WRITE (6, 500)
500 FORMAT (1H1, 1H)
WRITE (6, 500)
WRITE (6, 501)
501 FORMAT(1H1,40X,17H***DATA FOR MALES)
WRITE (6, 504)
WRITE (6, 504)
504 FORMAT (1H0,1H)
WRITE (6, 534) NUMALS
534 FORMAT(1H ,18HNUMBER OF MALES IS,I6)

4. The last output on one page is this pair of lines (centered):

DATA FOR CITIES
OF OVER 100,000 POP.

The next page is blank, then at the top of the following page are these lines (centered):
CITIES OF 100,000
OR LESS POPULATION

#blank line#
#blank line#
#blank line#

THE NUMBER IS###39

(Notice we are using, to the right here, the notation #blank line# to show a line that would be blank on the output paper. This is to help more accurately study the spacing between lines.)

The output statements producing this kind of output could be:
WRITE (6, 89)
89 FORMAT(1H0,50X,15HDATA FOR CITIES)
WRITE (6, 90)
90 FORMAT(1H ,50X,20HOF OVER 100,000 POP.)

(Remember that in centering a set of lines, the spacing of the whole set must be considered. Here the fact that the second line will extend past the end of the top line must be considered in deciding the spacing for the top line, if the combination of lines is to be centered.)

```
WRITE (6, 91)
91 FORMAT (1H1, 1H )
WRITE (6, 92)
92 FORMAT(1H1,51X,17HCITIES OF 100,000)
WRITE (6, 93)
93 FORMAT(1H ,51X,18HOR LESS POPULATION)
WRITE (6, 95)
95 FORMAT (1H0, 1H )
WRITE (6, 100) NUMCIT
100 FORMAT(1H0,51X,13HTHE NUMBER IS, I5)
```

Note that we can use a comma for the figure 100,000 here, since in this case this number is used in the label for categories of data, not as a constant in the program. Note also that this number is put into an H message here because these categories of population size will always be part of this program. In the last line, however, the number of cities is treated as a variable because presumably this will change when the program is used with different sets of data. Here the number of cities is really the number of cases, which is a variable in a program.

EXERCISES

See exercises 21–32 in Chapter Six of the *Workbook*.

H FIELDS USING APOSTROPHES

We said earlier that there are two ways to set up an H field. One is with the H itself, as we have been doing. The other way uses an apostrophe to show the beginning of a field, and another apostrophe to show the end of the field, like this:

'SUM='

Here the characters SUM=   again make up a field, but now we do not use the H or the number showing the length of the field. Rather, the opening and closing apostrophes do both these jobs: show that a Hollerith field is involved, and show the length of that field. Note that we still speak here of a Hollerith field, or H field, even though the letter H will not be present in this form. As this indicates, the field enclosed within the apostrophes has exactly the same characteristics as those we discussed earlier in connection with the H field; the only difference here is in the way we denote an H field and indicate its length.

Note something here very similar to what we earlier saw in connection with the print control character. That is, there are two versions of the print control character: one version uses the notation 1H followed by a 1, 0, or blank, and the other version uses the apostrophes, but again with the same 1, 0, or blank. In either form (regardless of whether we use the H or the apostrophes) the effect is the same. Precisely the same relationship holds for the two kinds of H fields we are discussing here.

Using apostrophes is obviously simpler in that it does away with the need to accurately count the number of characters in an H field. In effect, therefore, we started with the harder form of the H field first. There are several reasons for this. One is that beginning with the harder version means you should be able to pick up the easier one with relatively little difficulty. Also, the combination of H and a number keeps more clearly in view exactly what we are doing in an H field.

Furthermore, you should know about the version using H, because it is still in use. There are several reasons for this. One is that the version with apostrophes may not be accepted on some computers. The version using H was the earlier one, part of Fortran II. The version using the apostrophes is the later one, part of Fortran IV. Incidentally, here is an example of parts of the two versions of the language coexisting; the earlier version using H may also work on newer machines which are capable of handling Fortran IV.

Another reason for knowing and using the older form is that when reading a program it is often useful to see at a glance how long an H field is, and this is possible in the version using the H.

Since both kinds of H fields operate the same way, probably all we need do here is touch on a few major points from our earlier discussion, to familiarize you with the sight and the use of the apostrophes. Recall our example at the beginning of this chapter of writing out the value of SUM, and identifying that value with the characters SUM= on the output paper. We used this WRITE statement:

WRITE (6, 407) SUM

Using apostrophes for the H field, and still assuming the value of SUM to be 14.32, 407 FORMAT could now look like this:

407 FORMAT(1H0, 'SUM=', F5.2)

The result would again be this line of output, beginning at the left margin:

SUM=14.32

To get spaces between a message and a data value that message is identifying, we can again use either X or an over-wide field specification, or put the blank spaces in the H field itself, just as we did in our earlier version. For example, to print the characters SUM= and then leave five blank spaces before the printed value of SUM, we could use any of these FORMAT statements:

407 FORMAT (1H0,'SUM=',5X,F5.2)
407 FORMAT(1H0,'SUM=',F10.2)
407 FORMAT (1H0, 'SUM=#####',F5.2)

(Each # in the last statement indicates a space left blank in the FORMAT statement itself.)

Each of these FORMAT statements, coupled with the WRITE statement for SUM, would produce this line of output, beginning at the left margin:

SUM=#####21.43

In the first FORMAT statement, an X field provides the five spaces between the equal sign and the value. In the second FORMAT statement, the over-wide field specification for the value of SUM provides the spaces. In the third statement, the five blank spaces are provided in the H field itself, by having the closing apostrophe include five blank spaces after the = sign.

To get spaces *within* a message, we again include them in the H field, which here means inside the apostrophes, like this:

407 FORMAT(1H0, 'SUM = ', F5.2)

On paper this would produce the name SUM followed by a space, then by the equal sign, then by another space, before the value of SUM is printed. Both blank spaces here are provided by including them inside the apostrophes.

The apostrophes showing the limits of an H field do not appear on the output paper: just as, if we use the other version, the number and H preceding an H field do not appear on paper. Here we see on the output paper only what falls between the two ' signs.

To use this version of the H field in putting two messages in one FORMAT statement, say we want to write out the value of the locations named A and B, respectively, putting both values on the same line, and identifying each value. With the appropriate WRITE statement, we could use a FORMAT statement, like this:

500 FORMAT('0', 'A =##',F5.2, ', AND B =##',F5.2)

If A is 4.78 and B is 3.05, the resulting line of output, beginning at the left margin, would be:

A =###4.78, AND B =###3.05

Here the first two spaces after the characters A = are provided in that H field, and the third space before the 4 results from the field specification for A being one space wider than that value requires. The space after the 8 is provided at the beginning of the second H field, and the first two spaces after the B = are provided at the end of that H field. The third space before the 3 results from that data field being one space wider than the value of B requires. Note the comma after the 8. Because this comma comes inside the apostrophes of the second H field, it is treated as a character and not as part of the FORMAT punctuation.

To produce something like a row of asterisks, we merely enclose the desired characters inside the apostrophes. For example, to get a row of alternating spaces and asterisks 20 spaces long, we could write:

501 FORMAT (1H0, '* * * * * * * * * * ')

The twentieth space in the field would be the blank space before the closing apostrophe.

In short, everything we said about arranging, locating, and using H fields earlier holds for this form. We merely substitute the apostrophes for the H and the number showing length of the field. The FORMAT punctuation is also the same, with one exception: an H field using apostrophes ends with an apostrophe even when that field comes at the end of the FORMAT statement. For example, we could write:

500 FORMAT ('1', 'CROSS TABULATION')

Here the closing ' is needed, whereas in the version using H, there is nothing at the end of an H field if it is the last item in a FORMAT statement (except, of course, for the parenthesis closing the FORMAT statement itself).

To center the message in 500 FORMAT above, we can add the required X field before the H field, like this:

500 FORMAT('1',52X, 'CROSS TABULATION')

But note that to center a message means knowing how many blank spaces to leave on either side of it. And for this we must know how long the message itself is, so we can subtract this number of spaces from the total available on the line. This means that when working out the spacing of a line, we still may need to count the number of characters in an H field, even though this is not required for the H field itself when using apostrophes.

Finally, to skip lines or pages, we can use our apostrophes and the blank space in the H field, like this:

402 FORMAT('1', '   ')
403 FORMAT('0', '   ')
404 FORMAT('   ', '   ')

The first FORMAT statement would skip a blank page, the second would provide an extra two blank lines, and the third, an extra single blank line. In short, the above three FORMAT statements would be equivalent, respectively, to:

502 FORMAT(1H1, 1H)
503 FORMAT(1H0, 1H)
504 FORMAT(1H , 1H)

If a computer will accept both forms of the H field, they can be combined in the same FORMAT statement. For example, a print control character (which is actually a kind of miniature H field) using 1H can be followed by an H field using apostrophes, and vice versa.

EXERCISES

See exercises 33–44 in Chapter Six of the *Workbook*.

SOME ADDED NOTES ON OUTPUT

After this and the previous chapter, a number of things about output should now be apparent. First of all, if you had wondered about the use of H in the print control character, it should now be obvious that the print control character is merely an H field which is one character long, and which has been assigned to stand first in the FORMAT statement and control the spacing of the printer.

Secondly, it should now be clear just how precise we must be in arranging the output from a program. With a print control character we must tell the computer what to do with every line on a page (print on it or leave it blank) up to the last line printed on a page. We must also indicate when to leave a page and move to the next one unless we have no preference on this, in which case we do not use a print control character 1. In that event, the computer will continue down to the bottom of one page and then automatically move on to the next page.

Similarly, every space on a line, up to the last character printed on that line, must be provided for in the appropriate FORMAT statement.

Furthermore, we can see how complex it is to coordinate characters on different lines: for underlining, or to group several words on different lines into one heading, or to set up headings over columns, and so on. A great help with all such problems of spacing in output is to use graph paper, with each line having the number of spaces, or boxes, corresponding to the number of spaces on the line of output from your computer. This kind of graph paper is made specifically to help programmers lay out their output, even to the extent of having the spaces on the graph paper the same size as the spaces on the computer's output paper. If such paper is not available, make a crude version by combining the sheets of some other kind of graph paper to give the desired number of spaces on a line.

Arrange the output on the graph paper as you want it to appear, line by line and space by space, including empty boxes or spaces. Then write the FORMAT statement for each line according to the way the blanks and characters appear on your graph paper. (Remember that with over-wide field specifications the exact number of spaces left blank in a field depends on the number of spaces used by the value printed there. In this case what we usually do is align the data field itself on the graph paper: usually starting from the right side of a field, because we know there will be one or more characters at that edge of the field. Within data fields we can also line up decimal points, if we want to.)

Another thing that should now be apparent is that output with spacing, underlining, etc. can use a great number of output statements. Indeed, often a large part of a program will be concerned in some way with output. Obviously, therefore, one reason so many errors occur in output statements is that there are so many of these statements. Yet attempting to minimize the number of errors by minimizing the number of output statements means output that is simple (even crude) though the figures might be correct. Many programmers feel (particularly as they get more experience) that output should almost be something of a work of *art*, rather than a simple listing of figures. For one thing, other people will often see the output from a program, and there is some feeling that output should be labeled and separated in such a way that it will be virtually self-explanatory to someone who knows nothing about the actual working of the program. Also, of course, the output is the only visual product of what the computer does; therefore, in a sense, this is the only place to make the work *look good.*

A useful tip in connection with output is this: It is often convenient to cut output paper to the 8½ by 11 inch size that will fit in a standard notebook. This is merely a matter of finding out how many spaces can be used on a line without going more than 8½ inches from the left margin of the output paper, and how many lines can be used without going more than 11 inches down the paper. If you can keep your output in this upper left section of a page, you can clip the page(s) and include your computer output with other papers in a regular notebook, rather than needing a big separate folder for it. This has enough advantages so that it is worth experimenting with as you get more experience.

Also, there may be other special output features available; for example, getting one or more carbon copies of a set of output, or having the output printed on the kind of stencil or spirit master that can be taken off and put immediately on a duplicating machine. This is useful for wide distribution of a set of output; to a class, for example.

Finally, remember two things when you begin actually working with output. One is that we are assuming here 120 spaces on a line. Check with someone at your computing center on the number of spaces available per line on your computer.

Second, output as presented here may seem more complicated than it really is. There are a number of details to remember (concerned mainly with form) but the logic behind them is simple. As you gain experience, you should find that output becomes a pleasant, and even most challenging, part of a program. With each program you write, try to add another little touch: first getting a data value out, then identifying it, then adding a title, then underlining, and so on. You will soon find the look of your work, and your growing confidence, makes it all worth the extra trouble.

EXERCISES

See exercises 45–58 in Chapter Six of the *Workbook*.

Chapter Seven

ARITHMETIC

Instructing the computer to do arithmetic operations is much easier than nonprogrammers realize, and in a sense, even easier than doing an equivalent operation by hand. This is because if we want something like a square root, we need not know how to find a square root ourselves, we only need to know how to ask the computer to do it, which is quite simple.

ARITHMETIC STATEMENTS

Basically, the whole point of arithmetic on the computer is to get the result of a given operation stored in a separate location. Then to see that result, we put the name of that location in a WRITE statement. Or we can use that result later in the program by using the name of that location in a subsequent operation.

To do arithmetic on a computer we use what we call an *arithmetic statement*. An arithmetic statement can look something like a conventional mathematical equation. For example, this is an arithmetic statement:

$$A = B + C$$

On the left of the equal sign is the name of the location which is to receive the results of the arithmetic operation. On the right side of the equal sign there is an *arithmetic expression*, which tells the computer what operation to perform, and on which value(s).

An arithmetic expression is made up of one or more constants and/or variable names. If the expression contains more than one of these elements, then there are also *operation signs* included with them.

Arithmetic Operations

Operation signs, or *arithmetic operators,* are those signs which indicate addition, multiplication, and so on. They take their name from the fact that we use these signs to tell the computer what *operations* to perform, and when.

These signs are almost the same as those used in conventional arithmetic. In Fortran the plus sign tells the computer to add, and the minus sign shows subtraction. However, since X is one of the characters which Fortran uses in forming variable names, we avoid confusion by using an asterisk to indicate multiplication. Finally, division in Fortran is indicated by a diagonal line, or slash /. The reason for this is that each Fortran arithmetic statement is presented to the computer on a punched card. This means that each instruction must be written as one line, so the diagonal line, or slash, permits us to show division involving two values printed side by side.

Here is a comparison of the signs used in programming and those used in conventional arithmetic:

Conventional Arithmetic Sign	Fortran Operator	Meaning in Either Case
A + B	A + B	Add A and B
A − B	A − B	Subtract B from A
A × B or A.B or AB	A * B	A times B
$\frac{A}{B}$ or B/A or A/B	A / B	A divided by B

Differences Between Statements and Equations

Despite their similarities, however, there are several important differences between a Fortran arithmetic statement and a conventional mathematical equation. For one thing, on the left of the equal sign in Fortran there can be *only* a single variable name, like this:

$$L = K - 7 + N$$

This is because of another way in which an arithmetic statement differs from a mathematical equation: a different meaning for the equal sign. In regular math, the equal sign means that what is on one side of it is equal to what is on the other side of it. Thus to say $X = Y$ is to say that X and Y both have the same value. This is also, for convenience, the way we have been using the equal sign up to this point: as in showing the contents in a storage location which is known by a particular variable name.

Now, however, we turn to the real meaning of the equal sign in programming. This meaning is *Set equal to*. In programming, the equal sign instructs the computer to calculate the value of whatever is to the right of the equal sign, and store that value in the location known by the variable name which appears on the left of the equal sign. For example, consider this statement:

$$W = A + R$$

This tells the computer to add A and R and store their sum in W. If A was 12. and R was 7. this statement would result in the value 19. being stored in the location known by the variable name W.

Another way of looking at this is that the equal sign is used here to mean equal *after* the indicated operation has been performed, not *during* the operation, as would be the case in regular mathematics. In the example just above, W would have the value 19. *after* the statement adding A and R was executed; then, and only then, would W be equal to the sum of A and R. Up to the point of executing this statement, W might have any value, or no value at all; what concerns us is the value of W *after* the statement is executed.

Since only one variable name may appear to the left of the equal sign, if we were to write (wrongly) a statement like this:

$$X + A = B + Y$$

the computer would take the $X + A$ on the left of the equal sign as a variable name. This would not be an acceptable name because of the $+$ character and also because of the spaces.

For the same reason, a constant may never appear on the left side of the equal sign. For example, we might write:

$$A = 2.$$

However, we may *not* write:

2. = A

because the 2. here, appearing on the left of the equal sign, would be taken by the computer as the variable name it expects to find there. As we have seen, 2. is not an acceptable variable name because it does not begin with a letter, and also because it has a decimal point.

DEFINED NAMES

Another thing to remember about an arithmetic statement is that every variable name which appears on the right side of the equal sign must have a value assigned to it when that statement is executed. That is, all variable names on the right of an equal sign must be *defined*. Values must have been stored in the locations known by those names prior to this point in the program. When we say a variable name is *defined*, then, we mean that a value has been stored in the location bearing that name.

The reason for this requirement can be explained in two ways. One is that like an equation, an arithmetic statement can have only one *unknown* (except that here we would speak of *undefined*, rather than unknown). However, as we have seen, in programming the *unknown* must be on the left of the equal sign in an arithmetic statement, which means anything to the right of the equal sign must be *known*; that is, must have a value.

Looking at this a different way, we can say that the point of an arithmetic statement is to place in the location at the left of the equal sign a value equal to the value of the expression at the right of the equal sign. And for the computer to get a value for that whole expression on the right of the equal sign, every variable name in that expression must have a value. To illustrate, say we give the computer this statement:

M = N + L

For the computer to place the total of N and L in M, both N

and L must already have values at this point in the program. This, very simply, is why we say that every name on the right of an equal sign must have a value, even if that value is zero.

A name appearing on the right of the equal sign may have a value that was read into that location, or a value placed there by an earlier arithmetic statement. And a mixture of both kinds of values is possible in one arithmetic statement. Among other things, this allows us to use a series of arithmetic statements, each performing an intermediate step in a calculation, with the result of one step being stored in a location which is then used in the next step, and so on. We will show an example of this later in this chapter.

(If we do somehow get an undefined name on the right of the equal sign in an arithmetic statement, the computer may assign that name to some location and then use whatever is in that location in the arithmetic statement. This would in all likelihood mean a wrong result, with no indication that it is wrong. On the other hand, if the computer protects against using an undefined name, it would stop the program and indicate the name was undefined, as discussed in Chapter Five in connection with trying to write out the value of an undefined name.)

SUMMARY

We can sum up the operation of the arithmetic statement, and at the same time tie it in with what we have learned about other kind of statements, in this way. We have seen that when a variable name appears in a statement, this tells the computer to *do something* with the location bearing that name. When a variable name appears in a READ statement, this tells the computer to place a value in the location bearing that name. When a variable name appears on the left of the equal sign in an arithmetic statement, this also tells the computer to place a value in that location—except that now this value is not one read from a card, but is the value produced by performing the operation(s) indicated on the right side of the equal sign. Thus there is a relationship between putting a variable name in a READ statement and putting a variable name on the left of the equal sign in an arithmetic statement; both are ways of placing a value in the location bearing that name.

By the same token, we have seen that when we put a variable name in a WRITE statement, this tells the computer to go to that location, *take* the value there, and write it out. Putting a variable name on the right of the equal sign in an arithmetic statement also tells the computer to go to that location and take the value there; except that now what the computer does with that value is determined by any operation sign accompanying that variable name. Thus there is a relationship between putting a variable name in a WRITE statement and putting a variable name on the right of the equal sign in an arithmetic statement; in both cases the computer is instructed to go to the indicated location and do something with the value stored there. (In the arithmetic statement, as in the WRITE statement, the computer does not actually *take* a value from its location; rather, the value itself remains in that location, and the computer operates with an equivalent of that value.)

The fact that a constant can also appear in an arithmetic expression can be taken (in this view) as merely a part of telling the computer what to do with the contents of a storage location: add 2 to the value in that location, or multiply that value by 7, or whatever.

When we use one or more variable names, constants, and operation signs in an arithmetic expression, we say we are *symbolically* manipulating data values. That is, we are using variable names (this is one of the things the names do for us) to represent data values, and operation signs to represent relationships between those values. Through these symbols we tell the computer what actual operations to perform on the real values in the storage locations. So when we write:

$$A = B + C$$

we are manipulating symbols in such a way as to tell the computer what to do with the values stored in the locations named B and C, and where to put the result of this operation.

Finally, remember that to use the results of an arithmetic operation, we manipulate the name on the left of the equal sign after the results of that operation have been stored in that location. To see the results of the operation, we include the variable name in a WRITE statement which will put the results (our *answer*) out on paper. Or to use the results of the operation in a later arithmetic operation, we include this name in the expression on the right side of the equal sign in a subsequent arithmetic statement in the same program.

RULES FOR FORMING EXPRESSIONS

There are several rules for using operation signs in arithmetic statements: rules designed to make our meaning as clear as possible to the computer. One rule is that there must be a sign present to show each operation desired. In regular mathematics it is possible to put the letters A and B next to each other (as in AB) and to show by this that A is to be multiplied by B. Because of the way variable names are constructed in programming language, however, if the letters A and B appear right next to each other, the computer would see them as the variable name AB. Therefore, whenever we wish to multiply two quantities, we place an asterisk between them. So to multiply A and B on a computer, we write:

A * B

A second rule is that there may not be two of these signs in succession. In conventional math we might write something like:

A + — 4.

Here we would be using spaces to show that the + is the operation sign, whereas the minus sign here is part of the value of the constant —4., indicating a negative value. But we can not do this in programming, because the computer for the most part ignores spaces. So instead, we use parentheses, like this:

A + (—4.)

Similarly, to multiply A by —4., we write:

A * (—4.)

Another common rule is that decimal and integer values are not mixed in the expression on the right side of the equal sign. Thus we do not write:

$$X = A + M$$

because A is a floating point value, while M is an integer value. This rule affects both variables and constants, as the following examples show:

Not Acceptable	Acceptable
X = F + M	X = F + FM
K = X + N	K = LX + N
S = 3.0 + 3	S = 3. + 3.
L = 4 + 4.0	L = 4 + 4
M = A + 17	M = NA + 17
Y = N + 6.0	Y = CN + 6.0

The reason we do not usually *mix modes* in an arithmetic expression is that the computer performs arithmetic on the two types of values in different ways, and processes them in different parts of its system. However, it is possible to mix integer and floating point numbers *across* the equal sign. For example, if we have called for arithmetic to be done in decimal numbers, it is possible for a value produced by that calculation to be transferred to the area in the computer where integer numbers are stored. This would be done by means of the equal sign, which will store the results in the location known by an integer name. Consider this example:

$$N = A / C$$

This would divide A by C, and would store the result in N. But remember that any fractional part resulting from this division would be lost when the results were converted to integer form. In this example, say that A was 7. and C was 3. Then the value actually stored in N would be 2.

It is also possible to carry this process the other direction; that is, to store in a floating point location the results of arithmetic done with integer numbers. But here we must be careful in any division, because the truncation of any fractional part occurs at the *moment of division*. That is, when dealing with integer numbers, any remainder resulting from a division is instantly lost—even before the rest of the expression is evaluated. Integer numbers simply have no provision for keeping track of fractions under any circumstances.

This is important to remember. Many beginning programmers think that the truncation of fractions does not occur until a value is stored in a location carrying an integer name. This is not the case. And this means the order in which a series of operations is called for can actually make a difference in the answer produced. Consider these two statements:

N = 10 * 4 / 3
N = 10 / 3 * 4

In the first statement, the 10 multiplied by 4 gives 40. Divided by 3, this gives 13⅓. With the ⅓ truncated the value stored in N as the result of this first statement would be 13. In the second statement, dividing 10 by 3 produces the truncated value 3, which multiplied by 4 gives the value 12. So even using the same values and performing the same operations on them, the order in which the operations are carried out can influence the results when using integer numbers. Rather than worry about such things, it is safest to use only decimal numbers when divisions are involved except in special cases to be discussed later.

The fact that we can mix modes *across* the equal sign makes it possible to *convert* integer values to floating point, and vice versa. The reason for converting a value from integer to floating point is usually because we have a quantity which originally was integer, but which we want to use for arithmetic which may produce fractional parts. In this case we simply say something like:

FM = M

This stores in FM a value equal to the value of M, except that it is floating point. The original value of M remains where it is, so that we now have both integer and floating point versions of that value, to use wherever appropriate.

For the sake of using names that show what they represent, it is useful in such cases to use the same name for the floating point version, but to precede it by an F to make this name floating point. Then if we write this instruction:

FM = M

the name shows at a glance that the value in FM is the decimal *equivalent* of a value existing in integer form in the location known as M. If the letter F is reserved for this purpose of showing a floating point *conversion*, or equivalent, of a value which was originally integer, this can help in later reading of a program because it instantly shows the relationship between two variable names.

When we reverse the direction (that is, when we convert a floating point value to integer form) any fractional part of the floating point value is of course truncated when it is stored in the location known by the integer variable name. For example, if X is 17.9, then if we write:

NX = X

the value actually stored in NX will be 17. The truncation which occurs when the value is stored in NX does not affect the original value of X, which retains its fractional part. Note that here we are using the letter N to show an integer equivalent of a value which originally was floating point, just as we used an F to show the reverse relationship. (The reason for using N, rather than I, for this purpose, is because I can be easily mistaken for the digit 1.)

This truncation across an equal sign can be useful, because it allows us to get rid of the fractional part of a number. In advanced programming we can use this for a device to code things like income figures into categories, and also for automatic *rounding off* of fractions. For the most part, however, the safest procedure is to keep integer and decimal values separate, to avoid unintentional truncation which could destroy the accuracy of a program.

Some computers will *not* object to the presence of both integer and floating point values on the *same* side of the equal sign. However, do not rely on this. Sometimes a computer may let mixed modes slip by, other times an arrangement like this may be rejected. So the safest thing is not to mix the modes. Then there is no worry about what the computer might or might not do in a given case.

EXAMPLES

1. The following are valid arithmetic statements:

$$X = A * (-.5)$$
$$NX = R - FN$$
$$Z = NX \,/\, K$$
$$M = L \,/\, K$$

2. The following are not valid arithmetic statements:

M + N = L + K (Not a single variable name on left of equal sign)

B = C * −7.3 (Two operation signs in succession)

GAR = PLES − 1 (Mixed modes on right of equal sign)

2.7 = X (No variable name on left of equal sign)

3. In the left column below are some simple equations, as they might be expressed in mathematical form. Across from each equation, in the right-hand column, is the way that same set of relationships might be expressed in programming language.

X = R + S	X = R + S
Y = R × S	Y = R * S
Z = $\dfrac{R}{S}$	Z = R / S
L = J − K	L = J − K

EXERCISES

See exercises 1–4 in Chapter Seven of the *Workbook*.

PARENTHESES

Parentheses have several uses in arithmetic statements. One, indicated above, is to separate operation signs when there would otherwise be two signs in succession. Another is to show the order in which the operations in an arithmetic statement are to be carried out.

Without parentheses, the operations are carried out in this order: First the computer does all division and multiplications, beginning at the left of the expression and executing each division or multiplication as it moves toward the right. Then the computer returns to the left of the expression and performs each addition and subtraction in succession as it again moves to the right.

This sequence of operations, called the *standard order of operations,* is demonstrated in the following examples. The numbers above the operation signs show the order in which the operations would be carried out. In the first example, the division would be done first, then the multiplication, then the addition, and finally the subtraction.

$$\overset{\ 3\quad\ 1\quad\ \ 4\quad\ \ 2}{XL = A + R / SN - 7.2 * P}$$

$$\overset{\ 3\quad\ \ 4\quad\ \ \ 1\quad\ \ \ 2}{Q = 17. + SEP - REN * STAT / SIZE}$$

$$\overset{\ 1\quad\ 3\quad\ \ 4\quad\ 2\quad\ 5}{N = K * L - ML + J * M - JOB}$$

$$\overset{\ 4\quad\ 1\quad\ 5\quad\ 2\quad\ 6\quad\ 3\quad\ 7}{Z = P - S * W + T * R - Z / FN + 3.}$$

It is rare, however, that we want a sequence of operations carried out in exactly this order. More often, we want some additions and/or subtractions carried out *before* any division or multiplication. Or we want one particular addition performed before another one, and so on. For example, consider this equation, written in conventional notation:

$$X = \frac{A + B}{D + E}$$

When this is converted to a programming instruction, but without parentheses, it might be:

X = A + B / D + E

In this example, the division must be done *after* both additions are performed, otherwise the real result is:

$$X = A + \frac{B}{D} + E$$

Here, as in the case of the integer arithmetic discussed earlier, the order in which operations are carried out can make quite a difference in the results.

To precisely control the sequence of operations, we use parentheses to tell the computer what to do first, then second, and so on. The general rule is that everything *within* a set of parentheses will be done first. Then after all operations within parentheses have been performed, operations *between* sets of parentheses will be performed. For example:

R = Z * (A + B)

This will cause the addition to be executed first, because it is inside parentheses. Then the total of A and B would be multiplied by Z, and the result stored in R.

With two or more sets of parentheses, the sets will be evaluated from left to right in sequence. That is, all the operations inside the left-most set of parentheses will be executed, then all the operations in the next set, and so on. Having done this, the computer would then go back and perform the operations between the parentheses. For example:

Z = (A + B) * (C − D)

Here the plus and minus operations would be performed, then the multiplication. For another example:

Q = (A − B) + (F + M) / (C * D)

Here the operations within the parentheses would be performed first. Then the division between parentheses would be done before the addition between parentheses. The reason for this is that the signs *between* parentheses would be taken in the standard order described above: multiplication and division before addition and substraction.

To build more complex expressions, we simply use more parentheses. For example:

$$S = X / ((A + B) * (C + D))$$

In this case the parentheses around $A + B$ and those around $C + D$ are known as *innermost* parentheses. The order of operations in this case is that everything within innermost parentheses is done first. Then the computer goes to the next outer set of parentheses and performs all operations within them, and so on. In the example here, A and B would be added, and C and D added. Then, since these two totals are jointly surrounded by another set of parentheses, the multiplication between them would be carried out. Only after all this has been done would the division be executed.

This business of parentheses looks complicated, but it really is not. You will probably be surprised to find how quickly you develop a feeling for where parentheses should go: mainly because they are used on a computer much as they are used when we do arithmetic by hand. All the rules described above have the effect of making the computer do just what we would probably do in a similar case; that is, perform whatever operations are required to reduce the contents of each set of parentheses to a single value, beginning with the innermost set of parentheses and working outward. Within any set of parentheses, the computer will perform the operations in the standard order: multiplication and division, and then addition and subtraction, moving from left to right in each case. But remember that this order holds only for operations at a similar level of parentheses.

The following examples show, by means of numbers over the operation signs, the order in which the operations would be carried out. Note that the operations within the innermost parentheses are carried out in the standard order. Then the computer moves out to the next set of parentheses, performs the operations within them, and so on.

Also in these examples note the letters *under* the parentheses. These are used to show exactly what is meant by innermost parentheses, and next outer parentheses. Briefly, the innermost parentheses are those in which the opening and closing parentheses directly face each other across the contents of the expression. For example, in the expression:

$$((A + B) * 7.)$$

the innermost parentheses are those around A + B. The next outer parentheses are the others, which contain within them the expression (A + B). In the following examples, the small letter *a* indicates innermost parentheses, the letter *b* indicates the second order of parentheses, or the next outer parentheses, the letter *c* refers to yet the next outer parentheses, and so on.

$$
\begin{array}{c}
21435 \\
P = (((A - B * C) + (A + R)) / 17.) \\
cbaaaabc
\end{array}
$$

$$
\begin{array}{c}
1324 \\
S = ((RT - RS) * (X + Z)) * B \\
baaaab
\end{array}
$$

$$
\begin{array}{c}
1526374 \\
Q = (A - B) * (C + D) / (X - Y) * (V + W) \\
aaaaaaaa
\end{array}
$$

$$
\begin{array}{c}
132645 \\
Q = ((A - B)* (C + D)) / ((X - Y)* W) \\
baaaabbaab
\end{array}
$$

We use as many sets of parentheses as necessary to show precisely the order of a series of operations. There is no limit on how many parentheses may be used in one expression. We can use more parentheses than may actually be needed; that is, we can use parentheses where the meaning would be obvious even without them. This will not harm a program in any way. For example, we can write:

$$X = ((A + B) * Y)$$

In this expression, the outer parentheses are not necessary, but they do no harm.

For another example of this, we can write:

$$X = (A + B) - C$$

Here the parentheses around $A + B$ are not necessary. If they were not there the addition would still be performed before the subtraction, because this is the standard order of operations. But using the parentheses does show precisely what we have in mind for this expression. In this regard it may be useful when *we* read the expression even though not necessary as far as the computer is concerned. So the general rule is: If in doubt, or if it would add clarity, use extra parentheses.

However, make sure each set of parentheses is complete—that there is an equal number of left and right parentheses in each statement. A common error in programming is to miscount parentheses in a complex expression and not use all that are needed. In this case the program will not run. For example, we might have an expression like this:

$$X = ((((A - B) / C) * 5.) - 1.0) + A) / 16.5$$

As we write this statement, we add parentheses as needed: going back to the beginning to add a left parenthesis for each right parenthesis included in the body of the expression. As we get to the end of the statement we realize we need a parenthesis after the A so the addition there will be done before the division. But by this time there are so many parentheses at the front of the expression that the need for one more there is obscured. We would have to carefully count them to see that we have five right parentheses, but only four left ones. So when working with any complex expression it is useful to write it first on a sheet of paper. There we can count each pair of parentheses. We can even connect each pair with an overhead line, to make sure no parenthesis is left without a partner.

To illustrate two techniques for checking the parentheses, let us use the last statement pictured above. Using the technique of connecting each pair of parentheses by overhead lines, we end up with something like this:

$$X = (((\overline{(A - B)} / C) * 5.) - 1.0) + A) / 16.5$$

Figure 2. Connecting parentheses with overhead lines to check parentheses in an arithmetic statement.

Since we have one right parenthesis left over (indicated by the arrow) we obviously need another left parenthesis. This would send us back to the expression, to decide precisely where it should go.

If we numbered the parentheses, we would have something like this:

$$\begin{matrix} 4321 & & 1 & & 2 & & 3 & & 4 & & 5 \\ X = ((((A & - & B) & / & C) & * & 5.) & - & 1.0) & + & A) & / & 16.5 \end{matrix}$$

Since the totals do not match, we again obviously need another left parenthesis.

It is necessary to be this careful with parentheses for several reasons. One is the fact that if there are not equal numbers of left and right parentheses, the computer will discover this and will stop the program. Not knowing where a missing parenthesis is to go, the computer would not have complete instructions on the order in which it is to carry out the arithmetic operations in that expression. So rather than *guess*, the computer would return the program with a request that we clarify the meaning by adding the missing parenthesis.

Another reason for caution with parentheses is this: If the computer finds there are enough parentheses, and that they are used according to the basic rules, then the computer will execute an arithmetic statement without questioning whether it is the exact equivalent of any mathematical formula we have in mind. That is, the computer counts the parentheses to see that every one is part of a pair. It has no way of knowing whether the parentheses are in the proper places. This is the programmer's responsibility: to see that each parenthesis is really where he wants it to be to direct the sequence of the arithmetic operations in the right way. If we inadvertently put a parenthesis in the wrong place, thereby causing a series of operations to be carried out in an order we do not want, the program will produce faulty results. This is one form of what we call a *logic error:* against which the computer cannot protect us.

EXAMPLES

The following examples show how various statistical formulas might be translated into programming statements. The formulas have been taken from three statistics books: Blalock (1960); Freeman (1965); Siegel (1956).

Each formula is identified by the author's name and page of the book. Below the formula there appears a corresponding programming statement. For the sake of clarity, the variable names in each arithmetic statement resemble as much as possible the symbols in the corresponding formula. Note the use of F to create floating point names where division is involved.

4. Goodman and Kruskal's Coefficient of Ordinal Association: (Freeman, p. 83)

$$G = \frac{f_a - f_i}{f_a + f_i}$$

G = (FA − FI) / (FA + FI)

5. Kendall Rank Correlation Coefficient: (Siegel, p. 217)

$$T = \frac{S}{\frac{1}{2} N(N-1)}$$

T = S / ((FN * (FN − 1.)) / 2.)

6. Mann-Whitney Test: (Blalock, p. 199)

$$U = N_1 N_2 + \frac{N_2(N_2 + 1)}{2} - R_2$$

U = (FN1 * FN2) + ((FN2 * (FN2 + 1.))/2.) — R2

EXERCISES

See exercises 5–10 in Chapter Seven of the *Workbook*.

EXPONENTS

In addition to adding, subtracting, multiplying, and dividing, there remains another major operation: using exponents. An exponent, of course, is the number showing the power to which a base number is to be raised. In the familiar notation A^2, A is the base number, and 2 is the exponent showing that A is to be raised to the power of 2; i.e. squared.

To show an exponent in programming, we use two asterisks in succession, followed by the exponent. For example, to square the value A, we write:

A ** 2

Including an exponent in an arithmetic statement adds another kind of operation for the computer to perform on one or more data values, but in no way changes the operation of the arithmetic statement itself. For example, when we write:

A ** 2

thus telling the computer to square the value in A, there still must be on the left of the equal sign the name of the location in which the result of this operation is to be placed. Thus a whole statement which includes the operation of squaring might look like this:

X = A ** 2

The effect of this statement would be to place in X the square of the value in A. Remember that the results of operations indicated on the right side of the equal sign are of no use to us unless and until they are placed in a location named on the left of the equal sign.

The computer will not mistake this exponentiation sign ** for two consecutive multiplication signs. The rule that two operation signs may not appear in succession assures that when two asterisks appear next to each other, they must mean an exponent and not two multiplications.

An exponent may be a constant, as shown above. It can also be a variable name. Thus we can write:

$$X = A ** C$$

This will raise A to whatever power is indicated by the value of the name C at that point in the program. Finally, an exponent can consist of a whole expression. That is, we can write:

$$X = A ** (Z + Y - 7.)$$

The parentheses in this example have the same purpose described earlier: to show the order of operations in this expression. The standard order of operations calls for exponentiation to be done before anything else, even before multiplication and division. So if parentheses were not used here, the computer would give us the equivalent of:

$$X = A^z + Y - 7.$$

But since the entire expression $(Z + Y - 7.)$ is the exponent here, this value must be determined (this expression must be completely evaluated) before the exponentiation occurs. So we use parentheses to direct the computer to do the addition and subtraction before doing the exponentiation outside the parentheses.

Similarly, parentheses are useful in showing how this confusing expression is to be evaluated:

$$Z = A ** B ** C$$

If we want this to mean $(A^b)^c$, we write:

$$Z = (A ** B) ** C$$

However, if we want it treated as the equivalent of A^{b^c}, we write:

Z = A ** (B ** C)

Within the parentheses in an exponential expression, the standard order of operations holds: First inner exponents, if any, then multiplication and division, and finally addition and subtraction—in all cases done from left to right. Note also that as in any expression, an expression used as an exponent may have more than one set of parentheses, if this is necessary to show a particular order of operations. For example, we could write:

X = A ** ((B + C) * D)

Here the computer would add B and C and multiply this total by D with this whole value giving the exponent for A. The outer set of parentheses is necessary to make sure the whole expression is treated as the exponent of A. Within the expression itself, an inner set of parentheses is necessary to make sure that the addition of A and B occurs before anything is multiplied by C.

The computer makes the use of various kinds of exponents very simple. If a formula calls for a negative exponent, like $R = A^{-3}$, we simply write:

R = A ** (—3.)

This would give the equivalent of what would be written in mathematical notation as A^{-3} or $\dfrac{1}{A^3}$.

Note the parentheses used with the exponent —3. in the last statement above to avoid having two operation signs in a row. Since the two asterisks make up the one sign for exponentiation, when we speak of two signs here we are referring to ** and —.

A fractional exponent could be written either as:

Z = A ** .5

or as:

Z = A ** (1./2.)

Either would be the equivalent of $\sqrt{A}$, the square root of A. Note again the use of parentheses in the second statement here, to make sure that the indicated division in the exponent is done before the exponentiation itself. Without the parentheses, A would be raised to the power of 1, which would not change its value. This would then be divided by 2. So without the parentheses here we would get $\frac{A}{2}$ rather than $\sqrt{A}$.

If we need a cube root, we simply write:

X = A ** .3333333

or:

X = A ** (1./3.)

Since the computer cannot achieve the exact value of 1/3, either of these forms would be only an approximation, but one close enough for most of the values social scientists deal with.

Any value, including fractional or negative values, can be assigned to a variable name, and this name can then be used as an exponent. This would give the same kind of results as those shown here for constants. That is, while we can use 2 as an exponent, we can also set a name like POW equal to 2 and then use that name as the exponent. This is obviously useful when the exponential value can vary during a program.

With exponents, we find one exception to the idea of not mixing modes on one side of the equal sign. A floating point value may have an exponent which is either decimal or integer. Thus we could write:

X = A ** B
X = A ** N
X = A ** 2.
X = A ** 2

However, an integer number must have an integer exponent. Thus we can write:

K = M ** J
K = M ** 2

But we can not write:

K = M ** A
K = M ** 2.

The general rule, in other words, is this: Integer exponent with any value; decimal exponent only with decimal value.

The reason for this again is that the two types of numbers are treated in different parts of the machine, and in different ways. *The base value determines the mode of a value which includes an exponent.* Thus an integer exponent can be used as an exponent for integer values without change. If an integer exponent is also used with a decimal value, this exponent can be transferred to that area where floating point arithmetic is done, through the simple addition of a decimal point in the computer. But if a floating point value were transferred to an integer location for use as the exponent of an integer value, there would be truncation of any fractional part of the exponent.

This rule applies also for whole expressions used as exponents. In addition, the other rule governing expressions applies; that is, if an expression is integer, then every element in it must be integer, and if an expression is floating point, then every element in it must be floating point. Thus any of the following would be correct:

X = A ** (P − Q * S)

This is a floating point exponent for the floating point base value A. Every element in the expression used as the exponent must be floating point.

X = A ** (KD + J)

This is an integer exponent for the floating point base value A. Since the expression used as the exponent is integer, every element in the expression must be integer.

X = M ** (KD + J)

This is an integer exponent for the integer base value M. Since the exponent is integer, every element in it must be integer.

But these would not be correct:

N = L ** (P − Q * S)

This is a floating point expression used as the exponent for the integer value L. But an integer base number should have an integer exponent.

H = B ** (Z + N)

The exponent here could be either integer or floating point because it is used with a floating point base value. But the expression used as the exponent must be *either* integer or floating point, not mixed as it is here, with the floating point value Z and the integer value N.

Be careful that an integer expression used as an exponent does not contain a division. Here, as elsewhere, any remainder resulting from division with integer numbers would be truncated. If an exponent has a division in it, this exponent should be treated as floating point. This in turn means the base value for this exponent must also be floating point. In such a case, if the base value itself, or any other value involved, is integer, simply convert to floating point through the use of the equal sign. Then write the whole expression in floating point terms.

EXAMPLES

Each example here shows a formula and the programming equivalent.

7. Kolmogorov-Smirnov Test: (Blalock, p. 205)

$$\text{Chi-square} = 4D^2 \frac{N_1 N_2}{N_1 + N_2}$$

CHISQ = (4. * (D**2.)) * ((FN1 * FN2) / (FN1 + FN2))

An extra set of parentheses has been added here around D**2. This is for clarity only, because even without the parentheses, the order of operations calls for exponentiation before multiplication.

8. Kendall Coefficient of Concordance: (Siegel, p. 231)

$$W = \frac{S}{\dfrac{1\ K^2\ (N^3 - N)}{12}}$$

$$W = S\ /\ (((FK\ **\ 2.)\ *\ (FN\ **\ 3. - FN))\ /\ 12.)$$
$$\quad\quad\quad a\quad\quad\quad\quad\quad\quad\quad\quad a$$

An extra set of parentheses (those with an a underneath) is added in the denominator here for clarity, although without the parentheses the multiplication would still occur before the division, because the order of operations is left to right.

EXERCISES

See exercises 11–14 in Chapter Seven of the *Workbook*.

MATHEMATICAL FUNCTIONS

In doing arithmetic on the computer, we can also use certain mathematical functions. A *function* is the performing of a specific mathematical operation. For example, finding the square root of a value is a function.

Square Root

Since so many of the formulas used in social science contain a square root, we can use this to show how functions in general are employed in programming. Suppose we wish to find the square root of 25. We simply place this number in parentheses and precede it with the *name* (sometimes called the *symbolic name*) of the function. For the square root this name is SQRT. So to find the square root of the value 25., the expression would look like this:

SQRT (25.)

This would automatically calculate the square root of 25. and would produce the value 5. for this expression.

However, as with any arithmetic expression, the result would not be available to us unless it were stored in some location in the computer. Therefore, again we use the equal sign to tell the computer where to put the result of an operation: in this case, a square root. For example, we could write:

A = SQRT (25.)

This causes the computer to store, in the location named A, the value produced by taking the square root of 25. So after this instruction is executed, A has the value 5.

By the same token, if we have a quantity stored under some variable name, we insert the variable name inside the parentheses, and the computer finds the square root of the value stored in the location bearing that name. For example, say we have the value 9. stored in the location named Z. We tell the computer:

B = SQRT (Z)

After this statement is executed, B will have the value 3.

This is all there is to finding square roots in programming. This is part of why it is often said that programming requires less mathematical knowledge than doing an equivalent procedure by hand or with a desk calculator.

We have seen another way to get a square root: using 1./2. as an exponent. However, the SQRT function is probably used more, for clarity. The name SQRT clearly shows a square root is involved, whereas the exponent 1./2. can be mistaken for a simple fraction when we read a program.

The constant or variable quantity which appears inside the parentheses after the function name is called the *argument* of the function. An argument is simply that value on which the indicated operation is to be performed. For example, in this statement:

R = SQRT (S)

the value represented by the name S is the argument of the function.

The argument of a function (that is, the quantity inside the parentheses of the function) may be an expression, as well as merely a single value. If it is an expression, it may be as complex as necessary, in which case it follows all the rules described above for using parentheses to separate operation signs, to show order of operations, and so on. If the argument is an expression, the whole expression is enclosed in the set of parentheses associated with the function name, and these parentheses instruct the computer to perform all operations inside them before finally doing whatever operation is called for by the function name. So basically, the parentheses used with a function name have the same purpose as other parentheses: They show the function is to be performed last, simply by putting the function name outside the parentheses, and the argument inside.

Note that parentheses must be used with a function name, even if there is no question about the order of operations. That is, even when the argument is a single variable name, the use of the function itself requires one set of parentheses.

To illustrate the use of complex expressions as arguments of a function, let us begin by saying we want to find the square root of the sum of A and B. Since there is only one operation sign here, we need not use parentheses to show the order of operations in the expression itself. So here the only parentheses we need are those associated with the function name:

$$X = SQRT \ (A + B)$$

The computer here would add A and B, would find the square root of their sum, and would store this result in X. For example, if A had the value 9. and B had the value 16., this statement would store the value 5. in X.

To build a more complex expression in our example here, say we now wish to add A and B and multiply their total by C. Then we want to take the square root of the resulting value. In this case we obviously need parentheses in the expression itself to direct the computer to do the addition before the multiplication. Thus the expression used as the argument would be:

$$(A + B) \ * \ C$$

To find the square root of the value represented by this expression, we merely put parentheses around the expression and use the function name:

X = SQRT ((A + B) * C)
    f   f

The two parentheses with the small letter *f* under them are the parentheses which must be used whenever the function name is used. The other two parentheses are those required to show the order of operations within the expression which makes up the argument of the function.

Now say we have a program where we wish to add A and B, and also wish to add C and D. Then we wish to divide the former total by the latter total. Finally, we wish to take the square root of the resulting value. The expression here would be:

(A + B) / (C + D)

Using this as the argument for the square root function would give:

X = SQRT ((A + B) / (C + D))
    f   f

Again the small *f*'s show the parentheses associated with the function name itself.

A function may be part of a larger expression. For example, we can write:

X = SQRT(A) + B

Now assume we want to find the square root of this more complex expression:

(FN + 1.) * (FN − 1.)

Having found this square root, we want to add to it the value S, and store the resulting total in Q:

Q = SQRT((FN + 1.) * (FN − 1.)) + S

The square root function may also be inside the parentheses in a larger expression. For example, say we want to add the square root of A and the square root of B, and multiply the resulting total by T, with the overall result to be stored in X:

$$X = (SQRT (A) + SQRT (B)) * T$$

We can also use one square root function within the argument of another square root function. For example, we could write something like this:

$$X = SQRT (SQRT (A + B) + T)$$

This would first find the square root of $(A + B)$, then would add T to this value, and finally would find the square root of the resulting value, storing this square root in X.

Any floating point expression may be used as the argument of a function. The reason for saying floating point is illustrated by the square root function. The square roots of most values involve fractional parts. Because of this, the expression in which the function appears must also be floating point. If integer values are involved in such an operation, therefore, we simply use the equal sign to create floating point equivalents for them, and use these floating point values wherever necessary.

Absolute Value

Another function with some application in social science formulas is finding the absolute value of a number. This is the value of a number if its plus or minus sign is ignored.

To illustrate the idea of absolute value, say we subtract 6. from 10. The answer is obviously 4. However, we can also subtract 10. from 6., which gives an answer of —4. But in either case the *size* of the difference between the two numbers is 4. Thus when we disregard the sign, the *absolute* value of the difference is 4.

We use this absolute value function the same way we use the square root function. That is, we write the function name (in the case of the absolute function the name is ABS) and then follow it with parentheses which contain the argument, which for this function would be that quantity whose absolute value we want. Thus if we wrote:

X = ABS (—5.)

the value 5. would be stored in X, not the value —5.

If the argument inside the parentheses is a variable name, we can say something like:

X = ABS (W)

This would store in X the absolute value of W. That is, X would be equal to W *except* that X would always be a positive value, regardless of whether any given value of W was positive or negative.

As with the square root function, the expression used as the argument for the absolute value function can be as complex as necessary. There may be functions within functions, and this extends to the use of one kind of function within the argument of another kind of function. For example, the absolute value function could be used within the argument of a square root function, like this:

Y = SQRT (ABS (X))

One practical use of this stems from the fact that usually it is not possible to work with the square root of a negative number. If we should have a formula which requires the square root of a value which may at times be negative, we can use the ABS function to give the absolute value before the SQRT function is used. Remember that in doing a calculation by hand, we can ignore a minus sign when it appears, but that once a program starts running, we have no chance to make such adjustments. So when square roots are involved we can use the ABS function as a *filter* which will not let negative numbers through.

This is particularly important because on some computers the attempt to find a square root of a negative number will stop the program, but other computers may produce *garbage* for this value. The danger here is the same as in the case of creating too large numbers during a program: If we do not know a problem has occurred during the running of a program, then we will assume the results of the program are valid, when in fact they are not.

Other Functions

Square roots and absolute values are only two of the functions available in Fortran. Other mathematical tasks are handled by other functions. Some of these functions, and the jobs they do, are these, as listed in McCracken (1965) p. 136:

Function Name	Function
EXP	exponential
ALOG	natural logarithm
ALOG10	common logarithm
SIN	sine
COS	cosine
TANH	hyperbolic tangent
ATAN	arctangent

Most social scientists would have little occasion to use these functions, since they are not common in the statistics we use most. However, if the occasion should arise, these functions are used exactly as the square root and absolute value functions are used. The argument (that is, the value or expression for which the function is to be computed) is placed in parentheses after the name of the function. For example, to place in X the natural logarithm of the value represented by the expression A + B, we write something like this:

X = ALOG (A + B)

Similarly, to use the EXP function, we could write something like:

X = A * EXP (B − Q)

This would raise A to the power represented by the expression inside the parentheses following the name EXP. It would produce the equivalent of what would be written in mathematical terms as:

A^{b-q}

It would also produce the equivalent of what would be written with two asterisks as:

$$X = A ** (B - Q)$$

Thus there are two ways to work with exponents. The ** operator is probably the more widely used, but as with so many other things in programming, the choice is yours.

The rules for the expressions used as arguments for these functions, and for using the functions themselves in expressions, are the same as those discussed in connection with square roots and absolute values.

The functions listed above represent what are called *library* functions. This means they are provided in the overall system in the computing center, so we can use them simply by writing the appropriate name in a program. In addition, a computing center may build up a collection of other functions. These are simply ways of making it easier to do certain additional tasks that people in the computing center (or their customers) frequently want to do. So since one computing center may have more emphasis on one kind of job, while another center does a different kind of work more often, there will be some variation in the functions available at different computing centers. You can find out which functions are available at your computing center by asking the people who work there.

Even though you may not use any of these functions, you should have some idea about their names, because of another rule about variable names. This rule is that a variable name should not be the same as the name of a function, to avoid confusing the computer.

EXERCISES

See exercises 15–18 in Chapter Seven of the *Workbook*.

SIMPLIFYING COMPLEX EXPRESSIONS

When dealing with a complex formula, it is possible to break it into sections, evaluate the sections independently, store their results in *temporary* locations, and work out the final value using the intermediate values in these temporary locations.

A *temporary* location, as we speak of it in programming, is nothing more than a storage location usually being used for no other purpose in a program. We can assure that it is not being used for any other purpose by using a name unlike any other in the program. The computer then assigns this name to a location which has not been given a name. What we call a *temporary* location differs in no way from any other location; we merely use the word *temporary* to show that the value in such a location is, for example, an intermediate result which will be used in some subsequent operation in the program. The word *temporary* also suggests that this value probably will not be (although it could be) written out.

As an example of using temporary locations to break up an arithmetic expression into simpler pieces, consider this equation:

$$Q = \frac{R - F}{X - Y}$$

This could be programmed:

$$Q = (R - F) / (X - Y)$$

But we could also proceed by calculating the numerator and storing the result in a temporary location, using a name for this location that begins with T, to indicate the temporary nature of this value.

$$TNUM = R - F$$

Doing the same with the denominator would give something like:

$$TDENOM = X - Y$$

Then we could use these temporary variable names in another statement to produce the final value:

$$Q = TNUM / TDENOM$$

Either approach would give the same final value stored in Q. This step-by-step procedure has the advantage of reducing the complexity of an arithmetic statement. It gives, for example, fewer parentheses to count. But the disadvantage is that it means more variable names to keep track of.

PROTECTING AGAINST TOO LARGE VALUES

Our final note here in connection with arithmetic statements is one of caution against creating too large values in the course of the arithmetic. When we program a statistic on the computer, we should keep in mind the data and the kinds of values that might be produced as each arithmetic statement is executed for a particular set of data. If very large values might be generated during a program, it is sometimes possible t⌐ manipulate an arithmetic statement to keep values smaller than they would otherwise be. For example, if we have several additions and several subtractions, we might be able to do the subtractions before some additions, rather than doing all the additions first, letting a large total build up, and then doing the subtracting from that. Say we have a statement like this:

$$X = (A + B) - (C + D)$$

We could get the same effect with:

$$X = A - (C + D) + B$$

This second expression would avoid a value as large as the total of A and B. We could even go farther with this, by saying:

$$X = A - C - D + B$$

This would give the same end result, while avoiding as large a value as the total of C and D. Conversely, of course, remember the danger of creating too large a *negative* value through doing all the subtractions at once.

EXAMPLES

Each example shows a formula and a programming equivalent.

9. Contingency Coefficient: (Siegel, p. 197)

$$C = \sqrt{\frac{\chi^2}{N + \chi^2}}$$

C = SQRT (CHISQ / (FN + CHISQ))

10. Kendall Partial Rank Correlation Coefficient: (Siegel, p. 225)

$$Tau_{xy \cdot z} = \frac{AD - BC}{\sqrt{(A + B) \ (C + D) \ (A + C) \ (B + D)}}$$

TXYKZ = ((A*D)−(B*C))/SQRT((A+B)*(C+D)*(A+C)*(B+D))

11. Wilcoxon Matched-Pairs Signed-Ranks Test: (Blalock, p. 209)

$$Z = \frac{T - N(N + 1)/4}{\sqrt{N(N + 1)(2N + 1)/24}}$$

Z = (T − ((FN*(FN+1.))/4.))/SQRT((FN*(FN+1.)*(2.*FN+1.))/24.)

EXERCISES

See exercises 19–34 in Chapter Seven of the *Workbook*.

Chapter Eight

WRITING AND SUBMITTING A PROGRAM

With what we have seen so far it is possible to write and run a program (though it would be a simple program because we have not yet studied some of the things that give the computer its great flexibility and power). So, to get you started running programs as soon as possible, we will pause here to look at the actual physical process of preparing a program and giving it to the computer.

It is important to run programs early and often. This is the only way to actually become a skilled programmer, rather than someone who has *read about* programming. It is necessary to submit programs to the computer, get them back, find and correct any errors, give the program back to the computer, correct the next errors that show up, and so on. Even skilled programmers go through this process, and there is no substitute for it. So read this chapter, and then start running your own programs, even if you do nothing more at first than read in two values, add them, and write out the result.

To put the writing and submitting of a program into perspective, let us stress again that it is part of an overall process. This process starts with deciding what problem to work on, what kinds of data are needed and how to get them, what data processing and statistical techniques to use, and so on.

JOB NUMBERS

One of the first steps is to get a *job number* or *project number*. This is a number used to identify the programs each person runs, and used for bookkeeping purposes by a computing center. In a way, it is like the account number a store assigns a customer who opens a charge account there.

There are several kinds of job numbers. One is the student number, probably issued to a member of a formal programming class. With this number, the computer time for homework programs can be billed to that class, and hence charged to a budget for educational expenses. From the student's standpoint, the use of the computer here is free; it is considered an educational expense.

A second kind of job number is for people working on their own, outside a formal programming class. To obtain this kind of number, ask someone at the computing center how to apply for a job number. This may involve a form on which is entered the title of the project for which the computer will be used, and perhaps the amount of computer time desired (if this is not determined by the computing center itself). A beginning programmer might request anything from a few minutes to an hour, with the idea of applying for more time later on if needed.

This assumes, however, that the computing center makes *free time* available to *users*. Some places do; they prefer to be paid if the user has funds for the purpose, but they do not insist on it if he does not. If free time is available, it may be anything from a few minutes up to virtually unlimited use.

Other computing centers, however, charge for use of their computer. That is, if one is not a student in a programming class, so that use of the computer is paid for by an educational budget, then each bit of computer time must be paid for as it is used.

Since there is this variation, find out whether your computing center does make free time available to people outside formal programming classes. If not, it might be possible to make some other arrangement, such as taking more programming courses to get access to the computer.

If a student can receive free computer time, he may have to find an instructor to sign, as faculty sponsor, his application. For a student working on a thesis, his major professor or committee chairman would be a logical choice for this. For other students, perhaps a faculty advisor or interested faculty member will serve as sponsor.

Even if computer time is free, do not waste it. For one thing, it does cost money to run a computer, and somebody must foot the bill. Also, remember there are many programmers sharing the computer. If we waste its time (for example, leaving out a FORMAT statement simply through neglecting to check a new program before giving it to the computer) this would cause a needless delay in someone else's work. In short, even if it is possible to get as much computer time as needed simply by requesting it, it is still a privilege, and a resource to be treated with care.

There are things that can be done to minimize the amount of computer time used. One is to proofread programs before they are submitted, to catch such obvious errors as a missing parenthesis in a FORMAT statement. Then once a program is completely finished, it can be run in machine language form, rather than the original Fortran form which has to go through the translator each time.

STATEMENT AND DATA CARDS

As we have seen, a computer program is a series of individual statements. Each statement instructs the computer to perform one operation: to read, or compute, or write. Or like a FORMAT statement, it may give the computer information needed to do one of these things.

Each individual statement is punched on a separate card. This punching is done in a standard keypunch machine. The cards are then grouped in a *program deck*. It is this deck of cards which makes up the *program* we give the computer.

The punched cards used for this purpose are exactly the same as those we put data on. They have the same 80 columns. Furthermore, since these cards are punched in the same keypunch used for punching data cards, the numbers and letters and the other characters like plus and minus signs, parentheses, asterisks, and so on, use the same standard system of coded holes in the various card columns. And the computer reads these cards the same way it reads data cards; by electronically sensing the various arrangements of the coded holes.

Indeed, the only way the computer can tell the cards containing program instructions from the cards containing data is if we put the program cards first, separated from the data cards by a card which has some special notation on it, like the word DATA, or a dollar sign $. Then when the computer gets a program and the associated data cards, it considers the first cards it reads to be the program. Only when it gets to the card with something like DATA or $ does it begin considering the next cards as containing data. Different computing centers use different notations to enable the computer to know when it is leaving the program and getting to the data cards, so this is something else to check on locally.

Even though program cards and data cards are so similar, however, there are two superficial ways in which we humans often distinguish between them. One is verbal. If we take a blank card and punch data on it, we call it a *data card.* If we were to take that same card and punch a program statement or instruction on it, we would then call it a *statement card,* or perhaps a *program card.* So from here on we will refer to the punched cards containing program instructions as statement cards, to distinguish them from the punched cards which carry data for a program. Note, however, that this verbal distinction is strictly to help *us* keep track of the different uses we make of the cards; these words mean nothing to the computer, which responds only to what we put on the cards, and to the order in which we arrange the cards.

Also, as a further aid to us (not to the computer) it is common to reserve cards of one color for programming statements. This particular color may vary from computing center to computing center, so that one place may use only blue cards for statement cards whereas another may use only all-white cards for this purpose. The point of this is to make it easy to look at a set of punched cards and tell at a glance where the program ends and the data begins.

Furthermore, some of the cards designed to be used solely as statement cards may have special printing on them. For example, such a card may say *Fortran Statement Card* along the top. In addition, certain columns on statement cards are reserved for special purposes. For example, the statement number (like that used in numbering FORMAT statements) must go in certain columns. So as an aid to the human programmer, a card designed to be used as a statement card may have heavy vertical lines setting these columns off from the other columns. But remember that such words or lines on a card have no meaning to the computer. It responds only to the arrangement of the holes punched in the cards, and to the way the cards are arranged in the program. Thus in a pinch we could put program instructions on purple data cards, even though our computing center used white cards for this purpose. The human operators at the computing center might be disturbed by such a departure from a conventional color scheme, but the computer would be unaware of it. So too could we punch data on statement cards, if these were the only cards available at the moment.

THE PROGRAMMING FORM

Since certain columns on the statement card are reserved for certain purposes, it is advisable for beginning programmers to first write each statement on a programming form, which is designed to help locate each part of a statement in the proper column(s). Then the statement cards are punched from this form.

Figure 3 illustrates what a programming form might look like.

The general appearance of these forms may vary from one computing center to another, but they have in common the fact that they consist of a number of lines, with each line having 80 boxes or spaces corresponding to the 80 columns on a punched card. Each line on the form corresponds to one punched card, so one programming statement is written on each line. Lines may be skipped on the form for readability. This makes no difference in the actual program. That is, a blank line on the programming form does not mean a corresponding blank statement card must be put into the program deck itself. Rather, we punch a card only for each line on the

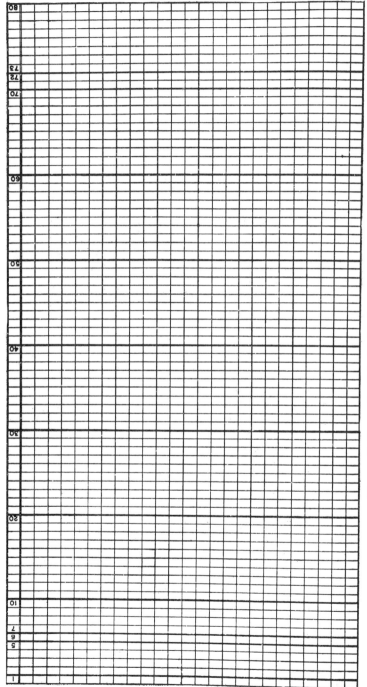

Figure 3. Example of the body of a programming form.

programming form on which something is written. What we may *not* do is decide that since one statement takes only part of a line, we will start a second statement on that line to save space on the form. Since statement cards are punched from this form, putting two statements on one line is an invitation to putting two statements on one card, and this the computer will not accept. So even a statement as short as:

A = B

must get a separate statement card, and hence a separate line on the programming form.

Figure 3 shows the lines and spaces that make up the body of a programming form. A form might also have space at one edge for the programmer's name, name of the program itself, and so on.

If some kind of standard programming form is not available, try to find a substitute (coding form, graph paper, or whatever). The only requirement is the 80 spaces per line, each space corresponding to a column on a statement card.

SPECIAL COLUMNS

On the sample form in Figure 3, certain columns are set off by darker lines. These columns have special purposes on the statement card, so they are clearly indicated on the programming form to make sure the various parts of each statement are properly placed on the form. This makes it easier to get the statements properly located on the statement cards themselves.

If you are using some kind of substitute for a programming form, you should initially draw in the heavy lines as shown in Figure 3. That is, draw a heavy vertical line after column 1, lines on both sides of column 6, and a line after column 72.

Comment Column

On the programming form, the heavy line after column 1 shows that this column has a special purpose on the statement card; it is what we call the *comment column*. In column 1 we indicate a *comment card*. If we put a C in column 1 of a statement card, the computer will ignore everything else that appears on that card, except that it will print the contents of this card in a *listing* of the program.

A *listing* is just what the term implies: a listing of what is on each card in a program. This listing is written out in the same characters used in writing the program. That is, it comes back in our programming language, not in the machine's own language.

There are several ways to get a listing of a program. One is from the computer itself. When a program goes into the computer, we can receive back (along with any output) a listing of what is on each statement card in the program. (Since this may require a special request to the computer, it is something else to check on at the computing center.)

Another way to get a listing of a program is to put it into one of the auxiliary machines in the computing center which prints out on paper the contents of a deck of punched cards.

The point of the comment card is that it lets us give messages to ourselves in a program: to give ourselves *comments*, as it were. In this way we can show the purpose of a program or section of a program, or even the purpose of a particular statement in a program. For example, we can begin a program with a comment card used as a *title card* to show the name or purpose of the program. This may not sound important now, but soon you will have written many programs, and you will want to be able to quickly identify any one of them. If the first card in the program is a comment card giving the name or title of the program, it is a simple matter to identify each program, regardless of whether you are looking at listings of programs, or at the program decks themselves.

At this point you may have a question about the relationship between the C or comment cards we are discussing here, and what we learned earlier about H fields. The difference is that a message in a C card shows up in a listing of the program, but *not* in the output. This means we can use C cards to say things about a program that we do not want to appear in the output. In other words, what the H field does for output, the comment card does within a program itself.

For an illustration of the difference between C cards and H fields, say that the first card in a program carries this message (assume the C is in column 1):

C   CORRELATION PROGRAM

This card would produce precisely this message in a listing of the program. However, to get this or a similar title in the *output*, to identify answers produced by the program, we must still use an H field in a FORMAT statement, like this:

WRITE (6, 200)
200 FORMAT(1H1,'CORRELATION PROGRAM')

Comment cards are also used in the body of a program to describe what its various elements do. C cards can be used to give just as detailed a description of the various steps in a program as desired, and any description is right in the program itself. One C card can show where data is read, another can show where calculations are done, another can show the output section, and so on. In a long program, with perhaps several separate input and output segments, a long series of calculations, etc. comment cards are really essential, so it is best to get in the habit of using them right away. When going back to a program later, these comment cards are very useful in refreshing one's memory about the various steps involved. Similarly, comment cards help other programmers follow the steps in a program. This is important when asking someone else to help find an error in the program.

Documentation

This describing each of the steps in a program, and showing its purpose, is known as *documenting* a program. Where the description is included within the program itself on comment cards, this is *internal documentation*. Then *external documentation* is writing a description of the program and its various sections in English, typed on a sheet of paper so that without going into the program itself, any potential user could tell what the program does and how the data are presented with it. Again, this kind of documentation can be made just as detailed as desired.

Special Comment Cards

A final note on comment cards is the fact that since their contents are ignored by the computer (except to be printed out in a listing of a program) we can do here something we also do with H fields: that is, we can put on a C card any character that is available on the computer. For example, a comment card with a row of asterisks on it is useful in separating the sections of a long program. In the listing of the program containing this card, the card itself will show up as a line of asterisks, thus visually separating one segment of the program from another.

Another similar device is a line of dashes on a comment card. But as with H fields, be careful of the force of the printer. To avoid having the paper cut, separate dashes by blank spaces here as well.

Still another useful device is to put a C in column one of a comment card, and then leave the rest of the card blank. This will produce an empty line in that position in the listing of the program. This is equivalent to using a blank H field to get extra spacing in output, except that a blank C card produces only one blank line in a listing of a program. So to skip two lines means using two blank C cards, to skip three blank lines means using three blank comment cards, and so on.

Regardless of how it is done, this kind of visual separation of segments of a program (along with titles or headings on comment cards for each segment) can really help in later reading the program.

Statement Number Columns

As we have seen, some statements, like FORMAT statements, use numbers. In the Fortran IV version we are using here, statement numbers go in columns 1 through 5 on the programming form, and correspondingly, in columns 1 through 5 on the statement cards themselves. This is a second use of column 1, but there is no conflict here. If there is a C in column 1, the computer will ignore everything else on the card, *except* to print it in the listing of the program. If a C does not appear in column 1, this means a card is being used for a regular statement. In this case, column 1 can be used for a statement number, along with columns 2 through 5.

If statement numbers are right-justified in these five columns (that is, using column 5 as the right margin for statement numbers) it is easier to read the numbers in looking at a listing of the statements. So put a one-digit statement number in column 5, a two-digit number in columns 4 and 5, and so on. (On a comment card, since its contents are ignored, except to be printed out, there must be a C in column 1, but columns 2 through 5 may be used for any purpose desired.)

Columns for the Statement Itself

For a moment we will skip over column 6 and move to column 7. This is where the body of a programming statement begins. The statement may use columns 7 through 72 inclusive. Any character in columns 73 through 80 would be ignored by the computer, so these columns can be used to consecutively number the program (the statement numbers themselves are not usually suitable for this) or some identification mark in these columns might show which program a statement card belongs to. (The heavy line after column 72 on the programming form shows that the body of a programming statement should not extend beyond this column.)

Continuation Column

It often happens that a statement is too long for one statement card. In this event, we simply continue the statement on another card, starting again in (or after) column 7 on this next card, which we call a *continuation card*. And to tell the computer that a card carries a continuation of a preceding statement, rather than a new statement, we put a digit in column six on the continuation card (that is, the card being used to continue a long statement). This use of column 6 is the reason this column is bordered by heavy lines on the programming form.

The first card which begins a long statement does not need a number in column 6. In the second card, which continues the statement, we can put a 2 in column 6 to show that this is the *second* card making up the statement. If a third card is necessary to continue the statement, we can put a 3 in column 6 of that card, and so on. Rarely will a statement require more than two continuation cards (a total of three cards, including the one beginning the statement). However, if more continuation cards should be needed, they are simply added, with successive numbers in column 6.

When a statement has a number (like a FORMAT statement) the statement number appears *only* with the first card which begins the statement.

In using continuation cards with FORMAT statements, an important thing to remember is this: Try not to go to a continuation card in the middle of an H field. Briefly, this is because blank spaces are significant in an H field. Once the computer starts on an H field, it keeps track of all blanks until it is told the H field has ended. For an illustration, say we come to column 66 on a FORMAT card, being in the middle of an H field, and find that the next word in the H field is too long to fit in columns 66 through 72, so we start the next word in column 7 of a continuation card. However, the computer, coming to column 66 on the first card, and knowing it is in an H field, would count columns 66 through 72 as blanks *within* the H field. If we are using the apostrophe form of the H field, this would mean a series of unwanted blanks in the middle of the H field. If we are using the form of the H field with the letter H and a number, there would be a further side effect: counting these left-over blanks at the end of the first card as part of the H field would mean the H field is longer than the number before the H indicates. This would be an error.

To avoid this kind of complication, then, the simple rule is: Do not go to a continuation card in the middle of an H field, *except* when the H field goes right up to column 72 of the first card, so that no extra spaces are left in going to column 7 of the second (continuation) card. Since blank spaces are not critical elsewhere, this problem does not arise in continuing arithmetic statements, field specifications, etc. from one card to another.

If a FORMAT statement uses a continuation card, the *output* printed according to that FORMAT statement still appears on one line, because it is still the closing parenthesis in the FORMAT statement that tells the computer to stop printing on one line of output. In other words, one FORMAT statement governs the printing of one line of output, even if the FORMAT statement itself is so long that it must be written on more than one card. (Remember, however, the limit on the number of spaces available on one line of output; if we assume 120 spaces per line, then a FORMAT statement, regardless of how many cards it requires, can not provide for more than 120 spaces in H fields, data fields, and blank spaces, combined.)

EXAMPLE

To sum up what we have said about the use of various special columns, Figure 4 is an example of a program written on a programming form. The program itself is of little import; it merely reads in five values, and finds and writes out their sum and average. The thing to concentrate on here is how the various statements are arranged on the programming form.

In this example, note the use of comment cards for internal documentation: that is, a C card gives the title of the program, and other C cards show what the different sections of the program do. Remember that the messages or characters on the C cards would show up in the program listing, but not in the output; the messages in 100 FORMAT and 101 FORMAT would show up in the output because they are in H fields in FORMAT statements.

Note also how blank C cards are used before and after each line of astericks, as well as elsewhere in the program. In a listing of the program, these blank C cards would result in an

```
C   ***  THIS PROGRAM FINDS THE SUM AND AVERAGE OF FIVE VALUES  ***
C     READ DATA
      READ (5,60) A, B, C, D, E
   60 FORMAT (5F10.0)
C     ***
C     FIND SUM AND AVERAGE
      Z = A + B + C + D + E
      AVE = Z / 5.
C     ***
C     WRITE RESULTS
      WRITE (6, 100)
  100 FORMAT (1H1, 'THIS PROGRAM FINDS THE AVERAGE OF FIVE VALUES ',
     2 'ENTERED UNDER THE NAMES A, B, C, D, AND E' )
      WRITE (6, 101) Z, AVE
  101 FORMAT (1H , 'THE SUM OF THE FIVE VALUES IS', F8.0,
     2 ' AND THE AVERAGE IS', F8.2 )
      END
```

Figure 4. Example of program written on a programming form.

extra (blank) line wherever they appear. (Remember that a blank line on the programming form does not in itself produce a blank line in the program listing; a blank line in the listing requires a blank C card.)

The body of each programming statement begins in column 7; however, the body of a statement could begin in a column after 7, because blank spaces before a statement are ignored.

Statement numbers are right-justified in columns 1 through 5.

The statement finding the sum of the five values is continued to a second card here; obviously, there would be room on the first of these cards to complete that statement, but the point here was to show how a continuation card could be used with such a statement.

Note how the continuation cards have been used for 100 and 101 FORMAT statements. The message in 100 FORMAT was broken into two H fields to avoid any problem of extra spaces in going to the continuation card. If we had continued the H field itself down to the second card, with the words located as they are here, the output would have included seven blank spaces (represented by the empty columns 66 through 72 on the first card in this statement) between the words VALUES and ENTERED on the output paper. (Remember that although two cards are used for this FORMAT statement, there would only be one line of output actually produced by this statement.)

At the same time, note that we would want one space between the words VALUES and ENTERED on the one line of output. We provided this blank space at the end of the H field on the first card.

In 101 FORMAT statement we also avoided going to a continuation card in the middle of an H field. There we provided at the beginning of the second H field for a blank space between the value for Z (the sum) and the beginning of the second message. (This FORMAT statement would also provide only one line of output.)

For comparison, Figure 5 is how a listing of this program might actually look as it came back from the computer.

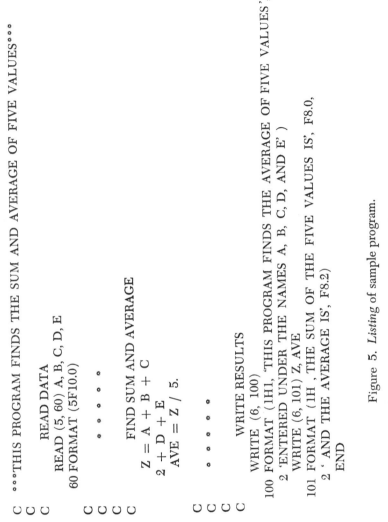

Figure 5. *Listing* of sample program.

For further comparison, Figure 6 is how the *output* from this program might look, given a value of 536. for Z (the sum) and a value of 107.2 for AVE (the average).

Note that the only things that would actually appear on the output paper for this program would be those messages contained in H fields in FORMAT statements, together with the data values themselves; anything on a C card in the program would not appear in the output.

THIS PROGRAM FINDS THE AVERAGE OF FIVE VALUES ENTERED UNDER THE NAMES A, B, C, D, AND E
THE SUM OF THE FIVE VALUES IS   536. AND THE AVERAGE IS   107.20

Figure 6. *Output* from sample program.

Finally, we spoke earlier of external documentation: that is, writing out in English a description of a program. For illustration, here is how we might describe this program, for external documentation:

> This program finds the sum and average of five values and writes both these figures out. Data are presented to the computer on one card, each value using a ten-column field, with no blank spaces between the fields. Each value must be right-justified in its field.

For complex programs, of course, the documentation would also be quite complex, but this example gives a general idea of how we would write up a description of a program so that someone else, reading this description, would know what the program does, and how to present his data to it.

BLANK COLUMNS

In our sample program on the programming form in Figure 4, empty spaces occur through the various statements. When the program cards are punched from this form, these empty spaces represent (and will become) blank columns on the statement cards.

Since some blank spaces have meaning (as in H fields and print control characters) one advantage of programming forms is that they help to specify blank spaces, and hence blank card columns. However, as programmers become more experienced, they often find ideas for programs occurring when there are no programming forms handy, and they end up writing programs on napkins, on backs of envelopes, or on any other scraps of paper handy.

In writing programs on plain paper, there are several ways of showing a blank space. One is to use a triangle. Since this is not used anywhere else in programming, it can show that a column is to be left blank when punching statement cards. Thus a print control character might be written like this:

1H△,

Another character sometimes used for this purpose is a lower case *b*, standing for *blank*. Since all letters used in programming are capitals, a lower case *b* is not a programming character. It can be used to give a print control character like this:

1Hb,

However, this can be confusing, because b can look like a 6, so sometimes the b is written with a slash: ƀ

Also, to avoid confusion, do not use a dash to show a blank space. This is easily mistaken for a minus sign.

Another character which does not appear in programming language, and therefore can be used solely to indicate a blank space, is a half-moon character lying on its side. This would give a print control character something like this:

1H◡,

Also, there is the # character we have been using here to show blank spaces. This character was chosen for this purpose because it is perhaps least likely to be confused with any other character. This, too, can be used to clearly show a blank space when writing a statement on a plain sheet of paper, like this:

1H#,

Except for the few places where they are critical, blank spaces can be used to advantage in writing statements. Some programmers indent certain sections of their programs five or ten spaces to show that certain statements belong together and are distinct from other segments of a program.

Also, it is useful to leave blanks at various other points within a statement. This has two purposes. One is to improve the readability of the program as it will appear in a listing. This is important, because in searching for errors in a program we read it over and over again. So rather than writing statements which crowd the characters together, like this:

A=B+C

it is useful to spread them out, like this:

A = B + C

Another reason for having blank spaces in statement cards

is to save time in correcting errors. Often a mistake will only be that a comma or parenthesis or operation sign was left out. If there are blank spaces in the statement involved, it is often possible to put that card in the keypunch, hit the space bar to move the card along to the appropriate place, and find there a blank space in which to insert the missing character. This saves repunching a whole statement. (For someone more experienced with a keypunch, a faster way to get to any given column on a punched card is to use the key intended for duplicating. It would save time if you get acquainted with this short cut as soon as possible, both in adding a missing character to a punched card, and in correcting wrong characters.)

KEYPUNCHING PROGRAMS

If not familiar with a keypunch, ask someone for instruction, because you should know how to use one. If you have done keypunching, but only straight numerical data, you will probably still need some instruction, because punching programs is more complicated, since programs use both letters and numbers. Learning to shift back and forth between numbers and letters rapidly takes some practice, but it is worth it, because this will allow you to punch your own programs when there is no one to do it for you.

However, other people may also punch some of your programs. Your computing center may offer a keypunching service. There may be a fee for this, even when the computer itself can be used free. But it is also possible that the center might punch your statement cards without charge, though this might be on a low priority basis.

Also, you may eventually have an assistant to do some of your keypunching. But some keypunchers, even those in a computing center, know little about programming itself, so you can not rely on them to correct any errors you might make, or even to guess what you mean if your handwriting is not clear. They can only do an accurate job of punching a program if it is written very clearly and precisely on a programming form.

For this reason, it is useful on these programming forms not only to show exactly what columns are to be blank, but also to use only capital letters. But even capital letters do not completely eliminate the possibility of misunderstanding. For example, a handwritten 2 can easily be mistaken for a handwritten Z. To avoid this, we conventionally write 2 as it would normally appear, but include a short horizontal line through the Z̶. Similarly, to distinguish between the letter O and the digit 0, we include a diagonal line through the letter Ø. Also, we can include a crossbar on the letter S̶ to distinguish it from the number 5. And we put crossbars on the top and bottom of the letter I to distinguish it from the digit 1.

Refer back to the program written on a programming form in Figure 4, and notice how we attempted to clearly distinguish between 0 and Ø, 1 and I, and so on. Be very careful in making these distinctions, because a common error for beginning programmers is getting similar-appearing characters mixed up in a program.

As an example of what can happen when two characters are mixed up, take zero and the letter O. The computer can distinguish between the two, of course, because the coded arrangement of holes for the two characters is different on a punched card. Thus if we want to start a variable name with the letter O, but inadvertently use zero, the computer would reject this as starting a variable name with a number, which is unacceptable.

Once an error like this has been made, it is very difficult to find, because the letter O and the digit 0 look so similar in a listing of a program. In reading a program, if we see something that *looks like* the letter O in a position where a letter should be, we assume it is an O, rather than zero, because the difference between them is so slight, perhaps only a slightly more angular shape for the letter O.

Conversely, we might have a letter where we should have a zero, as in writing the number 1O. The computer would object to this; it can not be a name because it starts with the number 1, but it can not be a number because it contains the letter O. And in hunting for this error, we could look at the characters

1O a dozen times and never notice that we have the letter O instead of a zero after the 1.

We are probably less likely to confuse the letter I and the number 1, but again, the two characters look enough alike so that if we have inadvertently written one in place of the other, we can easily overlook this error in reading the program.

In short, be extremely careful about getting certain letters and numbers mixed up. But even with care, this will probably happen a few times, particularly in early programs. The reason for this is that the letter O and the zero look much alike on a keypunch keyboard, and the same is true of I and 1. So until you have more experience in punching letters and numbers, you will probably hit the wrong key occasionally. Therefore, always remember that if an error is hard to find, it could be one of this kind. The solution is to look at a statement card itself to see whether a certain character is punched as a letter or number (the arrangement of holes in that column on the card shows this clearly).

PROOFREADING THE PROGRAM

When a program is punched on statement cards, it is a good idea to run the cards through the auxiliary machine which prints out a listing of what is on each card. Then this listing can be used to visually proofread the program, checking for any keypunching errors: characters left out, or transposed, or whatever.

Errors like this can keep a program from running, so it is a waste of computer time not to check for at least the most obvious ones before actually submitting a program to the computer. This proofreading is also useful when a program is changed enough to require considerable additional keypunching.

END CARDS

Once a program has been proofread, and any keypunching errors corrected, there are a couple of finishing touches required before submitting it to the computer. One has to do with any cards required to end the program. The procedure for this varies from place to place, but as an illustration, one common practice is to use two cards like these to tell the computer it has reached the end of a program:

RETURN
END

The exact procedure for ending a program is one of the things to ask about at the local computing center. However, regardless of their exact wording, these *end* cards come after all the other statement cards in a program. They tell the computer there are no more instructions to be executed in that particular program. Because of the variation, we will end programs here with a single card saying END.

CONTROL CARDS

When we give the computer the combination of program and data cards that make up a job, we may also need to give the computer information and instructions about the total job: telling it such things as where the program cards end and the data cards begin, where the job itself ends, whether to try and run the program or just look for errors in it, and so on.

These details may be given to the computer on separate cards, which control or direct the computer in *processing* or running a job. These particular cards are not part of a program itself; rather, they can be viewed as ways of giving the computer messages *about* a program. Because of their purpose, these cards may be referred to in various ways: with some computers, for example, they may be called *control cards* or *command cards*, and the information they contain may be referred to as control statements, or command statements, and so on. The logic of this, of course, is that these cards make up a language (separate from Fortran) which can be used to control, or command, the computer as it runs a program.

Because of the variation, all we will do here is describe a few cards of this kind, and show where and why they might be included in a job. The first card might be a *name* card, or ID card, with the programmer's name and job number. The ID card may also contain the title of the program and a date. Check at the computing center for the exact makeup of this card, the items included and the columns in which they are located.

There might also be a card which has this purpose: If a computer is capable of operating with several different languages, this card can tell it which language a program uses, Fortran, Cobol, or whatever.

Then there might be a card with a notation which tells the computer to start running a program. This could be something like the word EXEC (standing for *execute*) or the letter G (standing for *go*). The reason for this is that a computer may be set up so that it does not run a program unless specifically requested to do so.

This may seem odd, but there is a reason for it. As a program goes into the computer, it is translated into the machine language of that computer. During this process, the computer checks each statement for language errors, and if it finds none, it translates that statement into machine language. This overall process is known as *compiling*. If no error, is found, so that every statement is translated into machine language, a program is said to have *compiled*. On the other hand, if we say a program does not compile, this means that one or more language errors were found. Logically, that part of the computer system which does this checking and translating is known as the *compiler*.

If errors are found, the program is not run. But even if there are no errors, the computer can still stop at that point. Sometimes, particularly when checking a new program for errors, this is what we want: merely to see whether the program will compile. Therefore, when we do want a program to run (assuming it compiles) we can include in our control cards an *execute* card, containing a notation like EXEC or G. This card tells the computer to go ahead and execute (run) the program. This is where it proceeds to obey each of the instructions in the programming statements themselves.

The ID and execute cards would probably come before the program. Then after the program, and before the data, there would probably be a card telling the computer that the program itself ends at this point and that the next cards encountered are those containing the data to be used with the program. As indicated earlier, this card might carry a special notation like a dollar sign, or the word DATA.

Next come the data cards. These cards may contain either real data, or (in the first few runnings of a program) test data used to be sure the program is working properly.

Finally, there will be an *end-of-file* card, or *end-of-job* card, or something comparable. This tells the computer it has encountered the end of the data for this program. Do not confuse this with the END card in the program itself. Both are necessary: one to show the end of a program, the other to show the end of the job (*job* meaning both program and data).

It should be emphasized again that there can be variation from one computing center to another in the makeup of these cards used to give the computer information about a job being submitted to it. The important thing for our purposes here is that you know such cards are used, and roughly what their purpose is. Remember that before running a program you should ask your instructor (if in a programming class) or someone at your computing center about the cards used there for this purpose: the makeup (and perhaps color) of each card, and where it is placed relative to your program deck and data cards. Since these added cards are so important (probably a program will not run without them) many people at the computing center (including other programmers you may meet there) should be familiar with them.

If a programmer has two or more jobs to give to the computer at the same time, each may be considered by the computer as a completely separate job, requiring its own set of control cards. In this event, make up each job separately, then submit each one separately (though at the same time, if desired) to the computer in the manner described just below. (If several jobs are to be submitted to the computer at the same time, it is probably safest to treat each job as a completely separate unit, giving it its own control cards. However, there may also be a provision for combining several jobs into one, so that they share one or more control cards, such as an ID card or end-of-job card. This is also something to check at your computing center.)

SUBMITTING THE PROGRAM

To submit a program to the computer, all the cards (the program cards, then the data cards, and the control cards giving instructions to the computer about the job) are assembled and perhaps fastened with rubber bands. The actual process of submitting this program to the computer (or more accurately, to the people who run it) is something else that varies from one computing center to another. At one center programs may be dropped into a tray, to be periodically picked up and taken into the computer in the *machine room.* Somewhere else each program may be handed to a clerk who puts a ticket on the program and hands back a stub to be used when calling for the program. Another arrangement might be to leave the program in a box near your office, with a messenger periodically taking a group of programs to the computing center and bringing them back when they are finished. Again, because of the variation, check on what arrangements your computing center uses for submitting programs and getting them back.

A program returns from the computer as it went in, with the cards in the same order, probably fastened together by rubber bands, and with output from the program perhaps wrapped around the program and secured by a rubber band, or folded and tucked under the rubber bands that hold the cards together.

In this printed output are several things. One is probably a complete listing of the program, including all the comment cards, and with the characters on the control cards appearing at the appropriate points. For example, the information on the ID card, the first card the computer reads in a job, could make up the first line in this listing.

Then, if the program contained no language errors, and otherwise worked properly, this listing will be followed by any output called for in the program.

DEBUGGING

On the other hand, if the computer found errors in a program, there will be some indication of these errors, probably identified both as to where they occur in the program, and the kind of error involved. These indications of errors are often called *error* messages, or *diagnostics*. The computer indicates *where* the error occurred in one of several ways. One way is to reprint the incorrect statement in the error message part of the output. Another way is to assign consecutive numbers to the statements showing up in the listing of the program. These numbers, *independent of any statement number* in the program, are printed opposite the statements to which they apply. Then in the error message section is a notation that the statement bearing the *listing* number (*not* program statement number) so-and-so had an error.

If there are errors present, and often there will be, even for expert programmers, then comes the debugging process. The computer will help in this by indicating not only where an error occurred, but also what kind of error it was. The error message may be written out, as when the computer prints something like *comma missing,* or *undefined name,* or *illegal character.* Or the computer may give only an error code number. This number refers to what is called an *error code book* or *error message book.* In this book (or in this portion of a programming manual) various errors are listed, each identified by a number. Upon seeing an error code number in the results that come back from the computer, look up this number in the listing of error messages to find the kind of error committed. For example, there might be a number like F18 in an error message coming back from the computer. Looking up this number in the error code book, we might find it followed by the entry, *Improper Variable Name.*

A personal copy of this listing of error messages may be available either from the computing center or from the computer manufacturer. Also, a copy should be available in the computing center.

Also, an error may be indicated by something in the output

from a program itself. For example, we indicated in Chapter 5, in discussing output, that if a field specification provides too few spaces for the value to be printed in that data field, the computer may show this by printing a row of asterisks or something comparable in that data field. This indicates something wrong about that data field just as clearly as if the computer printed an error message about it.

However, a complication here is the fact that a computer may also print a row of non-numerical characters in a data field to show that the variable name whose value is to be printed in that field is in fact undefined. For example, if we have the variable name DAT in a WRITE statement, but have not placed a value in that location, then when the computer tries to print out a value for DAT, it will find DAT is undefined, and might indicate this by printing something like a row of asterisks in the data field intended for the value of DAT.

So if you see a row of asterisks, X's, etc., in a data field in a line of output, first make sure that the field specification for that field provides enough spaces for the value to be printed there. If the field specification is correct, then check to make sure the variable name associated with that data field is defined. In practice, this can mean first changing the field specification to provide more spaces in that data field, and giving the program back to the computer. If the row of *garbage* characters still appears in that data field, this may mean the variable name associated with that data field is undefined when it appears in the WRITE statement. Correcting this kind of error means going through the program to make sure that each variable name appears either in a READ statement, or on the left of the equal sign in an arithmetic statement.

Sometimes an error is so difficult to find, even with a hint as to where it is and what it is, that we are convinced the computer itself has made a mistake. This can happen, of course, because even computers are not perfect; after all, they are made by people. Since there is a possibility of *machine error*, however remote, if an error is not found after a few minutes hunting for it, give the program back to the computer. If there is a machine error, the same mistake should not show up next time because the malfunction responsible for it would probably be corrected during routine maintenance of the machine. If the error shows up repeatedly, therefore, it is almost certainly a programming error.

One thing to keep in mind in looking for errors is the fact that so many are somehow involved in the input/output processes. There may be an error in a READ or WRITE statement, or a FORMAT statement. Also, more often than might be expected, the programming statements will be correct, but there is an error in the *data* itself which causes a mismatch between data and FORMAT field specification. For example, a decimal point may have inadvertently been punched in a data column which is supposed to contain a digit. Another common error, particularly for beginning programmers, is mixing integer and decimal values in an arithmetic expression. Also, variable names may be incorrectly constructed, or commas or parentheses may be missing or wrongly placed.

So far here we have been speaking of *grammatical* errors: that is, errors in the programming language, errors in the way statements are constructed, errors like too many or too few parentheses, improper names, and so on. These errors the computer will usually find for us, although occasionally one will slip by so that we learn about it only when the results of a program seem suspicious. But as we have stressed several times, a program may run with no language errors, but it may contain errors in logic. Various possible errors of this kind have been referred to in the past few chapters. These are not faults in *how* we give the computer instructions; rather, they are errors in *what* we tell it to do. For example, we may have a minus sign in a statement which really requires a plus sign. The computer has no way of knowing this is a logic error. After all, the statements:

$$A = X - B$$
$$A = X + B$$

are both correct *from the standpoint of the language.* Therefore the computer will accept whichever one appears.

The fact that the computer can give no indication of them

makes these logic errors the hardest to find. And if the computer will give no warning of logic errors, we must protect against them ourselves. Some logic errors, of course, will give themselves away. For example, we may know a correlation value can only fall between 1.0 and —1.0. If we get a result for this correlation of 427.2, we know there was a logic error in the program.

But if a result were .2 when it really should have been .7, this would give no obvious warning of anything wrong. Therefore, always use *test data* to check out a new program, or a program which has been substantially changed.

One way to get this test data is to make up a small set of figures, work out the statistic or procedure by hand, and then give these same figures to the computer and see if the computer gets the same results you got by hand. Another approach sometimes possible is to take from a statistics textbook the data used to illustrate the particular statistic being programmed. Punch these figures on data cards, give them to the computer, and see if the answer produced by the program is the same as the textbook's.

With either approach, there is a warning. Because of the time involved in working out a complex problem by hand, there is a tendency to use small amounts of test data. But it may happen that a program which works perfectly with a small set of test data does not work with larger sets of data. That is, a program might work well with test data from 30 cases, but foul up completely on real data for 300 cases.

We have already discussed one possible reason for this. During the course of its calculations on a large sample the computer may produce a value which exceeds the largest number permissible, whereas this would be less likely with a small set of test data. This is particularly a danger with a statistic using factorials.

Later we will see other reasons why the computer could give valid results with one size sample, and wrong answers with another size sample. Here we are offering only an indication of how thoroughly a new program must be tested before we can have real faith in it.

However, even though errors may occur with some size samples but not with others, or may be logic errors that are hard to find, we still have a very useful defense against them, a technique you should *quickly* get in the habit of using. This is to liberally sprinkle temporary WRITE statements through a new program. For example, in a long series of calculations, include after each step a WRITE statement which will show the results of that intermediate step. This gives a much better chance of spotting a logic error at the point where it occurs. As a matter of fact, some programmers even include such a WRITE statement immediately after the input statements which read data into the computer. Since this brings at least a portion of the data right back out, it is a way of checking that the computer begins its calculations with the data it is meant to have.

Put these temporary output statements on cards of a different color from the rest of the program. Then when the program is finally working as desired, it is easy to go through it and pull out all these temporary cards. This procedure is *very strongly* recommended, because it can save immense amounts of time hunting for errors.

Having found and corrected all the errors that show up after one running of a program, the process of submitting the program is repeated. If more errors show up the next time the program comes back, correct these errors and resubmit the program, and so on.

HANDLING THE PROGRAM

Finally, all the *bugs* are out and the program is running exactly as desired, giving you a tool well worth the time invested in it. At this point, get a deck of cards containing the machine language version of the program: the object program. This is the version of the program which does not need to be translated each time it is used, and therefore will save considerable computer time if used in future runs of the program. This deck of cards is produced by the computer. The exact procedure for getting this version of a program is something else to check at the computing center.

Now put the original Fortran program deck in a card drawer, under pressure, so the cards will not warp. In its place, after any initial control cards, place the new machine language deck, add the data and any other control cards, and submit this set of cards as you did the set containing the original Fortran program. (It may be necessary to make a change in the control cards, the cards giving information to the computer about the program, to tell the computer that it is now using a machine language program deck. This is also something to check at the computing center.)

Do not get rid of your Fortran language deck, however, for several reasons. One is that you may want to make subsequent changes in your program, even though it is running properly now. These changes will be made with the Fortran deck. Furthermore, since machine languages differ from computer to computer, you might need this Fortran deck if you move to another computer. A new computer could take this Fortran deck and translate it into the machine language of that computer. However, any machine language deck you had might be meaningless to a new computer, because the new computer (that is, the computer at the place to which you move) might use a different machine language.

The final note in this connection has to do with a way of identifying program decks, while at the same time protecting against the possibility that a deck may be dropped or otherwise mixed up. Remember that although a program is a way of communicating with the computer, human beings serve as intermediaries. They take a program to the computer, and operate the appropriate controls. Since they are subject to human error, they, like anyone else, can drop cards, mix up or misplace a program deck, and so on.

As indicated earlier, we could put a set of consecutive numbers in columns 73 through 80 on the program cards, so that if a deck were ever mixed up, it could be quickly restored to order with a card sorter, or even by hand. But this is not the entire solution, for two reasons. One is that it would be almost impossible to keep the numbers in consecutive order because of all the changes and improvements which are almost inevitable in any program. Secondly, these numbers on the cards themselves would not indicate, in just glancing at a deck of cards, whether it was mixed up. Therefore, we need something that will alert us instantly and unmistakably when a deck of cards is out of order.

This procedure is recommended: With a felt-tip pen, make a bright, straight, diagonal line across the top of the program deck. Since this line is drawn across the tops of the cards, we can tell, simply by looking at it, whether the cards are in order. If they are not, the line will not be as straight and true as when it was drawn.

Use the felt pen also to write various items of information on the top of decks of cards, both program and data cards. You can more quickly pick your program out of a pile of returning programs if you have written your name on the top of the deck. Also, you may eventually find yourself with drawers full of programs, so it is useful to write something on each program deck that will identify that program. For example, if you have written a program to do frequency distributions, write across the top of the program deck (in addition to the diagonal line and your name) the letters FREQ DIST. Then when you open a drawer to look for one particular program, you can quickly pick it out from among all the others. Do this for machine language decks as well as for the original Fortran decks.

Finally, another very useful practice is to make a duplicate of each program deck as that program begins to reach its final form. This involves running the program through the *reproducer,* a machine which produces an exact duplicate of any set of cards put into it. (Cards which are *reproduced* usually will not have the kind of printing which the keypunch puts along the top of each card it punches. Without this printing, it is very difficult to read the contents of a punched card, so after reproducing a new program, or data, deck then put the new cards in a machine called the *printer,* or *interpreter,* which will print along the top of each card just what is on that card.)

Then if the original program deck should be mixed up, or have cards torn, or be lost, simply pull out this duplicate deck of cards. Make another copy of this duplicate deck, and you again have a working copy and a spare or back-up copy. This will protect against losing all the time and effort that went into writing a program should the original cards that contain it be torn or lost. Also take this same precaution for decks of data cards to protect against possibly having to repunch a whole set of data.

EXERCISES

See exercises 1–4 in Chapter Eight of the *Workbook*.

Chapter Nine

TRANSFER OF CONTROL AND
DECISION-MAKING

So far we have assumed the computer takes the statements in a program in consecutive order: the first statement, then the second, then the third, and so on through the program. And indeed, one basic rule of programming is that the computer *always* goes to the next statement in line, *unless* instructed otherwise.

However, this consecutive order does not provide for the kinds of *decisions* required in many of our procedures; and these procedures are full of decisions, even though we do not usually recognize them as such. For example, even something as simple as a frequency distribution means the computer must decide which response category each data value belongs to.

Basically, decision-making on a computer usually amounts to telling the computer to do one thing or another, depending on the value of a variable name; that is, depending on the value stored in the location bearing a particular name. When we say the computer does one thing or another, we mean it executes one statement *or* another, or goes to one segment of a program rather than to another.

The fact that decision-making sends the computer from place to place within a program is why we speak of decision-making, broadly, as part of the *transfer of control* in a program. The word *control* here refers to the fact that a program controls the computer's actions: telling it what arithmetic to do, when and where to read data, and so on. So if we send the computer from place to place within a program, we are, in effect, transferring control of the computer from one part of that program to another.

UNCONDITIONAL GO TO

The simplest way of transferring control from one point to another within a program is a statement called the *unconditional GO TO*. This statement consists of the words GO TO, followed by the number of some other statement in the program, like this:

GO TO 88

When the computer hits this GO TO statement, it will then be sent to the statement having number 88 in the program.

This means, of course, that somewhere else in the program there must be a statement numbered 88. This is a second use of statement numbers, along with the FORMAT numbers discussed earlier. Everything we learned in connection with FORMAT statement numbers applies to the use of numbers with other statements in a program; that is, statement numbers need not be consecutive, nor in order, and they go in columns 1 through 5 on the cards containing the statements (right-justified in those columns, so that the number 88 here would appear in columns 4 and 5 of its statement card).

We call this kind of statement an *unconditional* GO TO because it *always* sends the computer to that same point in the program indicated by the statement number following the GO TO. Thus the statement:

GO TO 88

always sends the computer to statement number 88 in the program, wherever that may be. Therefore, we say the unconditional GO TO is *not* a decision-making statement, but *is* a transfer of control statement.

An unconditional GO TO can send the computer to any other statement in a program, except that it may not send the computer to a FORMAT statement. This means that if we say:

GO TO 88

the statement having the number 88 may be anywhere in the program (before or after the GO TO statement) and that statement 88 may be any kind of statement except that it may not be a FORMAT statement.

The reason for this exception is that the GO TO must send the computer to a statement which will *do something.* If the computer were sent to a statement which merely gave it information (like a FORMAT statement) what would it do when it got there? So a GO TO can only send the computer to a statement which tells it to do something: to read a data card, or print a line of output, or do a calculation, or even GO TO yet another point in the program. These statements which tell the computer to do something are called *executable* statements. That is, they give the computer an instruction which is to be executed; they do not merely give it information.

If an unconditional GO TO sends the computer to a later statement, the statements in between are not picked up. That is, the computer will not return to execute those statements it jumped over (unless there is some provision elsewhere in the program for this).

THE CONTINUE STATEMENT

Sometimes we want to send the computer to a point in a program where there is no executable statement handy. In this case we can supply one. This is the CONTINUE statement. This statement consists merely of that word:

CONTINUE

This kind of statement is executable in that it tells the computer to do something; yet it is what we might call *passive* because it instructs the computer to do nothing more than move down to the statement following the CONTINUE, so it does nothing to really change the course of a program in any way.

When given a number, a CONTINUE statement serves as an executable statement to which the computer can be sent from somewhere else in the program. For example, we could write:

```
    GO TO 104
    X = Y + Z
    A = B + C
104 CONTINUE
    E = F + G
```

This sequence would send the computer over the first two arithmetic statements directly down to statement 104. This satisfies the requirement that the computer be sent from a GO TO to an executable statement.

DEVICE TO ILLUSTRATE FLOW OF CONTROL

When control of the computer moves from one part of a program to another, we speak of the *flow* of control through the program. In the following examples we introduce a device we will use to illustrate the flow of control from point to point within a program. We put a lower case letter at the right margin opposite each statement. We can pretend these letters are in columns 73 to 80 on a statement card: those columns which are ignored by the computer and therefore are free for whatever notation we wish to put there.

These lower case letters will be in order. That is, the first statement in a series will have the letter *a* opposite it at the right margin. The second statement will have the letter *b*, the third statement the letter *c*, and so on. We will then use these letters to show which statements in a series would be executed. (Statement numbers are not suitable for this, because not all statements have numbers.)

EXAMPLES

Notice in these examples how the CONTINUE statements are used.

In each example, the computer would begin at the first

(top) statement in the sequence, and move down, although it may later be sent back to the beginning of the sequence, as first happens in Example 7.

Each example here will not make much sense in terms of the actual sequence of statements. Particularly, as the computer jumps from one statement to another, it will appear that the statements in between would never be executed, and therefore should not be included. We will take care of this problem later; here we are simply making up statements to show where the computer would go under certain conditions.

1. Here the computer would jump from statement *a* directly to statement *c*:

GO TO 224	(a)
A = 0.	(b)
224 CONTINUE	(c)

2. In this sequence the computer would execute the first statement, *a*, then jump to statement *c*, then move on to statement *d*:

GO TO 419	(a)
418 A = B / C	(b)
419 A = (B / C) ** 2	(c)
CONTINUE	(d)

3. Here the computer would execute statements *a* and *b*, then jump down to execute statements *e* and *f*:

CONTINUE	(a)
GO TO 481	(b)
B = C ** 2.	(c)
480 B = C − 1.	(d)
481 CONTINUE	(e)
B = A + 1.	(f)

4. In this sequence, the computer would go from statement *a* directly to statement *e*, and then to statement *g*:

GO TO 502	(a)
CONTINUE	(b)

501 C = A + 1.	(c)
GO TO 1000	(d)
502 GO TO 1000	(e)
C = A − B	(f)
1000 CONTINUE	(g)

5. Statements executed in this sequence would be *a*, *f*, and *g*:

8214 GO TO 8216	(a)
8215 A = B	(b)
GO TO 1000	(c)
8217 A = C	(d)
GO TO 1000	(e)
8216 A = D	(f)
1000 CONTINUE	(g)

6. Statements executed in this sequence would be *a*, *d*, *e*, *f*, and *h*:

GO TO 4	(a)
2 A = 10.	(b)
GO TO 92	(c)
4 CONTINUE	(d)
A = 12.	(e)
GO TO 92	(f)
6 A = C	(g)
92 CONTINUE	(h)

7. In this sequence the computer would execute statements *a*, *b*, *c*, and *d*. Statement *d* would send the computer back to statement *a* to begin the sequence over again.

88 CONTINUE	(a)
X = SQRT (AVAL)	(b)
Y = SQRT (BVAL)	(c)
GO TO 88	(d)

8. In this sequence the computer would execute all the statements *except e*. Statement *g* would send the computer back to statement *a* to begin the sequence again.

62 CONTINUE	(a)
SUM = A + B	(b)

FNCASE = NCASE	(c)
GO TO 40	(d)
AVE = FNCASE / SUM	(e)
40 SUMSQ = SUM ** 2	(f)
GO TO 62	(g)

9. In this sequence, the computer would execute statements *a, b, c, g* and *h,* then would return to statement *b* to begin executing that part of the sequence again.

404 CONTINUE	(a)
83 R = 1. −Z	(b)
GO TO 71	(c)
80 R = 1. + Z	(d)
GO TO 71	(e)
81 R = Z ** 2	(f)
71 CONTINUE	(g)
GO TO 83	(h)

10. In this sequence the computer would execute statements *a, b, j, k, l,* and *m,* and then would return to statement *a* to begin the sequence again.

60 CONTINUE	(a)
GO TO 5	(b)
P = Q * T	(c)
CONTINUE	(d)
GO TO 68	(e)
P = Q / T	(f)
GO TO 69	(g)
P = Q ** 2	(h)
68 CONTINUE	(i)
5 CONTINUE	(j)
69 CONTINUE	(k)
CONTINUE	(l)
GO TO 60	(m)

EXERCISES

See exercises 1–16 in Chapter Nine of the *Workbook.*

COMPUTED GO TO

The unconditional GO TO is too limited to be of any use in a program by itself. Its main value is in connection with a statement which does have a true decision-making capability. The simplest of these is also a GO TO statement, but one called a *computed GO TO*. Thus there are two forms of GO TO: an unconditional GO TO and a computed GO TO.

A computed GO TO (which is also called a *conditional* GO TO) does not actually compute anything, in the sense that an arithmetic statement does. Rather, the word *computed* here refers to the fact that this kind of statement, in a sense, forces the computer to *compute* its next move. Specifically, the computer is forced to decide where it will go next in the program, a decision it makes on the basis of the value of a specified variable name.

We can also say that this kind of statement sends the computer to one of several places in the program, depending on the *condition* (that is, the *value*) of a variable name. This is why we also call this kind of GO TO a *conditional* GO TO.

Form of Computed GO TO

The computed GO TO has this form:

GO TO (100, 200, 300), NAMVAR

Each of the numbers within the parentheses is the number of a separate statement in the program containing this GO TO. The number 100 refers to statement 100 in the program, the number 200 refers to statement 200 in the program, and so on. At the end of the statement is the variable name the computer uses in making its decision. The statement numbers in the parentheses are separated by commas, and there is also a comma after the closing parenthesis and immediately before the variable name. Remember this latter comma because it is easily overlooked in writing a computed GO TO. Spaces between the various elements of the statement are ignored.

Operation of the Computed GO TO

The point of the computed GO TO is that it sends the computer next to *one* of the statements indicated by the numbers inside the parentheses. Conversely, in leaving a computed GO TO, the computer must go to one of the statements whose numbers appear inside the parentheses. The question (the *decision*) is: To which one?

We answer this question by giving the computer a value for the variable name which appears at the end of the computed GO TO. If the value of the variable name is 1, the computer goes next to the statement whose number appears in the first (number *one*) position inside the parentheses. Similarly, if the value of that name is 2, the computer goes next to the statement whose number appears in the number two (or *second*) position inside the parentheses. A value of 3 for the variable name sends the computer next to the statement whose number appears third inside the parentheses, and so on. The reason the computer, upon leaving a computed GO TO, can go to only one of those statements indicated inside the parentheses is because the variable name following the parentheses can have only one value at a given point in the program.

Look again at the example of the computed GO TO:

GO TO (100, 200, 300), NAMVAR

This tells the computer to go to the location named NAMVAR, and use the value stored there in deciding where to go next in the program. If the value in NAMVAR at this point is 1, the computer is to go next to statement 100. If the value of NAMVAR is 2, however, the computer is to go next to statement 200, and so on.

If we tell the computer what to do for a data value which fails to show up, this is all right. For example, the above computed GO TO provides for values ranging from 1 through 3. But what if no 3 shows up?

This presents no problem. The general rule of decision-making is to provide a route for the computer to take for any data value which *might* occur at a decision-making step. But if one of these values does not show up, all that happens is that the computer does not take the corresponding route. So in the computed GO TO pictured above, if NAMVAR never had the value 3 for a particular set of data, the computer simply would never go to statement 300 as that set of data is processed. (But note that if we use the statement number 300 in the computed GO TO, there must be a statement with that number somewhere in the program.)

The same thing is true even if several of the values provided for in the computed GO TO fail to show up. For example, if only values of 1 showed up in NAMVAR in the computed GO TO above, this is still all right. The important thing is that we have told the computer what to do *if* values of 2 or 3 should appear in NAMVAR.

This means, therefore, that if we are not absolutely sure what values may occur in the variable name in a computed GO TO, we should err on the side of giving the computer too many, rather than too few, alternatives. Preferably, of course, we know the range of values for each variable being processed, but occasionally we may not be sure. Rather than sifting through a whole data deck to see if a certain value does show up, it is easier (within limits) to set up any decision-making step so that if the value does occur the computer knows how to respond to it. If it does not appear, nothing is lost by having an additional few statements in the program.

The value for the variable name in the computed GO TO may have been read into the location bearing that name, or it may have been placed there by an earlier arithmetic statement, where the variable name appeared on the left of the equal sign. Thus for the computed GO TO we are using for an example here, we could have this:

```
    READ (5, 40) NAMVAR
 40 FORMAT (I1)
    GO TO (100, 200, 300), NAMVAR
```

Or we could have this:

```
    NAMVAR = N + M
    GO TO (100, 200, 300), NAMVAR
```

Just as simply as this, we have the computer making decisions. But right at the outset we should emphasize that this kind of decision is hardly what we would call decision-making in human terms. For us, a decision is something we make in the *absence* of complete information. The computer, on the other hand, can only make a *decision* when it is given complete information. It can *decide* nothing unless it is told precisely what to do under every possible circumstance, or for every data value that might possibly appear. If we were to give the computer a piece of data, but had not told it what to do when that particular data value appears, the computer would be helpless.

To illustrate this, look again at the computed GO TO:

GO TO (100, 200, 300), NAMVAR

This statement tells the computer what to do if NAMVAR has a value of 1, 2, or 3. But if NAMVAR were to have the value 4 when the computer reached this computed GO TO, the computer would have no idea what to do next. It might quit in frustration, or, if it tried to go on anyway, it might execute some other statement chosen virtually at random and would produce garbage.

Several important points to remember about this kind of GO TO are the same as in the case of the unconditional GO TO. One is that the statement numbers inside the parentheses may refer to statements anywhere in the program. One could be at the beginning, one at the end, one in the middle, and so on. Also, regardless of where these statements are in the program, when the computer jumps to one of them it then begins executing the following instructions in consecutive order.

Finally, a computed GO TO may send the computer only to the kind of executable statements discussed in connection with the unconditional GO TO. That is, they must be statements telling the computer to do something, not merely statements which give it information, like a FORMAT statement. This means we can also give a CONTINUE statement a number and use it here just as we used it with the unconditional GO TO.

The statement numbers inside the parentheses of a computed GO TO may differ from those shown here, depending on which statements are to serve as possible *next stops* for the computer. Also, there will be variation in how many statement numbers appear inside the parentheses, depending on how many outcomes there are for the decision: that is, how many different values are possible for the variable name after the parentheses. Finally, any variable name may be used in the computed GO TO, as long as it is an integer name, as in our examples here.

LIMITS OF COMPUTED GO TO

The reason for requiring an integer name in the computed GO TO is because the values assigned to that name must be integer. This is because for each value of the variable name there must be a corresponding position inside the parentheses. For example, if the value assigned to the variable name is 1, the computer knows it is to go next to the statement whose number appears first in the parentheses. If the value of the variable name is 2, the computer goes next to the statement whose number appears second in the parentheses. But what if the variable name had a value of 1.5, or 0.2?

For the same reason, the value assigned to the integer variable name in the computed GO TO should not be negative: there are no negative positions inside the parentheses. If a value to be used in a computed GO TO may be negative, use the absolute value function to make sure the value actually placed in the variable name is positive.

Finally, of course, the value of the variable name must not be zero because there is no zero position inside the parentheses.

In sum, therefore, we can say that the value of the variable name in the computed GO TO must be an integer number greater than zero.

Another limitation of the computed GO TO is the range of values that can be used in making a decision. For each *possible* value of the variable name, there must be a statement number in the corresponding position inside the parentheses of the computed GO TO. If the variable name might have a value as large as 9, then we include nine statement numbers inside the parentheses.

But what if we wanted to make a decision based on the value of a census figure, which could be as large as a million or more? We could hardly have a million statement numbers inside the parentheses of a computed GO TO.

Yet despite its limitations, the computed GO TO still has real value for certain purposes in programming. And we will see in the next section how we make decisions with values we cannot handle in a computed GO TO.

EXAMPLES

In these examples we use the letters at the right margin to show which statements in a series would be executed for a given value of the variable name in a computed GO TO. Note that in each example, the computed GO TO (and any statements prior to the computed GO TO) are executed for every value of the variable name. The variation in which statements are executed begins after the computed GO TO.

11. We have this program segment:

GO TO (31, 32, 33), K	(a)
31 L = 10	(b)
GO TO 500	(c)
32 L = 20	(d)
GO TO 500	(e)
33 L = 30	(f)
500 CONTINUE	(g)

Value in K	Statements Executed
1	a,b,c,g
2	a,d,e,g
3	a,f,g

The left column here shows each value for K. Since the computed GO TO has only three statement numbers in its parentheses, K can only have, for this GO TO, the values of 1 through 3. To the right of each value, under the heading

Statements Executed, are the small letters identifying the statements that would be executed in this sequence for this value of K. For example, when K has the value 1, statements *a*, *b*, *c*, and *g* are executed: the computed GO TO statement, then statement 31 and the unconditional GO TO following 31, and finally, the 500 CONTINUE statement.

12. We have this program segment:

GO TO (427, 428, 429, 430), NSEND	(a)
427 A = C ** 2	(b)
GO TO 400	(c)
428 A = C + 1.	(d)
GO TO 400	(e)
429 A = B ** 2	(f)
GO TO 400	(g)
430 A= B + 1.	(h)
400 CONTINUE	(i)

Value in NSEND	Statements Executed
1	a,b,c,i
2	a,d,e,i
3	a,f,g,i
4	a,h,i

13. We have this program segment:

GO TO (42, 44, 46, 48), NVAL	(a)
48 M = NVAL ** 2	(b)
GO TO 47	(c)
44 M = NVAL * 2	(d)
GO TO 47	(e)
42 M = NVAL + 1	(f)
GO TO 47	(g)
46 M = NVAL − 1	(h)
47 M = N	(i)

Value in NVAL	Statements Executed
1	a,f,g,i
2	a,d,e,i
3	a,h,i
4	a,b,c,i

14. We have this program segment:

READ (5, 15) NVAL	(a)
15 FORMAT (I1)	
GO TO (10, 11, 12, 13, 14), NVAL	(b)
10 NVALX = N + 1	(c)
GO TO 88	(d)
11 NVALX = N + 2	(e)
GO TO 88	(f)
12 NVALX = N + 3	(g)
GO TO 88	(h)
13 NVALX = N + 4	(i)
GO TO 88	(j)
14 NVALX = N + 5	(k)
88 CONTINUE	(l)

Note that we have not given a small letter to the FORMAT statement here, since it is not an executable statement. That is, we are using the small letters to show which statements would be executed for a given value of NVAL, and the computer does not execute a FORMAT statement; it merely uses the FORMAT statement for information.

Value in NVAL	Statements Executed
1	a,b,c,d,l
2	a,b,e,f,l
3	a,b,g,h,l
4	a,b,i,j,l
5	a,b,k,l

15. We have this program segment:

100 READ (5, 47) N,J,K	(a)
47 FORMAT (I1, I2, I3)	
GO TO (60, 70, 80), N	(b)
60 L = J ** 2	(c)
GO TO 100	(d)
70 L = K ** 2	(e)
GO TO 100	(f)
80 L = J + K	(g)
100 CONTINUE	(h)
101 CONTINUE	(i)

Value in N	Statements Executed
1	a,b,c,d,h,i
2	a,b,e,f,h,i
3	a,b,g,h,i

16. We have this program segment:

```
60 READ (5,6) NCASE                        (a)
 6 FORMAT (I1)
   GO TO (86, 87, 88, 89), NCASE           (b)
86 L = 1                                   (c)
   GO TO 60                                (d)
87 L = 2                                   (e)
   GO TO 60                                (f)
88 L = 3                                   (g)
   GO TO 60                                (h)
89 L = 4                                   (i)
   GO TO 60                                (j)
60 CONTINUE                                (k)
```

Value in NCASE	Statements Executed
1	a,b,c,d,k
2	a,b,e,f,k
3	a,b,g,h,k
4	a,b,i,j,k

17. We have this program segment:

```
   READ (5, 48) NORM                       (a)
48 FORMAT (I1)
   L = M                                   (b)
   GO TO (101, 102, 103), NORM             (c)
101 L = N                                  (d)
   GO TO 103                               (e)
102 L = J                                  (f)
103 CONTINUE                               (g)
```

Value in NORM	Statements Executed
1	a,b,c,d,e,g
2	a,b,c,f,g
3	a,b,c,g

Notice here that if NORM has the value 3, the effect of the

computed GO TO is to leave L with the value given it in statement *b*. This illustrates a common use of the CONTINUE statement.

18. We have this program segment:

READ (55, 5000) K, J	(a)
5000 FORMAT (2I1)	
M = J + K	(b)
GO TO (61, 62, 63, 64, 65), M	(c)
65 X = A	(d)
GO TO 110	(e)
64 X = D	(f)
GO TO 110	(g)
63 X = C	(h)
GO TO 110	(i)
62 X = B	(j)
GO TO 110	(k)
61 X = E	(l)
110 CONTINUE	(m)

Value in M	*Statements Executed*
1	a,b,c,l,m
2	a,b,c,j,k,m
3	a,b,c,h,i,m
4	a,b,c,f,g,m
5	a,b,c,d,e,m

Note here that the arrangement of the statements in the program makes no difference; the critical relationship is in the position of the statement numbers in the computed GO TO. Since statement number 61 is first in the computed GO TO, the value of 1 in M would send the computer to statement number 61 *wherever* that statement appears in the program.

EXERCISES

See exercises 17–26 in Chapter Nine of the *Workbook*.

IF STATEMENT

The computed GO TO is too limited for many of the decisions we want to make on the computer. Data values not appropriate for the computed GO TO can be handled with another form of decision-making statement, called the *IF statement*. Since this involves a comparison of two values, we speak of an *arithmetic IF*.

Form of the IF Statement

The IF statement looks like this:

IF (A — B) 100, 200, 300

The statement begins with the word IF, followed by parentheses containing an expression with two elements. After the parentheses are three statement numbers, separated by commas, but in the IF statement there is no comma after the parentheses. Spaces between the various items are ignored.

Operation of the IF Statement

The point of the IF statement is that it compares the two elements within the parentheses, and then, depending on the result of that comparison, it sends the computer next to one of the statements whose numbers appear after the parentheses.

The elements inside the parentheses (the two values being compared) may be either floating point or integer, but both must be of the same mode. Both may be variable names, or one may be a constant. A variable name used in an IF statement may have a value computed earlier in the program, or a value read into the location bearing that name.

These are acceptable pairs of elements inside the parentheses of an IF statement:

IF (R — ST)
IF (N — K)
IF (R — 2.)
IF (L — 5)

Also, a whole expression may be used as an element in the parentheses:

IF (R — (A ** B))
IF ((X + Y) — .01)
IF ((N — K) — M)
IF (100 — (NK * MK))

If an expression is used, all the rules for constructing expressions apply, such as not mixing modes, and using parentheses to show order of operations. Also, the IF statement requires its own outside set of parentheses, along with any others that may be used.

However, a word of advice is this: If a complex expression is involved in an IF decision, reduce that expression to a single value in an arithmetic statement and then use that value in the IF statement. For example, this expression might be involved in a decision:

(X + Y) * Z

This could make an IF statement like this:

IF (((X + Y) * Z) — B) 70, 80, 90

The decision involved might be clearer if we did this:

A = (X + Y) * Z
IF (A — B) 70, 80, 90

The reason for this advice is that in writing an IF statement we are concerned about the different parts of the program to which it will send the computer, and it seems to help if the comparison in the IF statement is as simple as possible; that is, includes as few variable names as possible.

The comparison in the IF statement takes the form of a subtraction. As the sign indicates, the second value inside the parentheses is always subtracted from the first. Obviously there are three possible outcomes of this operation. If the first value is greater than the second, the result is a positive value. If the second value is larger than the first, the result is negative. Finally, the values may be equal.

Another way of looking at this is to say the expression inside the parentheses is evaluated with respect to zero. To illustrate this, say we have this comparison in an IF statement:

$$(A - B)$$

If A is greater than B, then the result of $A - B$ is greater than zero: i.e. positive. If A is less than B, then $A - B$ produces a value less than zero: i.e. negative. Finally, if A equals B, then $A - B$ produces a result of zero: i.e. equal to zero. In this sense we can say the expression within the parentheses is tested against (or evaluated in terms of) zero.

Therefore, we speak of the three *outcomes*, or *results*, of the expression in the parentheses as these:

1. The first value is smaller than the second.
   A negative *condition* or result.
2. The first value is larger than the second.
   A positive condition or result.
3. The values are equal.
   A condition or result of equality.

Each of these three outcomes, or results, sends the computer to a different point in a program—to one of the points indicated by the three statement numbers following the parentheses. For this reason, the statements whose numbers appear in the IF statement must be the kind of executable statements we discussed in connection with the computed and unconditional GO TO statements.

Since there are three possible outcomes of the expression inside the parentheses of the IF statement, and also three points in the program to which the computer can go as it leaves an arithmetic IF statement, how do we arrange for a particular outcome to send the computer to a particular statement?

The positioning of the statement numbers in the IF statement is the critical factor here, just as it was in the computed GO TO. Very simply, we tell the computer this:

If the comparison in the IF statement produces a negative result, go next to the statement whose number appears in the *first* position after the parentheses.

If the comparison produces a positive result, go to the statement whose number appears in the *last* position after the parentheses.

If the comparison produces a condition of equality, go to the statement whose number appears in the *middle* of the three numbers.

Needless to say, we do not actually give the computer these instructions in so many words in a program. What happens is that when we put an IF statement into a program, the computer *understands* that these instructions apply, or that these instructions are *implied* when we write the IF statement.

Look again at the IF statement:

IF (A — B) 100, 200, 300

Here, if A is *less* than B, the computer will go to statement 100 in the program, and will execute that statement and any that follow it. In the same way, statement 200 (and any program segment that statement introduces) will be executed *only* when A and B are *equal*. Similarly, the computer will go to statement 300 when A is greater than B.

For example, say A has the value 5. and B is 3. If we use those names in this IF statement:

IF (A — B) 100, 200, 300

The computer would go next to statement 300. $A - B$ here produces a positive value, and this sends the computer to the statement whose number appears in the third position after the parentheses.

A shorthand way to keep in mind this relationship between the comparison in the parentheses and the statement numbers after the parentheses is this: Pretend the second value is a reference point against which the first value is being evaluated. Then simply ask: Is the first value less, or equal, or greater? These three conditions correspond, in order, to the first, second, and third positions after the parentheses. In our example here:

IF (A — B) 100, 200, 300

We can say:

> If A is less than B, go to 100.
> If A equals B, go to 200.
> If A is greater than B, go to 300.

Ultimately this boils down to a catchphrase like this: *Less,* first position; *equal,* second position; *greater,* third position.

Remember the relationship between the way the two values are arranged inside the parentheses, and the way the three statement numbers are arranged following the parentheses. That is, we could reverse the positions of the two values in the parentheses, but if we wanted the computer to respond the same way to the comparison of these values, then we would also have to reverse the first and third statement numbers after the parentheses. To illustrate this point, compare these two IF statements:

> IF (A — B) 100, 200, 300
> IF (B — A) 300, 200, 100

In the first statement, if A is greater than B, the result of the expression is positive, sending the computer to statement number 300. In the second IF statement, if A is again greater than B, the result is negative (because the positions of A and B have been reversed in the parentheses). Since number 300 has correspondingly been moved to the first position, this statement would again send the computer to statement number 300. In either of these IF statements, then, the fact that A is greater than B would send the computer next to statement number 300.

But what if we changed the positions of A and B in the two versions of the IF statement, but did *not* change the statement numbers correspondingly? For the answer to this, consider these statements:

> IF (A — B) 100, 200, 300
> IF (B — A) 100, 200, 300

In the first statement here, A being greater than B would send the computer to statement number 300. But in the second statement, A being greater than B would send the computer to statement number 100.

Therefore, keep in mind that the arrangement of values inside the parentheses is directly related to the way the statement numbers are arranged after the parentheses. Both points are involved in constructing an IF statement that will send the computer where it is to go under a given set of data values.

As with the computed GO TO, the statements to which the IF statement sends the computer may be anywhere in the program: either above the IF statement, or immediately below it, or far below it.

Also like the computed GO TO, the statement numbers used in an IF statement will differ, depending on where we want the computer to go next in the program as it leaves the IF statement. Unlike the computed GO TO, of course, there may be only three statement numbers in the IF. Also, the variable names used in the IF statement will differ, depending on what names are used for the values involved in an IF decision.

Zero Understood

For convenience, if one of the items inside the parentheses is the constant 0 (zero) it need not actually be written in the program. For example, say the variable name DAT is to be compared with zero. The IF statement could be written this way:

IF (DAT — 0.) 40, 42, 44

But it could also be written this way:

IF (DAT) 40, 42, 44

The same holds when dealing with integer values.

In short, if an IF statement has only one variable name inside the parentheses, this means the value of zero is understood, and that the variable name is being compared with zero. This in no way changes the operation of the IF statement, which works exactly *as though* the constant zero was present in the parentheses *in the second position.*

In this shortened form, therefore, if the variable name in the parentheses has a value greater than zero, the computer goes next to the statement whose number appears in the third position after the parentheses. If the variable name has a value less than zero (i.e. negative) the computer goes next to the statement whose number appears first after the parentheses. If the variable name has a value of zero, then the computer goes next to the statement whose number appears second after the parentheses. So this form really offers merely a more convenient way of writing an IF statement when a value is being compared with zero.

Negative Values in IF Statement

It is possible that negative values will show up in the IF comparison. For example, some time in comparing A and B we might be dealing with values like these:

A = 5.   B = −17.

This presents no problem if we remember either of two rules. One is that a positive number is *greater* than a negative number, regardless of their absolute sizes. *Greater* here means *more positive*, its meaning in the IF comparison. To illustrate, let us use the above values of A and B in an IF statement:

IF (A − B) 100, 200, 300

The above two values for A and B respectively would send the computer from this IF statement to statement 300, because A (a positive value) is *greater* or *more positive* than B (a negative value).

Now say A has the value −17., and B is 5. Again we have this IF statement:

IF (A − B) 100, 200, 300

Here the second value (B is positive) would be greater than the first (A is negative) sending the computer next to statement 100.

When two negative values are involved, the rule is that the smaller negative number is the *greater*, because it is closer to zero and therefore is closer to a positive value. To illustrate, let us now give A and B these values:

A = —2.   B = —50.

This IF statement:

IF (A — B) 100, 200, 300

would send the computer to statement 300 now, because A is greater than B here. That is, A is *less negative* than B, or A is *closer to zero* than B, or A is *closer to a positive value* than B.

The second rule for handling negative numbers in the IF comparison (an alternative to the approach above) is that when a negative number is subtracted, the two minus signs cancel each other out, so that the second value in the parentheses is actually added to the first value. For example, let A again equal —2. and B equal —50. Then the statement:

IF (A — B) 100, 200, 300

actually means:

IF (—2. — (—50.)) 100, 200, 300

and this equals:

IF (—2. + 50.) 100, 200, 300

So the result of this comparison would be positive, again sending the computer to statement 300.

In sum, to avoid trouble with comparisons involving negative numbers, remember either of the two rules:

1. A small negative number is greater than a large negative number, by virtue of being closer to zero.
2. Two minus signs equal a plus sign.

Negative numbers in an IF comparison are probably rare in social science programming, but they can occur, with negative correlations and negative rates of change as two examples.

BRANCHING

As a final note, look at a simple picture (Fig. 7) of an IF statement here.

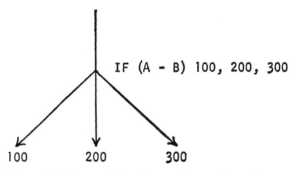

Figure 7. Picture of decision-making as branching.

This picture shows why the process of decision-making is also often referred to as *branching*. The possible routes out of an IF statement can be viewed as something like branches emanating from a central trunk. So we also call decision-making statements (computed GO TO and IF) *branching statements,* and we call the different parts of a program to which the computer may go from a decision statement *branches.* In Figure 7 above, for example, we might say there are three branches out of the IF statement, with each of the statements indicated (statements 100, 200, and 300) representing the beginning of one of those branches.

EXAMPLES

19. We have this program segment:

IF (K — NCASE) 40, 50 60	(a)
40 R = A	(b)
GO TO 100	(c)
50 R = 13.	(d)
GO TO 100	(e)
60 R = L	(f)
100 CONTINUE	(g)

Values of K and NCASE	Statements Executed
K is 5 and NCASE is 10	a,b,c,g
K is 1000 and NCASE is 1000	a,d,e,g
K is 99 and NCASE is 98	a,f,g

Here the left column, headed *Values,* shows values of the two variable names in the IF statement. In the right column, under the heading *Statements Executed,* are shown the statements in the sequence that would be executed for the pair of values on that same line. For example, if K is 5 and NCASE is 10 in the IF statement, then statements *a, b, c,* and *g* in this segment would be executed. On the second line, however, we see that if K is 1000 and NCASE is 1000, the computer would execute statements *a, d, e,* and *g.* The third line shows the statements that would be executed if K is 99 and NCASE is 98.

20. We have this program segment:

IF (XA — YB) 78, 79, 75	(a)
75 X = XA ** 2	(b)
GO TO 12	(c)
79 X = SQRT (XA)	(d)
GO TO 12	(e)
78 X = XA —1.	(f)
12 CONTINUE	(g)

Values of XA and YB	Statements Executed
XA is 4. and YB is 7.	a,f,g
XA is 498. and YB is .06	a,b,c,g
XA is 41. and YB is 41.	a,d,e,g

21. We have this program segment:

IF (ZA — TX) 40, 40, 60	(a)
40 GOP = TX	(b)
GO TO 60	(c)
60 CONTINUE	(d)

Values of ZA and TX	Statements Executed
ZA is 6. and TX is 4.	a,d
ZA is 5.6 and TX is 10.	a,b,c,d
ZA is 7. and TX is 7.	a,b,c,d

22. We have this program segment:

GO TO 60	(a)
101 X = RA	(b)
GO TO 62	(c)
60 CONTINUE	(d)
61 IF (R — RA) 100, 102, 101	(e)
62 CONTINUE	(f)
102 X = 1.	(g)
GO TO 105	(h)
100 X = —1.	(i)
105 CONTINUE	(j)

Values of R and RA	*Statements Executed*
RA is 46.25 and R is 46.25	a,d,e,g,h,j
RA is —.01 and R is 0.	a,d,e,b,c,f,g,h,j
RA is 1642.3 and R is .0001	a,d,e,i,j

23. We have this program segment:

GO TO 55	(a)
490 X = L	(b)
GO TO 75	(c)
55 IF (L — MA) 471, 490, 472	(d)
472 NSIZE = MA ** 2	(e)
GO TO 75	(f)
471 FL = L	(g)
75 CONTINUE	(h)

Values of L and MA	*Statements Executed*
L is —70 and MA is —70	a,d,b,c,h
L is 14 and MA is —26	a,d,e,f,h
L is —14 and MA is —12	a,d,g,h

24. We have this program segment:

R = 0.	(a)
GO TO 1185	(b)
1620 P = 1.	(c)
GO TO 1603	(d)
1185 IF (XL — B) 1620, 1421, 1422	(e)
1603 CONTINUE	(f)

1422 R = R + 1.		(g)
GO TO 9000		(h)
1421 T = B / 3.		(i)
9000 X = T / R		(j)

Values of XL and B	Statements Executed
XL is 16. and B is 27742.3	a,b,e,c,d,f,g,h,j
XL is 5.1 and B is 5.1	a,b,e,i,j
XL is 47.5 and B is —2.1	a,b,e,g,h,j

25. We have this program segment:

IF (Z — TU) 428, 429, 429	(a)
429 Z = Z ** 2	(b)
GO TO 6000	(c)
428 Z = (Z ** 2.) — 1.	(d)
6000 CONTINUE	(e)

Values of Z and TU	Statements Executed
Z is 12.001 and TU is 12.002	a,d,e
Z is 12.001 and TU is 12.001	a,b,c,e
Z is 12.001 and TU is 12.	a,b,c,e

26. We have this program segment:

GO TO 55	(a)
911 X = 16	(b)
GO TO 503	(c)
55 IF (NAM — NOT) 427, 503, 911	(d)
427 Y = NAM ** 2	(e)
GO TO 17	(f)
503 A = 12	(g)
17 CONTINUE	(h)

Values of NAM and NOT	Statements Executed
NAM is 5826 and NOT is —4	a,d,b,c,g,h
NAM is 2 and NOT is 10	a,d,e,f,h
NAM is 0 and NOT is 0	a,d,g,h

27. We have this program segment:

GO TO 98	(a)
68 SIX = SIGA + SIGB	(b)
GO TO 500	(c)

```
69 SIX = SIGB                              (d)
   GO TO 500                               (e)
98 IF (SIGA — SIGB) 69, 68, 400           (f)
400 SIX = SIGB — SIGA                      (g)
500 CONTINUE                               (h)
```

Values of SIGA and SIGB	*Statements Executed*
SIGA is .01 and SIGB is .01	a,f,b,c,h
SIGA is .16 and SIGB is .00428	a,f,g,h
SIGA is .04 and SIGB is .09	a,f,d,e,h

EXERCISES

See exercises 27–38 in Chapter Nine of the *Workbook*.

Chapter Ten

COUNTING AND SUMMING

We will begin our discussion of uses of decision-making statements with the computed GO TO, since it involves only one variable name.

FREQUENCY DISTRIBUTION

One important use of the computed or conditional GO TO is in a frequency distribution. For an illustration of this, say that in a survey we have a question about the sex of the respondents. The responses on the question are coded so that 1 represents male and 2 represents female. For each respondent the code value for sex is punched in column 4 of his or her data card. In analyzing the data from our survey, we want to find out how many of the respondents are male and how many are female, which means finding out how many 1's and 2's show up in the data for this question.

A frequency distribution, of course, is nothing more than counting how often each kind of response value shows up in the data. It may help in understanding how we do this counting on a computer if we first look at other ways of doing the same thing.

If we were doing a frequency distribution on our sex data here by hand, we could write on a sheet of paper a label for the category MALE and another label for the category FEMALE. Then as we went through the data, each time the number 1 appeared we would make a mark opposite the label MALE. For each 2, we would put a mark opposite the label FEMALE.

If we had a small (for simplicity) sample of twenty cases, when we were done our results might look something like this:

MALE   *///////////*   (11)
FEMALE   */////////*   (9)

If we were doing this frequency distribution on a counter-sorter, we would use our data cards which each have a 1 or 2 punched in column 4, the column assigned to the question on sex. Each card with a 1 in this column would fall into bin number 1 on the sorter; each card with a 2 would fall into the second bin. Then the number of cards in each of the two bins shows the number of responses in each category, and hence, the number of males and females, respectively, in our sample.

If we do this frequency distribution on the computer, we still need some place to keep track of the number of responses of each kind that show up. Doing it by hand, we used a sheet of paper. Doing it on a counter-sorter, we used the bins. On a computer, we use storage locations, one for each category of the variable, just as on a sheet of paper we used one line for each category, and on a counter-sorter we used one bin for each category.

Since each storage location needs a name, so we can refer to it in the program, we set up two category names just as we did on the sheet of paper, except that for the computer we make these names integer because this is a counting operation in which fractions of responses are not possible. The names we use are these:

NMALES
NFEMAL

Since a frequency distribution means counting the number of times a given data value shows up, we must find a way of counting in the location named NMALES the *number* of 1 responses in the data, and counting in NFEMAL the *number* of 2 responses. On paper we did this by making a mark each time a given value showed up, and then counting the marks. On a counter-sorter, we did it by having cards fall into the appropriate bins, and then counting the cards.

On the computer we do it by telling the computer that every time a value of 1 shows up, the computer is to add one to the contents of NMALES, and to add one to the contents of NFEMAL every time a 2 shows up.

Updating

This *adding one* is known as *updating*, which makes use of the meaning of the equal sign: *Set equal to*. For a general illustration, say we had this statement:

$$M = M + 1$$

The effect of this is to increase the value in M by one. For example, say that before this statement is executed, M equals 3. In executing this statement:

$$M = M + 1$$

the computer adds 1 to the value of M. This makes M now equal to 4. This new value of 4 is stored in the location known as M, superseding the value of 3 that was there until this point, which is why the meaning *set equal to* for the equal sign is so important. Obviously, M does not equal M + 1. But M can be *set equal* to the value M + 1, which means adding 1 to the value of M.

This little technique has a variety of uses for the social scientist, including serving as the basic mechanism of the frequency distribution we are doing now. This is how we tell the computer to add one to the appropriate storage location every time a given response value appears in the data.

In so doing we are counting the number of each kind of response, which is why this procedure is also known as *counting*, and each storage location (or its name) used in this kind of operation is known as a *counter*.

In our example of a frequency distribution here, counting the number of 1's in the data means that every time a 1 shows up, we want the computer to execute a statement like this:

$$NMALES = NMALES + 1$$

This adds one to the value that was previously in NMALES. The value of NMALES is *updated* by one, in other words. And since the value of NMALES is raised by one each time the response value 1 appears in the data, at the end of the program the final value of NMALES shows how many times the value 1 appeared in our data. This in turn tells us how many *male* responses showed up in the survey.

Similarly, whenever the response value 2 appears in the data, the computer is to execute this instruction:

NFEMAL = NFEMAL + 1

Since the value of NFEMAL is increased or updated by one every time the value 2 appears in the data, at the end of the program the final value of this variable name shows how many 2 responses (meaning females) appeared in the data. At the end of the program, therefore, instead of a sheet of paper with marks on it, or a set of bins with punched cards in them, we have as our result a pair of storage locations with respective values in them, like this:

NMALES has the value 11
NFEMAL has the value 9

When we write out these values, the resulting figures in the output show us the number of males and females, respectively, among our respondents.

The core of this process is obviously the decision the computer must make with each data item: deciding which storage location to update (to increase by one) for that data item. This is where the computed GO TO enters.

Remember that when a data value is 1, we want this statement executed:

NMALES = NMALES + 1

When a data value is 2, we want this statement executed:

NFEMAL = NFEMAL + 1

So we use a computed GO TO to send the computer to either statement, depending on the value of the variable name in the GO TO.

Both statements must have numbers, so they can be referred to in the computed GO TO. Let us use the number 10 for the statement updating NMALES, and 20 for the statement updating NFEMAL. And since we want the computer to update NMALES when a 1 shows up in the data, we put the number 10 first inside the parentheses of the computed GO TO. Since the variable involved in this decision is sex, we could use the name NSEX, giving us this computed GO TO:

GO TO (10, 20), NSEX

If the value of NSEX is 1, the computer would go next to statement 10, where it would add one to the total in NMALES by executing this statement:

10 NMALES = NMALES + 1

Similarly, for a value of 2 in NSEX, the computer would go next to this statement:

20 NFEMAL = NFEMAL + 1

where it would add one to the total in NFEMAL.

Note that the statement numbers have been chosen to help make the program easier to follow. That is, the numbers were chosen to indicate something about the data values which would send the computer to the various statements. Each statement number here equals ten times the data value that would send the computer to that statement. At the same time, the related sizes of these statement numbers suggest they are both possible outcomes for one decision statement. Both these ends (showing the data value that would send the computer to a given statement, and showing that the statements are both possible outcomes of a single decision) could also be satisfied by these pairs of statement numbers:

100, 200
11, 21

They would not be achieved by numbers like these:

497, 2053

In short, while statement numbers can be chosen arbitrarily, we may as well make them work for us, in the same way that we can use variable names that show what they stand for.

Zeroing Out

Before actually counting anything in the locations named NMALES and NFEMAL, however, there is a precaution we must take. If we were doing a frequency distribution by hand, we would use a clean sheet of paper so that only the marks reflecting responses in *our* data would be counted in the totals. Similarly, when using the counter-sorter we would make sure no cards were left in its bins before running our deck of cards through. The equivalent operation on a computer is known as *zeroing out*.

To zero out a location we use a statement telling the computer to set that location equal to zero (or to place the value zero in that location). So we could zero out our two locations this way:

NMALES = 0
NFEMAL = 0

Regardless of any value either location might have had prior to these statements, after these statements were executed both locations would have the value zero. Whenever a location is used for counting or updating, first zero it out to be sure that only the figures in a given set of data are reflected in the total accumulated there.

There remains merely the question of getting the data values one by one into the name NSEX in the computed GO TO. For this we use a READ statement, which is executed once for each respondent (that is, once for each data card).

The program segment to zero out the storage locations, read the data items one at a time into NSEX, update the proper storage location for each item, and then go back and read another data item, could look like Figure 8.

```
C     ZERO OUT STORAGE LOCATIONS
      NMALES = 0                                    (a)
      NFEMAL = 0                                    (b)
C     READ DATA VALUES ONE BY ONE
1000 READ (5, 90) NSE.                              (c)
  90 FORMAT (3X, I1)
C     * * * * * * * * * *
      GO TO (10, 20), NSEX                          (d)
  10 NMALES = NMALES + 1                            (e)
      GO TO 1000                                    (f)
  20 NFEMAL = NFEMAL + 1                            (g)
      GO TO 1000                                    (h)
```

Figure 8. Program segment for frequency distribution.

Note the placement of the statements on these printed pages. Since we are not using programming forms, pretend the C's on the comment *cards* show the location of column 1, with statement numbers and statements located relative to this column 1. Also pretend that the lower case letters at the right margin are in columns 73 and beyond on the respective statement cards.

In this program segment, the computer first zeroes out the two storage locations. Then it begins reading from the data deck we give it along with the program. This deck contains 20 cards, one for each respondent, with the sex code value punched in column 4 on each card. Say that the first respondent is male, so the first value read into NSEX is 1. This sends the computer from the GO TO down to statement 10, to add 1 to the contents of NMALES. At this point, then, NMALES has the value 1.

Moving from the arithmetic statement (the computer moves in consecutive order unless instructed otherwise) the next statement (f) is the GO TO sending the computer to statement 1000. Statement 1000 is the READ statement, so the computer reads another value for NSEX. This value is taken from the second card in the data deck. The reason for this, of course, is that after reading one data value from the first card, the computer encountered the closing parentheses in the FORMAT statement, which told it to leave that card. So the next time the computer executes the READ statement, it reads from the next (second) card.

Say the second respondent is female, so the value now read into NSEX is 2 (remember that a value read into a location replaces any value there previously). At the computed GO TO the value 2 in NSEX sends the computer directly to statement 20, where it updates NFEMAL. This location, having started at zero, now has the value 1. Leaving statement 20, the computer encounters the statement which sends it back to statement 1000 to read another data value, and so on.

Note that the sequence can have two (or more) statements saying:

GO TO 1000

because this is not repeating a statement number. There is only one statement numbered 1000; that is, only one statement with the number 1000 in the statement number columns 1 through 5. This is similar to the fact that there can be several WRITE statements using the same FORMAT statement number, and thus referring to the same FORMAT statement.

REVIEW OF THE COMPUTED GO TO

Having seen the computed GO TO working, let us pause to review what this kind of statement does, and what it *means.*

As simple as it looks, we have here a classic example of decision-making on a computer. The computer executes one of several possible actions by going to one of several statements in a program, and it does this according to the value of a specified variable name. But the key to understanding decision-making on a computer (in this simple example, as well as with more complex decision-making statements) is to recognize that the computer does not actually *decide* anything at all. It merely reacts to *conditions:* that is, to data values.

Basically the decision involved in the computed GO TO is really nothing more than the kind of decision made by a counter-sorter. We do not usually extend to counter-sorters, as we do to computers, the accolade of *thinking machine.* Yet a counter-sorter makes a *decision* with each data card fed into it. It *decides,* in effect, which of its bins it must drop that card into. It makes this *decision* on the basis of the hole in that particular column on the card it has been told to look at during a particular run of cards.

For example, say we give a counter-sorter our deck of data cards with the sex code values punched in column 4. We want the cards sorted according to sex, so we set the sorter to read on column 4. For each card, the sorter must decide whether to drop it into bin 1 or bin 2, and it makes this decision on the basis of the number (hole) in column 4.

Since column 4 is where we punched the sex code values, we can say that for this deck of cards, column 4 *represents* the sex variable. Further, we can say that in making its decision on the basis of the value in column 4, the sorter is actually deciding on the basis of a value of this variable, *sex.*

Exactly the same thing is true of the computer. If we give this same data deck to a computer, we *set* it to read column 4 by giving it this FORMAT code:

(3X, I1)

The computer would then take, from each card in turn, the value in column 4, and place it in NSEX. Therefore, we can say the storage location named NSEX also *represents* the variable *sex,* and corresponds to column 4 on the data card. Since we use the variable name NSEX in the GO TO which determines which storage location to update, we can say the computer is also making its decision on the basis of the variable *sex.*

For a computer, we might sum up this relationship between variable, variable name, and decision this way: A variable name refers to a location which contains the value of a variable; when the computer makes a decision based on the value of that name, this decision is actually based on the value of that variable at that particular time.

Therefore, *to connect a decision in a computed GO TO to a particular variable,* we read a value for that variable into the variable name in the computed GO TO. This is comparable to telling the counter-sorter what variable to use in sorting cards by telling it which column to look at. Do not be mislead by the seeming difference that on a computer a value is placed in a storage location before being involved in a decision.

The only real difference between a computer and a counter-sorter in *decision-making* is that for the most part the latter has permanent criteria for a decision, whereas with the computer the criteria can be made to vary. That is, if a counter-sorter finds the value 1 in the column it is reading on a data card, that card (if being sorted) goes into bin 1. In the computer, however, we can arrange the criteria so that the data value 1 will cause the computer to do whatever we want done next.

To continue the analogy, when we use a location in the computer in which to count the number of 1 responses in a set of data, this location is comparable to the bin numbered 1 on a counter-sorter. On the counter-sorter, any time a 1 shows up in a deck of cards (in the column used for sorting) that card falls into the bin marked 1. On the computer, every time a 1 shows up in a set of data, one is added to the contents of the location assigned to that response value. Therefore, the updating of a computer storage location is exactly equivalent to a data card falling into a bin on the counter-sorter.

Each location used in counting the number of responses in a category also represents a variable. But each *counting location* represents a *category* of the variable. For example, in our program segment in Figure 8 above, the locations named NMALES and NFEMAL also represent sex, but rather than representing the variable as a whole, as NSEX does, each of these locations represents a category of that variable: male or female.

Remember, however, that this relationship between storage location and response category exists *only* because of the way we arrange the arithmetic statements doing the updating, and the order in which the statement numbers appear in the parentheses of the computed GO TO. That is, the location named NMALES represents (is used to count) the category of males *only* because the number of the arithmetic statement updating NMALES appears first in the parentheses, so that the code value 1 (representing male) will send the computer to that statement. There is nothing magic in our decision to assign a particular location to a particular category of a variable. This does not happen simply because we will it, but rather because of the way we arrange the elements of the program.

To illustrate this, say we had this sequence:

```
    GO TO (10, 20), NSEX
 10 NFEMAL = NFEMAL + 1
    GO TO 1000
 20 NMALES = NMALES + 1
    GO TO 1000
```

The value 1 in NSEX here would cause the computer to update NFEMAL, which is where we *said* we want to count the number of *females*. Thus if we take the contents of NFEMAL as representing the number of females (after it had accumulated a count of 1's, representing males) we would have another kind of logic error.

The point is, *we* must arrange the elements of the program so as to get each kind of data value counted in the location where we want it counted. This, like anything else on a computer, happens only because we cause it to happen, through the way we handle the various statements involved.

ARRANGING UNCONDITIONAL GO TO'S

Unconditional GO TO's can be combined with decision-making statements in a variety of ways to accomplish a given purpose. For example, instead of using an unconditional GO TO to send the computer directly back to the READ statement after it has updated a counting location, as we have been doing in our program to count males and females, we could use this arrangement:

```
1000 READ (5, 90) NSEX
  90 FORMAT (3X, I1)
     GO TO (10, 20), NSEX
  10 NMALES = NMALES + 1
     GO TO 999
  20 NFEMAL = NFEMAL + 1
 999 GO TO 1000
```

Here, for a value of 1 in NSEX, the computer will go to statement 10, but then instead of jumping directly back to the READ statement, it would skip down to statement 999, and from there it would be sent back to the READ statement.

However they are arranged, unconditional GO TO statements are vital to the decision-making process because they help direct the computer *away* from the options *not* chosen in a decision. Indeed, a very common logic error is to leave out one or more of the unconditional GO TO's needed in connection with a decision.

To illustrate this aspect of decision-making, let us see what would happen if we left out the unconditional GO TO's from the frequency distribution segment we have been working with here. The result would be something like this:

```
1000 READ (5, 90) NSEX
  90 FORMAT (3X, 11)
     GO TO (10, 20), NSEX
  10 NMALES = NMALES + 1
  20 NFEMAL = NFEMAL + 1
```

These statements are grammatically correct, but this segment would give us wrong results: specifically, it would count the number of males in NMALES, but it would count the *total* number of responses in NFEMAL.

To see why, let us do something we often do when hunting for logic errors in debugging real programs: We follow a data item step by step through the program until we see something happening to it that we do not want. In effect, we *imagine* a running of the program; we *run* it in our mind, pretending we are the computer. This technique has weaknesses: we are not as logical as the computer, so we may overlook a logic error, and in a long program, we are less able than the computer to keep track of all the data values. But the technique can be useful, as we will see here.

If we say again that the first data item read in is 1, the first value for NSEX is 1. At the decision statement, since NSEX has the value 1, the computed GO TO sends us next to statement 10, which adds one to the storage location known as NMALES.

Now we move to the next statement (remembering that in the absence of a statement transferring control elsewhere, the computer moves statement by statement in consecutive order). But wait: The next statement is the one which adds one to the storage location named NFEMAL. We do not want this to happen, because our data value was 1, not 2. So as the segment stands here, without the unconditional GO TO's, when it reads a data value of 1 it would not only add one to NMALES as we want it to, it would also add one to NFEMAL because it would also execute the second arithmetic statement.

For a data value of 2, of course, the computer would execute statement 20, but not statement 10, because the computer does not go back to execute statements it jumps over unless instructed to do so, and there is no statement here telling the computer to do this. The result, then, is that NMALES would end up with the total number of males, but NFEMAL would end up with the total of both males *and* females.

This is why we need an unconditional GO TO after the first arithmetic statement: to tell the computer that after it has executed that statement for a data value of 1 it is to skip statement 20.

The second unconditional GO TO is also necessary, of course, to send the computer back to the READ statement after statement 20 is executed. Without this GO TO, after executing statement 20 the first time, the computer would not go back to the READ statement, meaning it would read no more data.

In sum, the proper combination of GO TO statements sends the computer to whichever statement updates the storage location corresponding to any given data value, and then causes it to return to the READ statement. This is how we produce in the computer that single response we want for each data value, and how we prevent the computer from making any other response.

CONTROLLING NUMBER OF REPETITIONS WITH IF

Even with the unconditional GO TO's properly arranged, however, we still have a problem in our program here. Eventually the computer will read the last item of data. This data item will again send the computer from the computed GO TO to the appropriate arithmetic statement to update the appropriate storage location. Then the unconditional GO TO associated with that arithmetic statement will send the computer back to read another data value. But since it has just read the last piece of data, the computer will find no more, and therefore will immediately stop the program. (Always remember that a program stops if the computer is asked to read a piece of data which is not there.) But we would not want the program to stop yet because we want something else done: we want the results written out.

We need some way, then, to tell the computer exactly how many data items to read before moving down to write out its results. We do this by telling the computer to count the number of times it executes the READ statement, continually compare this figure with the number of items in a set of data, and when the two are equal, stop reading data and go on to some other point in the program. Thus we combine two procedures, counting and comparing.

For this second use of counting, we choose a name, say KOUNT, an integer name because here again fractions are not possible. We zero out this *counter variable:*

KOUNT = 0

Then we tell the computer to update this counter each time it executes the READ statement. We do this by putting after the READ statement this arithmetic statement:

KOUNT = KOUNT + 1

Thus at any given point the value in the counter KOUNT equals the number of times the READ statement has been executed.

Finally, we tell the computer to compare each successive value of this counter against a number we have given it: the number of items of data in the set it is working on. When the counter has a value equal to this *limiting value,* or *test value,* the computer is to move to another point in the program.

To make the comparison, we use an IF statement, with the

arrangement of the statement numbers after the parentheses telling the computer whether to go back to the READ statement again, or move on to another part of the program.

To illustrate this technique, let us add it to our frequency distribution segment which uses the sex data for twenty respondents.

```
C     FREQUENCY DISTRIBUTION PROGRAM
C     ZERO OUT STORAGE LOCATIONS AND COUNTER
      NMALES = 0                                    (a)
      NFEMAL = 0                                    (b)
      KOUNT = 0                                     (c)
C     READ DATA VALUES ONE BY ONE
 1000 READ (5, 90) NSEX                             (d)
   90 FORMAT (3X, I1)
C     COUNT REPETITIONS
      KOUNT = KOUNT + 1                             (e)
C     * * * * * * * * * *
C     UPDATE RESPONSE CATEGORIES
      GO TO (10, 20), NSEX                          (f)
   10 NMALES = NMALES + 1                           (g)
      GO TO 900                                     (h)
   20 NFEMAL = NFEMAL + 1                           (i)
  900 IF (KOUNT - 20) 1000, 1001, 1001              (j)
C     WRITE RESULTS
 1001 CONTINUE                                      (k)
      WRITE (6, 99) NMALES, NFEMAL                  (l)
   99 FORMAT (1HO,I5,' MALES AND ', I5,' FEMALES')
      END
```

Figure 9. Program for frequency distribution.

In this program, the computer would read the first item of data, and then would immediately add one to the value in KOUNT. So now, having started at zero, KOUNT is 1. The computer goes next to the GO TO, and from there moves down to update the storage location corresponding to the value of NSEX at this point. If this first data value was 1, the computer would execute statement 10, then jump over statement 20 to the IF statement. Since the value of KOUNT is now 1, the comparison in the IF statement produces a negative result; that is, the first value in the parentheses is less than the second. This means the computer goes next to the statement indicated by the number in the first position after the parentheses. This is statement 1000, the READ statement. So the computer goes back to execute the READ statement a second time, then immediately adds one to KOUNT, so the value in KOUNT is now 2. If the second data value was 2, the computer would move from the computed GO TO to statement 20, and then down to the IF statement again. The value of 2 now in KOUNT is still less than 20, so the negative result of this comparison would again send the computer back to execute the READ statement once more.

Now say the READ statement is being executed for the twentieth time. Since KOUNT was updated each time the READ statement was executed, after this 20th execution of the READ statement, when KOUNT is again updated, its value would now become 20. After moving from the computed GO TO to update the appropriate storage location, depending on the value of this last data item, the computer again reaches the IF statement. Now that KOUNT is 20, the result of the comparison in the IF is equality, which sends the computer to the statement whose number appears second in the IF statement. This is the CONTINUE statement leading into the output section.

REDUCING OUTCOMES OF IF

This little program contains several features that will also show up in much larger programs. The one most directly related to decision-making is the fact that we used the number 1001 in both the second and third positions in the IF statement.

The last statement number in the IF gives the computer a route to take in the event that KOUNT has a value greater than 20 when it enters this IF. But as we arranged the program, it is impossible for KOUNT to have a value larger than 20 at this statement; as soon as KOUNT *is* 20, the computer is sent out of the sequence which includes the IF. It is sent down to the WRITE segment, and there is nothing there that would send the computer back up to add to the value of KOUNT.

In short, since KOUNT cannot be higher than 20, the IF comparison here cannot produce a positive result, which means it is impossible for the computer to be directed anywhere by the last statement number following the parentheses in the IF statement. In this case we are using only two of the three possible outcomes of the IF comparison: the negative and equal conditions. The last statement number following the parentheses is there only because the rules require it. This is why we used the number 1001 there as well as in the second position. Since the positive condition cannot occur, it makes no difference what number we put in the last position among the three statement numbers following the parentheses. In this case that number is a *dummy*, and the only requirements for it are that it refer to some statement in the program, and that it refer to an executable statement because of the rule that a decision-making statement can send the computer only to an executable statement.

Because of these requirements, it is common to repeat a statement number for the dummy number, as we have done here. This guarantees that the dummy number refers to an executable statement in the program. And because it means that only two *different* statement numbers appear after the parentheses, it also has the advantage of telling us, when we look at an IF statement, that the IF is being used for only a two-way branch.

When we repeat a statement number like this to set up an IF statement with just two branches, we can create out of the original conditions (positive, negative, or equal) three kinds of two-way branches:

1. *Positive* versus *not positive* (i.e. negative or equal)
2. *Negative* versus *not negative* (i.e. positive or equal)
3. *Equal* versus *not equal* (i.e. positive or negative)

This point is illustrated in the following three IF statements:

IF· (A — B) 90, 90, 100

This means that if A is greater than B, the computer goes next to statement 100. But if A is *either* less than B or equal to B, the computer goes to statement 90:

IF (A — B) 80, 81, 81

This statement means that *only* if A is less than B would the computer go to statement 80. Otherwise it would go to statement 81:

IF (A — B) 900, 901, 900

This statement means that *only* if A and B are equal will the computer go to statement 901. If they are *not* equal, it will go to statement 900.

FLEXIBILITY WITH CONTINUE STATEMENTS

Another point to note in our frequency distribution program in Figure 9 above is the use of a CONTINUE statement before the WRITE statement. Why not use the statement number on the WRITE statement itself, and send the computer directly there, rather than use a CONTINUE statement? The result would be the same and we could save a statement.

The answer is that an extra CONTINUE statement like this provides greater flexibility in a program. Specifically, it allows us to add or delete parts of a program without having to move statement numbers from one statement to another, which would mean repunching statement cards.

For example, what if we wanted to add another statement before the WRITE statement here; a statement that would be executed *after* the computer leaves the frequency distribution segment, but *before* it executes the WRITE statement (1)? Say we wanted to add a WRITE statement which would print a label or heading over the output, like this:

WRITE (6, 98)
98 FORMAT (1H1, 'NUMBER OF MALES AND FEMALES')

Now we could insert this WRITE statement very simply after 1001 CONTINUE, and it would be executed before the WRITE statement (1). If the existing WRITE statement (1) had the number 1001, however, we would have to take that number off that statement, which means repunching that statement card. The way it is now, however, with the number 1001 on a CON-

TINUE statement, we can arrange statements after that point in the program any way we want without having to change any statement number.

In short, when sending the computer from place to place in a program, it is often convenient to send it to a CONTINUE statement. Then changes in *working statements* (those which actually perform some operation) can be made without having to worry about transferring statement numbers from one statement to another.

GENERALIZING CONTROL OF THE COUNTER

The other major fact about the frequency distribution program in Figure 9 above is that it would be limited to a sample of twenty cases. However, the point of writing a program is to be able to use it with a number of different sets of data. To illustrate, say we later wanted to use this program with a sample of 250 cases. In order to tell the computer how many times to execute the READ statement for that data, we need the number 250 in the IF statement. Now this would mean going into the program to change the constant 20 in the IF statement to the constant 250.

However, for a number of reasons it is not wise to go into a program to make changes like this. For one thing, it must be done with the Fortran program deck, which takes more computer time than the machine language deck which does not need translating. Also, every time we go into a program there is a new chance of error, of mixing up statement cards, etc.

So rather than going into a program to change it for each new set of data, we try to arrange the program so such changes can be made from the outside. For example, when we use our frequency distribution program here with a new sample, having other than 20 cases, we want to give the computer a value for the second position in the IF statement, but we want to do this from *outside* the program, and *as* we give the computer a new set of data.

We do this by using a variable name, rather than a constant, in the second position in the IF statement. Through a READ statement, we can assign that name a different value each time we use the program.

The variable involved here is of course the number of cases in a sample, because we want this to control the number of repetitions, or *iterations*, of the reading and frequency distribution process. The name we choose for this variable, then, is NCASE.

Since we want to change the value in NCASE for each sample, we must read a value into NCASE each time we use the program with a new set of data. This means adding a new READ statement for NCASE that will be executed only *once* each time the program runs. Thus this READ statement must go *before* the one now carrying the number 1000. We then put the name NCASE in the IF statement in place of the constant 20. Then for each set of data we give the computer for this program, the value of KOUNT will be continually tested against the number of cases in *that* set of data.

If we add the READ statement for NCASE, and put this variable name in the IF statement, our program looks like Figure 10.

Say we give this program a set of sex data for a sample which has 250 cases. These 250 items of sex data are to be read, each from a separate card. We would put the value 250 in the first three columns of a separate data card and put this card before the cards containing the sex data (which are again punched in column 4 on each card, to match 90 FORMAT).

From this first card, the computer would read the value 250 into NCASE. Then the computer would execute the READ statement and the frequency distribution segment consisting of statements *e* through *k* 250 times. Since KOUNT is updated each time the READ statement is executed, after 250 items of data have been read, KOUNT is 250, at which point the comparison (KOUNT−NCASE) for this sample produces a result of equality, which sends the computer down to statement 1001.

If we wanted later to use this program with another sample, this one having 900 cases, we merely give the computer the value 900 for NCASE by placing this value on the card the computer reads *first*.

When we arrange a program so that we can give it (from

```
C     FREQUENCY DISTRIBUTION PROGRAM
C     ZERO OUT STORAGE LOCATIONS AND COUNTER
      NMALES = 0                                        (a)
      NFEMAL = 0                                        (b)
      KOUNT = 0                                         (c)
C     READ NUMBER OF CASES
      READ (5, 80) NCASE                                (d)
   80 FORMAT (I3)
C     READ DATA VALUES ONE BY ONE
 1000 READ (5, 90) NSEX                                 (e)
   90 FORMAT (3X, I1)
C     COUNT REPETITIONS
      KOUNT = KOUNT + 1                                 (f)
C     * * * * * * * * * *
C     UPDATE RESPONSE CATEGORIES
      GO TO (10, 20), NSEX                              (g)
   10 NMALES = NMALES + 1                               (h)
      GO TO 900                                         (i)
   20 NFEMAL = NFEMAL + 1                               (j)
  900 IF (KOUNT − NCASE) 1000, 1001, 1001               (k)
C     WRITE RESULTS
 1001 CONTINUE                                          (l)
      WRITE (6, 98)                                     (m)
   98 FORMAT (1H1, 'NUMBER OF MALES AND FEMALES')
      WRITE (6, 99) NMALES, NFEMAL                      (n)
   99 FORMAT (1H0, I5,' MALES AND',I5,' FEMALES')
      END
```

Figure 10. *Generalized* program for frequency distribution.

outside the program) different values to tailor it to different sets of data, we say we *generalize* the program. This means we make that program general; that is, we do ñot specifically limit the program to one set of data by putting into the program as constants things which are unique to one set of data, like the number of cases. Rather, we are able to suit the program to different sets of data *without* changing any of the statements in the program itself.

Obviously, generalizing a program goes beyond merely changing the number of cases; here, for example, we would also eventually want to be able to change 90 FORMAT for each set of data. We will do this eventually, but it is more complex than merely changing number of cases, and *number of cases* is a good place to begin getting used to the idea of generalizing a program as much as possible.

Note that the first thing in this program is zeroing out the various storage locations involved in counting. The reason for putting these zeroing out statements at the very beginning of the program is that they are so easy to forget. Zeroing out statements do nothing dramatic, yet they can be vital to assuring that a program ends up with accurate counts. And since it is so easy to forget these statements when we start thinking about more complex things, we should take care of any zeroing out statements before doing anything else.

In the frequency distribution program in Figure 10, also note one more feature: We added a WRITE statement (m) to provide a title for our output. This is to show (after our earlier discussion) that since we used a CONTINUE statement for number 1001, we can add an additional statement in this position without having to change any statement numbers.

EXPANDING NUMBER OF CATEGORIES

When a variable has more than two categories, we simply use more storage locations, and arrange the computed GO TO accordingly. For example, say a variable has five response categories, meaning data values of 1 through 5. We decide to count the number of 1's in the data in a location named KAT1, count the number of 2's in KAT2, and so on. Thus to update the respective storage locations when the appropriate data values show up, we use these statements:

```
11 KAT1 = KAT1 + 1
12 KAT2 = KAT2 + 1
13 KAT3 = KAT3 + 1
14 KAT4 = KAT4 + 1
15 KAT5 = KAT5 + 1
```

Since we are counting the number of 1's in the data in KAT1, the statement number 11 must be located in the GO TO so that a value of 1 sends the computer next to statement 11. This means putting the number 11 first in the parentheses. Since we are counting the number of 2's in KAT2, the number 12 goes second in the parentheses, and so on.

If we read each data value in turn into a location named NVAR, and use this name in the computed GO TO, the frequency distribution segment for this data might look like Figure 11.

- - - - - - - -
zeroing out segment
- - - - - - - -

```
C     READ NUMBER OF CASES
      READ (5, 1100) NCASE
1100 FORMAT (I3)
C     READ DATA
130 READ (5, 1101) NVAR
1101 FORMAT (7X, I1)
C     UPDATE COUNTER
      NREP = NREP + 1
C     UPDATE RESPONSE CATEGORIES
      GO TO (11, 12, 13, 14, 15), NVAR
   11 KATI = KATI + 1
      GO TO 110
   12 KAT2 = KAT2 +1
      GO TO 110
   13 KAT3 = KAT3 + 1
      GO TO 110
   14 KAT4 = KAT4 + 1
      GO TO 110
   15 KAT5 = KAT5 + 1
110 IF (NREP − NCASE) 130, 140, 140
140 CONTINUE
```

- - - - - - - -
output segment
- - - - - - - -

Figure 11. Sequence for frequency distribution with five categories.

The rows of dashes in Figure 11 are an important device we will use from time to time to represent one or more statements we are passing over at the moment. The rows of dashes show there are, or will be, statements in the positions indicated by those dashes. It may be that we are discussing a long program, but are only interested in a certain portion of it at a particular time, as is the case here. Then we can quickly and easily indicate the other parts of the program with dashes. For example, here we are interested in the READ statements and frequency distribution statements in the program, so for our purposes here we can indicate the zeroing out statements and the WRITE statements by rows of dashes, to show that there are other statements in those positions, but that at the moment we are not concerned with those statements.

EXERCISES

See exercises 1–16 in Chapter Ten of the *Workbook*.

COLLAPSING CATEGORIES

A related use of the computed GO TO is to collapse categories in the course of a frequency distribution. To illustrate this, say we have a set of 35 data items representing responses on this attitude item:

The national political leaders are doing a good job.

Say the responses on this item come in the conventional five categories, ranging from Strongly Agree to Strongly Disagree, with each category assigned a code value. These code values are punched on data cards in column 8.

The categories and code values are:

Strongly Agree   1
Agree   2
Don't Know   3
Disagree   4
Strongly Disagree   5

Now say we want to *collapse categories*: that is, get a combined count of two or more related categories under one general heading. Here, say we want a combined count of the number of Strongly Agree and Agree responses under the general heading *Agree*, and a combined count of the last two categories under the heading *Disagree*. The Don't Know category will be treated separately.

A question here might be why we should have the computer doing this collapsing of categories; why not do it in coding or punching the data? The reason is to retain on the data cards all the information available, which allows us to do many more things with one set of cards. For example, if we keep the original code values for all five categories on the data cards, we can get a count for each of the five categories, and we can also have the computer collapse, or combine, the data values into fewer but broader categories, as we are doing here, *using the same set of data cards.*

Thus if we keep data in as much detail as possible on the data cards, we can use the information for a variety of purposes without having to repunch data cards each time. Indeed, one of the advantages of the computer is that it can easily handle the time-consuming chores necessary with more detailed data (as in keeping track of more categories) and at the same time can quickly collapse categories if desired, to give us a more condensed view of the data. So as a general rule, when using a computer, get, and keep, the data in as much detail as possible: exact years of education, or exact income figures, for example, rather than merely in categories such as *high, medium,* or *low.*

In collapsing categories, we follow the general procedure for the frequency distribution, with one exception. Instead of counting the number of times each data value appears, we want to count the number of times any one of a *set* of data values appears.

Here, for example, counting the Strongly Agree and Agree responses together means counting how often the values 1 *or* 2 appear in the data. Similarly, counting Disagree and Strongly Disagree responses together means counting how often the values 4 *or* 5 appear. Since Don't Know responses are being treated as a separate category, 3's will be counted separately.

Again the counting is a matter of updating the appropriate storage location for each data value. Here, because we want to collapse the figures into three categories, we use three locations for the counting. Remember that although the original data values can range from 1 through 5, which in turn means five statement numbers in the computed GO TO, we only want *three* separate counts, which means only three storage locations for counting.

To use names which show what they refer to, the name for the location in which we count the number of Strongly Agree and Agree responses combined will be NAGREE. The name for the location in which we count the number of Don't Know responses will be NDKNOW. The name for the location in which we count the number of Disagree and Strongly Disagree responses combined will be NDISAG.

To update the storage locations, we use these statements:

```
11 NAGREE = NAGREE + 1
12 NDKNOW = NDKNOW + 1
13 NDISAG = NDISAG + 1
```

In programming terms, the logic problem is this: If a data value is 1 *or* 2, we want the computer to update the storage location named NAGREE: that is, to execute statement 11 shown above. We accomplish this by putting the number 11 in the first *and* in the second positions inside the parentheses of the computed GO TO.

We can do this because this is not repeating a statement number; it is merely telling the computer that if a value of 1 shows up at the computed GO TO, the computer is to go next to statement 11, and that if a value of 2 shows up at the computed GO TO, the computer is *also* to go next to statement 11. For a value of 3 we want statement 12 above executed, to update NDKNOW, which is where we are counting the number of Don't Know responses. Therefore we put the number 12 in the third position inside the parentheses. Since we are counting Strongly Disagree and Disagree responses combined in NDISAG, we want statement 13 above executed whenever a 4 *or* 5 arrives at the GO TO, so we put the number 13 in the fourth *and* fifth positions inside the parentheses.

For this data, the computer, in deciding in the computed GO TO on which location to update, makes its decision on the basis of a political attitude. Therefore, let us use the variable name NPOLAT in the computed GO TO. The computed GO TO thus looks like this:

GO TO (11, 11, 12, 13, 13), NPOLAT

The fact that the number 11 appears twice, in the first and second positions in the parentheses, is how we *collapse* the categories of Strongly Agree and Agree; that is, how we combine both data values of 1 and 2 in updating the category NAGREE. If NPOLAT has the value 1, indicating a response of Strongly Agree, the computer would go next to statement 11. If NPOLAT is 2, indicating a response of Agree, the computer would also go to statement 11. Thus both values 1 and 2, indicating responses of Strongly Agree and Agree respectively, would be counted in NAGREE. Similarly, a value of 4 *or* 5, representing Disagree and Strongly Disagree, respectively, would send the computer next to statement 13, to update the category NDISAG, thus counting in that location the number of Disagree and Strongly Disagree responses. A value of 3 in NPOLAT would cause the computer to update NDKNOW.

In repeating statement numbers in the GO TO like this, we are, in effect, reducing the number of outcomes of the decision statement, just as we reduced the number of outcomes of an IF statement from three to two by repeating a statement number. A very important difference, however, is this: When we repeat statement numbers in the IF, one of the numbers repeated may be a dummy, meaning the computer could never arrive at an outcome in the IF comparison that would correspond to the position of the dummy number. In our GO TO here, however, none of the repeated numbers is a dummy: all represent routes the computer can take. Repeating statement numbers here merely means that there are several different values which can cause the computer to take the same route out of the GO TO.

For a complete program, we add statements to zero out the storage locations before counting in them, a READ statement to read the data values one by one into NPOLAT, and the necessary unconditional GO TO statements.

Finally, we add a counter, which we call NREP, and an IF

statement to control the number of times the READ statement is executed. We use the variable name NCASE to tell the computer how many items of data to read in a given set of data. The result looks something like Figure 12.

```
C    FREQUENCY DISTRIBUTION PROGRAM
C    INCLUDES COLLAPSING CATEGORIES
C    ZERO OUT
         NAGREE = 0                              (a)
         NDKNOW = 0                              (b)
         NDISAG = 0                              (c)
         NREP = 0                                (d)
C    READ NUMBER OF CASES
         READ (5, 2100) NCASE                    (e)
 2100 FORMAT (I3)
C    READ DATA VALUES ONE BY ONE
  230 READ (5, 2101) NPOLAT                      (f)
 2101 FORMAT (7X, I1)
C    UPDATE COUNTER
         NREP = NREP + 1                         (g)
C    UPDATE RESPONSE CATEGORIES
         GO TO (11, 11, 12, 13, 13), NPOLAT      (h)
   11 NAGREE = NAGREE + 1                        (i)
         GO TO 210                               (j)
   12 NDKNOW = NDKNOW + 1                        (k)
         GO TO 210                               (l)
   13 NDISAG = NDISAG + 1                        (m)
  210 IF (NREP − NCASE) 230, 240, 240            (n)
  240 CONTINUE                                   (o)
         WRITE (6, 2180)                         (p)
 2180 FORMAT (1H1, 'POLITICAL ATTITUDE DATA')
         WRITE (6, 2181) NAGREE                  (q)
 2181 FORMAT (1H0, I5, ' AGREE RESPONSES')
         WRITE (6, 2182) NDKNOW                  (r)
 2182 FORMAT (1H0, I5, ' DO NOT KNOW RESPONSES')
         WRITE (6, 2183) NDISAG                  (s)
 2183 FORMAT (1H0, I5, ' DISAGREE RESPONSES')
         END
```

Figure 12. Frequency distribution program with collapsing categories.

Let us use the small letters at the right margin to show the statements that would be executed in this program for different data values. Statements *a* through *e* would be executed once, regardless of what values were read into the program. So beginning with the READ statement *f*, if this brought in a value of 1 *or* 2, the computer would execute statements *g* and *h*, then statements *i* and *j*. Statement *j* would send the computer to the IF statement *n*. If the value of NREP here was less than 35 (the value we read into NCASE for this set of data) the computer would go back to READ statement *f* for another piece of data. If a 4 *or* 5 were read in, the sequence of statements, beginning with the READ statement, would be the following: *f*, *g*, *h*, *m*, and *n*. At statement *n*, if NREP was less than NCASE, the computer would return to execute the READ statement again. If a data value was 3, the computer would execute these statements: *f*, *g*, *h*, *k*, *l*, and *n*, and back to the READ statement if NREP were less than NCASE.

Table IV below summarizes the statements, from *f* through *n*, inclusive, which would be executed for each different data value read into NPOLAT.

Note that in the program in Figure 12 we used the words DO NOT KNOW, rather than DON'T KNOW, in 2182 FORMAT. This is to avoid using an apostrophe in an H field which is itself indicated by apostrophes. Unless specially handled, using an apostrophe *within* an H field like this may confuse the computer.

EXERCISES

See exercises 17–30 in Chapter Ten of the *Workbook*.

SUMMING

Summing is closely related to counting and updating, in that summing also uses the meaning of the equal sign: *Set equal to.*

TABLE IV
STATEMENTS EXECUTED IN THE PROGRAM IN FIGURE 12,
FOR DIFFERENT VALUES OF NPOLAT

Meaning of Data Value	*Data Value In NPOLAT*	*Statements Executed*
Strongly Agree	1	f, g, h, i, j, n
Agree	2	f, g, h, i, j, n
Don't Know	3	f, g, h, k, l, n
Disagree	4	f, g, h, m, n
Strongly Disagree	5	f, g, h, m, n

The Summing Statement

We have seen that to count we use a statement like this:

NTOT = NTOT + 1

Each time this statement is executed, the value of NTOT is increased, or raised, by 1. But this is only because we use the constant 1 in showing what is to be added to NTOT.

Now what if we replaced the constant 1 with a variable name whose value could change as different data values were read into it, like this:

NTOT = NTOT + NVAL

When this statement is executed, NTOT is increased by whatever is the current value of NVAL. This statement tells the computer to set the location named NTOT equal to whatever is *now* in NTOT *plus* whatever is currently in the location named NVAL. So NTOT is given a *new* value which is equal to its prior value plus the current value of NVAL. This new value replaces the value that was in NTOT up to this point, and remains the value of NTOT until such time as we do something to change the value of NTOT again.

To illustrate with a few figures, say that the value of NTOT at a particular point is 17, and the value of NVAL is 9. When the computer executes this statement:

NTOT = NTOT + NVAL

the sum of the values on the right of the equal sign (that is, the sum of the values of NTOT and NVAL) is 26. Then, because of the equal sign meaning *set* equal to, the computer, in executing this statement, puts the value 26 in the location indicated by the name on the left of the equal sign. Since this name is also NTOT, *after* this statement is executed, NTOT has the new value 26.

Now say we place (read) a new value in NVAL, the value 4. Then we tell the computer to execute this summing statement again. This time, because the value of NTOT is now 26, the sum of the values of NTOT and NVAL on the right of the equal sign is 30. So this execution of the summing statement would set NTOT (the name on the left of the equal sign) equal to 30.

The key to understanding this kind of operation is that (odd as it may seem) the *use* of the name NTOT on the right of the equal sign is in a sense unrelated to the *use* of the name NTOT on the left of the equal sign. This is because of the way an arithmetic statement works, and particularly because of the meaning of the equal sign which appears between the two names NTOT.

Remember that when a name appears on the right side of the equal sign, this tells the computer to go to the location bearing that name, see what value is stored in that location, and do with that value whatever is indicated by the arithmetic operator(s) accompanying that name. Doing this with all the elements on the right of the equal sign gives the computer a value for the full expression there. Then the equal sign tells the computer to put this value in the location whose name appears on the left of the equal sign.

Therefore, when the same name appears on both sides of the equal sign in a summing statement, the computer treats the location bearing that name in two different ways, and at two different times, during the execution of that statement. First that name (on the *right* of the equal sign) is treated as showing the location of a data value to be used in working out the results of the arithmetic expression. Then, once the computer has a value for that expression, it puts that value into that same location because that name also appears on the *left* of the equal sign. And this new value replaces the value that was in that location prior to the execution of this summing statement. So when a variable name appears twice in a summing statement, this merely means the computer puts a value into a location from which a value was just used; but the putting occurs *after* the using because of the equal sign between the two appearances of the name.

This explanation of what happens during summing also applies to updating, or counting, which is merely a special kind of summing, though we did not describe it in these terms earlier. When we use a statement like this:

NREP = NREP + 1

to update a counter, the computer first gets a value for the elements on the right of the equal sign. This means it sees what value is stored in the location named NREP, and then, because of the plus sign and 1, adds one to this value. Then because the name NREP also appears on the left of the equal sign, the computer puts this new value back into NREP, replacing the value there previously. So while the updating statement seems merely to increase the existing value of NREP by 1, it is really creating and storing a whole new value in that location: a value which consists of the old value plus 1.

Summing In a Program

Summing on the computer is merely a matter of having a *summing statement* executed over and over again, each time with the variable name after the plus sign having the value of a different item of data. We say the effect of this is to *accumulate* the total of all these values in the location whose name appears to the left of the equal sign. Because the storage location named at the left of the equal sign thus ends up with the sum of a set of data, we refer to a location like this as a *summing location*.

Obviously, then, the basic procedure of summing consists of two parts. One is a statement to read values one at a time into a variable name. The other part is an arithmetic statement like this:

$$NTOT = NTOT + NVAL$$

This statement is repeated over and over again, once for each value read into the variable name here represented by NVAL. As the summing statement is executed repeatedly, it adds each value in turn to the total accumulating in a summing location, which in the statement above is named NTOT.

For a complete summing operation, therefore, we put a READ statement and a summing statement together in a sequence which also includes a counter and IF statement, and a variable name whose value shows the number of times this sequence is to be repeated for a given set of data. When this sequence has been repeated the specified number of times (that is, the specified number of data values have been read and added to the total accumulating in the summing location) the IF statement tells the computer to stop reading and summing, and go on to some other step: writing out the sum, or finding the average of the values, or whatever.

Using the variable name NVAL, the summing location NTOT, and KTR as a counter, a complete summing program could be as simple as that illustrated in Figure 13.

```
C    SUMMING PROGRAM
        NTOT = 0                              (a)
        KTR = 0                               (b)
C    READ NUMBER OF CASES
        READ (5, 30) NCASE                    (c)
     30 FORMAT (I3)
C    READ DATA
     80 READ (5, 40) NVAL                     (d)
     40 FORMAT (I1)
        KTR = KTR + 1                         (e)
C    SUMMING STATEMENT
        NTOT = NTOT + NVAL                    (f)
        IF (KTR - NCASE) 80, 90, 90           (g)
     90 CONTINUE                              (h)
        WRITE (6, 100) NTOT                   (i)
    100 FORMAT (1H0, 'THE SUM IS', I10)
        END
```

Figure 13. Basic summing program.

To briefly illustrate how this program works, say we give it these five items of data, in this order:

4
3
9
6
2

Each value is in column 1 of a separate data card. Before these cards is one with the digits 005 in the first three columns; this is the value to be read into NCASE.

After reading the value for NCASE, the computer reads the

value 4 from the first data card into NVAL, and then adds this value to the total accumulating in NTOT. Since NTOT began at zero (the result of the zeroing out statement), after the first execution of statement *f*, the value in NTOT is 4.

KTR was updated immediately after the READ statement was executed, so it now has a value of 1. The IF comparison thus sends the computer back to read into NVAL the value 3 from the second data card. This value (3) is added to the total presently in NTOT (4). After this second execution of statement *f*, therefore, NTOT now has the value 7.

Since the counter value is now 2, the IF statement sends the computer back up to read the value 9 from the third data card. The third execution of statement *f* adds this value of NVAL (9) to the total now in NTOT (7) so that the value of NTOT now becomes 16.

The fourth repetition of the READ/add sequence adds the value 6 to the sum (16) now in NTOT. Finally, the fifth repetition adds the value 2 to the total accumulating in NTOT. After the fifth repetition of the READ/add sequence, KTR equals the value read into NCASE, so the computer goes next to statement 90 and on to write out the sum of the data values, which for these five values would be 24.

Finding Average Score

For a practical application of summing, say we want a program which will read in a set of scores and find an average. Say the scores are for some test where values can range from 0 to 100, with no fractions. Say also that the test is given to great numbers of people: all the freshmen at a university, for example, or all the employees at a large company, so that the sample size can be in the thousands. Here is our first real introduction to the power of programming: With virtually the same program that finds an average for five cases, we can also find an average for 5000. Basically, then, what the computer really does is magnify the effect of the work we do: but magnify it by a factor of thousands.

Say that each score is in columns 7, 8, and 9 of a separate data card. Each of the scores will be read, in turn, into a location named SCORE. The reason for using a floating point name, although we said the scores themselves would be integer (no fractions) is the size factor. Any one score would not be too large for an integer name, but with thousands of scores their sum might exceed the size limits of an integer summing location. So to use the larger values possible with a floating point name, we call the summing location TOTSCR. And this means that for the location into which each of the scores will be read in its turn, we also need a floating point name, so we do not mix modes in the summing statement. So we call this location SCORE.

Thus our summing statement could look like this:

TOTSCR = TOTSCR + SCORE

This program to find the average score is constructed like our earlier simple summing program, except that here we add statements to get an average once the sum has been accumulated.

```
C    PROGRAM TO FIND AVERAGE SCORE
         TOTSCR = 0                                    (a)
         KTR = 0                                       (b)
         READ (5, 1000) NCASE                          (c)
   1000 FORMAT (I6)
     50 READ (5, 1001) SCORE                           (d)
   1001 FORMAT (6X, F3.0)
         KTR = KTR + 1                                 (e)
         TOTSCR = TOTSCR + SCORE                       (f)
         IF (KTR − NCASE) 50, 51, 51                   (g)
     51 CONTINUE                                       (h)
         FNCASE = NCASE                                (i)
         AVESCR = TOTSCR / FNCASE                      (j)
         WRITE (6, 2000) AVESCR                        (k)
   2000 FORMAT (1H1, 'AVERAGE SCORE IS', F20.2)
         END                                           (l)
```

Figure 14. Basic program to find average.

For 1001 FORMAT here we are assuming the data are in columns 7 through 9 of the respective data cards, with no decimal points or decimal parts punched in the data cards. If decimal points or fractional parts were present (as with scores on another kind of test) 1001 FORMAT could be changed accordingly.

In this program, the number of cases is first read into NCASE. Then the computer reads the first score into SCORE, and after updating the counter, adds this first score to TOTSCR. At the IF statement, the computer is then sent back to read the second score, from the second data card, into SCORE. At the summing statement, this second value is added to the total accumulating in TOTSCR, then the IF statement sends the computer back to read the score from the third data card, and so on.

This process continues until the computer has read a score for each case, at which point KTR equals NCASE, so the IF statement sends the computer down to statement *i* to create a floating point equivalent for number of cases to use in statement *j*, which finds the average, which is then written out in statement *k*.

TREATING DATA AS INTEGER OR FLOATING POINT

Since we said the scores used here did not have decimal parts, it would also be possible to read the individual scores into an integer location, like NSCORE, using an integer field specification in 1001 FORMAT. Then after the READ statement we could use an extra statement to get the necessary floating point equivalent for the summing statement, like this:

```
- - - - - - -
- - - - - - -
      READ (5, 1001) NSCORE
1001 FORMAT (6X, I3)
      SCORE = NSCORE
      TOTSCR = TOTSCR + SCORE
- - - - - - -
- - - - - - -
```

Assuming that each of the scores in the data used with this program consists only of one to three digits in the specified columns, this would give us the same values read into the computer, and the same total in TOTSCR.

This is an important point because it illustrates two useful features of programming. One is that often a data value can be treated either as floating point, or as integer, depending on what we want to do with it. The exception to this would of course be values with decimal parts we do not want to lose. These values must be treated as floating point, to avoid truncation.

The second point illustrated here is the way we can often shift from one mode to another in a program, so that we are not limited in what we can do by the way data values are initially read in.

But remember that while we have this flexibility, we use it only when there is good reason to, because it can involve extra statements. For example, in our program for finding the average score here, if there is no reason for using an integer name like NSCORE, we can read each value directly into the floating point name SCORE, and save the extra statement (and computer time) needed to convert each value from integer to floating point.

This ability to treat a value as integer *or* floating point, *if* it has no fractional part we want to keep, also holds true for number of cases and for counter variables. Probably the only reason for using integer names for these values is that it is simply conventional, because they so clearly involve counting, like the counter variable KTR here, or number of cases, where fractions are not possible.

EXERCISES

See exercises 31–34 in Chapter Ten of the *Workbook*.

A CONCLUDING NOTE

At this point you have seen the basic processes in a computer in their simplest form. In the next book in this series you will be introduced to the concept of *array*, and shown how this enables us (through the computer) to process large quantities of data quickly and with relatively few programming statements. With that next book you should soon have practical programs for a number of procedures used in social science, procedures involving one or two variables, and at the nominal and interval levels of measurement: procedures such as frequency and percentage distributions, standard deviation, one- and two-sample *t*-tests, and Pearson's *r*.

In sum, you have now learned the most basic things about a computer; the next step is to learn how these things are applied to large quantities of data in a way that will be of direct use in your research.

BIBLIOGRAPHY

1. Alluisi, Earl A.: *Basic Fortran for Statistical Analysis.* Homewood, Illinois, Dorsey, 1967.
2. Anderson, Decima M.: *Computer Programming: Fortran IV.* New York, Appleton-Century-Crofts, 1966.
3. Blalock, Hubert M.: *Social Statistics.* New York, McGraw-Hill, 1960.
4. Dial, Eugene O.: *Computer Programming and Statistics for Basic Research.* New York, American Book Company, 1968.
5. Farina, Mario V.: *Fortran IV Self-Taught.* Englewood Cliffs, New Jersey, Prentice-Hall, 1966.
6. Freeman, Linton C.: *Elementary Applied Statistics.* New York, Wiley, 1965.
7. Lee, R. M.: *A Short Course in Fortran IV Programming.* New York, McGraw-Hill, 1967.
8. McCammon, Mary: *Understanding Fortran.* New York, Crowell, 1968.
9. McCracken, Daniel D.: *A Guide to Fortran IV Programming.* New York, Wiley, 1965.
10. Price, Wilson T.: *Elements of Basic Fortran IV Programming.* New York, Holt, Rinehart and Winston, 1969.
11. Siegel, Sidney: *Nonparametric Statistics for the Behavioral Sciences.* New York, McGraw-Hill, 1956.
12. Veldman, Donald J.: *Fortran Programming for the Behavioral Sciences.* New York, Holt, Rinehart and Winston, 1967.